SUN TZU

BILINGUAL CHINESE AND ENGLISH TEXT

# THE ART OF WAR

孫子兵法

To my brother

# Captain Valentine Giles, R. C.,

in the hope that

a work 2400 years old

may yet contain lessons worth consideration

to the soldier of today,

this translation

is affectionately dedicated

# SUN TZU

BILINGUAL **CHINESE** AND **ENGLISH** TEXT

# THE ART OF WAR

孫子兵法

With a new foreword by **John Minford**
Translated by **Lionel Giles**

**TUTTLE** Publishing
Tokyo | Rutland, Vermont | Singapore

## "Books to Span the East and West"

Tuttle Publishing was founded in 1832 in the small New England town of Rutland, Vermont [USA]. Our core values remain as strong today as they were then—to publish best-in-class books which bring people together one page at a time. In 1948, we established a publishing outpost in Japan—and Tuttle is now a leader in publishing English-language books about the arts, languages and cultures of Asia. The world has become a much smaller place today and Asia's economic and cultural influence has grown. Yet the need for meaningful dialogue and information about this diverse region has never been greater. Over the past seven decades, Tuttle has published thousands of books on subjects ranging from martial arts and paper crafts to language learning and literature—and our talented authors, illustrators, designers and photographers have won many prestigious awards. We welcome you to explore the wealth of information available on Asia at www.tuttlepublishing.com.

Published by Tuttle Publishing, an imprint of Periplus Editions (HK) Ltd.

www.tuttlepublishing.com

Copyright © 2008 Periplus Editions (HK) Ltd.
Paperback edition Copyright © 2016
Periplus Editions (HK) Ltd.

Library of Congress Control Number: 2007935319

ISBN 978-0-8048-3944-0 (HC)
ISBN 978-0-8048-4820-6 (PB)

First edition
27 26 25 24 23
14 13 12 11 10 9      2306VP

Printed in Malaysia

Distributed by

North America, Latin America & Europe
Tuttle Publishing
364 Innovation Drive, North Clarendon
VT 05759-9436 U.S.A.
Tel: 1 (802) 773-8930; Fax: 1 (802) 773-6993
info@tuttlepublishing.com
www.tuttlepublishing.com

Japan
Tuttle Publishing
Yaekari Building, 3rd Floor, 5-4-12 Osaki
Shinagawa-ku, Tokyo 141 0032
Tel: (81) 3 5437-0171; Fax: (81) 3 5437-0755
sales@tuttle.co.jp
www.tuttle.co.jp

Asia Pacific
Berkeley Books Pte. Ltd.
3 Kallang Sector #04-01, Singapore 349278
Tel: (65) 6741-2178; Fax: (65) 6741-2179
inquiries@periplus.com.sg
www.tuttlepublishing.com

TUTTLE PUBLISHING® is a registered trademark of Tuttle Publishing, a division of Periplus Editions (HK) Ltd.

# CONTENTS

FOREWORD
    The Art of War: A Classic for our Times ....................... vii

PREFACE.................................................................. xxvii

INTRODUCTION
    Sun Tzŭ and His Book.................................... xxx
    The Text of Sun Tzŭ..................................... xlvii
    The Commentators........................................ li
    Appreciations of Sun Tzŭ................................ lvii
    Apologies for War......................................... lix
    Bibliography................................................. lxiv

## Part One: The Art of War

COMPLETE CHINESE TEXT AND ENGLISH TRANSLATION
    Chapter 1  Laying Plans.................................... 2
    Chapter 2  Waging War .................................... 6
    Chapter 3  Attack by Stratagem ....................... 10
    Chapter 4  Tactical Dispositions...................... 14
    Chapter 5  Energy............................................ 17
    Chapter 6  Weak Points and Strong.............. 21
    Chapter 7  Maneuvering................................. 27
    Chapter 8  Variation of Tactics ...................... 32
    Chapter 9  The Army on the March ................ 35
    Chapter 10 Terrain........................................... 42

Chapter 11  The Nine Situations ..................................... 47
Chapter 12  The Attack by Fire ...................................... 57
Chapter 13  The Use of Spies .......................................... 60

## Part Two: **Critical Notes and Commentaries**

Chapter 1   Laying Plans .................................................. 66
Chapter 2   Waging War ................................................... 71
Chapter 3   Attack by Stratagem ................................... 76
Chapter 4   Tactical Dispositions .................................. 82
Chapter 5   Energy ............................................................ 86
Chapter 6   Weak Points and Strong ............................. 93
Chapter 7   Maneuvering ................................................ 101
Chapter 8   Variation of Tactics ................................... 112
Chapter 9   The Army on the March ............................. 119
Chapter 10  Terrain ........................................................... 133
Chapter 11  The Nine Situations ..................................... 142
Chapter 12  The Attack by Fire ...................................... 169
Chapter 13  The Use of Spies .......................................... 177

# FOREWORD

## The Art of War: A Classic for our Times

This extraordinary little book is one of the oldest, shortest and most frequently translated of all Chinese classical texts. In this respect, it stands in the same category as those two other venerable scriptures, *The Book of Changes* (*Yijing* 易經), and *The Way and Its Power* (*Daodejing* 道德經). Since probably the fifth century BC, *The Art of War* has been one of the key texts of Chinese strategic thinking. Widely read in Japan since the eighth century, it has also since the eighteenth century held a deep fascination for the Western reader. Napoleon is reputed to have possessed a copy of the earliest (1782) French translation by the Jesuit, Père Jean-Joseph-Marie Amiot (1718-1793). It has also exerted a huge influence in the modern Chinese world. Both Chiang Kai-shek and Mao Zedong are known to have studied the book carefully, and Chiang was an avid collector of *Art of War* editions. As for Mao, he learned many lessons from Master Sun, applying them to the dialectics of guerrilla warfare, and himself writing in December 1936: "Some people are good at knowing themselves and poor at knowing their enemy, and some are the other way around. There is a saying in the book of Sun Tzŭ, the great military scientist of ancient China, 'Know the enemy, know yourself, and victory is never in doubt, not in a hundred battles,' which refers both to the stage of learning and to the stage of application, both to knowing the laws of the development of objective reality and to deciding on our own action in accordance with these laws in order to overcome the enemy facing us. We should not take this saying lightly."[1]

---

[1] Mao Zedong, "Problems of Strategy in China's Revolutionary War", *Selected Works*, vol. 1. For the original, see *Mao Zedong xuanji* 毛澤東選集 (Beijing, 1969), p. 166. See also the excellent

In the twentieth century, the relevance of Sun Tzŭ was widely acknowledged across the globe. During the Second World War, an English version was produced for the Royal Air Force, with the admonition: "Master Sun is fundamental and, read with insight, lays bare the mental mechanism of our enemy (the Japanese). Study him, and study him again. Do not be misled by his simplicity." We are told that American soldiers fighting in Iraq and Afghanistan are provided with a copy. The great historian of Chinese science, Joseph Needham, called Sun Tzŭ's *The Art of War* a "unique masterpiece of military thinking,"[2] and went on to compare its extremely modern "psychological emphasis" on the "duel of minds" with the work of twentieth-century "praxiologists" ("those who study the spring of individual action and conduct"), such as Parsons and Shils.[3] Needham's summary of the book remains one of the most intelligent and succinct.

The military historian B. H. Liddell Hart (1895-1970) wrote in 1963: "Sun Tzŭ's essays on 'The Art of War' have never been surpassed in comprehensiveness and depth of understanding... The need [for a fresh translation of Sun Tzŭ] has increased with the development of nuclear weapons, potentially suicidal and genocidal. It becomes all the more important in view of the re-emergence of China, under Mao, as a great military power."[4] Liddell Hart's own principles of strategy, as seen in his study *Strategy: the indirect approach*, often reflect his reading of Sun Tzŭ:

> In strategy the longest way round is often the shortest way there; a direct approach to the object exhausts the attacker and hardens the resistance by compression, whereas an indirect approach loosens the defender's hold by upsetting his balance.

---

study and translation by Brigadier General Sam Griffith, US Marine Corps, *Sun Tzu: The Art of War* (Oxford, 1963), especially part six of the Introduction, "Sun Tzu and Mao Tse-tung." This book was based on the author's Oxford D. Phil. Dissertation. In addition to his military background, Griffith had the good fortune to be supervised in his work by the prominent scholar Wu Shichang, then teaching at Oxford.

[2] Joseph Needham and Robin Yates, et al., *Science and Civilisation in China*, vol. 5, part vi, *Military Technology* (Cambridge, 1994), p. 18.

[3] Talcott Parsons, and Shils, E. A., *Toward a General Theory of Action* (Harvard, 1951).

[4] Foreword to Griffith's *Sun Tzu: The Art of War* (Oxford, 1963).

He also claimed, in Sun Tzŭ-like vein, that:

> The profoundest truth of war is that the issue of battle is usu-
> ally decided in the minds of the opposing commanders, not in the
> bodies of their men.[5]

At the same time, Sun Tzŭ's book has become prescribed
reading internationally for students in Management Studies. "By
using the principles of Sun Tzŭ and competing more creatively,
business leaders will be able to avoid the huge casualties of corporate downsizing caused by dull strategic thinking."[6] The legendary
Japanese entrepreneur (and founder of Panasonic) Konosuke
Matsushita (1894-1989) wrote: "All our staff members must read
Master Sun's *Art of War* and apply its teachings flexibly so that my
firm will flourish."[7] And flourish it did. In her popular book *The
Asian Mind Game: A Westerner's Survival Manual*, Chin-ning Chu
devotes a whole chapter to Sun Tzŭ. She tells the story of the great
Japanese warrior Minamoto Yoshiie (1041-1108), who while on
his way to attack a rival's fortress, "observed a flock of wild geese
rising in disordered flight from a forest through which he must
pass. Because he had studied Sun Tzŭ's *Art of War*, he knew that
these birds had probably been flushed out by an army preparing
an ambush for him. He was able to lead his army around the ambush and surprise and destroy this enemy." [8]

In China today, new books on Sun Tzŭ are appearing all the
time. One of the most distinguished and prolific *Art of War*
scholars is Professor Li Ling, who lectures regularly on this
subject to large classes at the prestigious Peking University. His
most recent book on the subject is already in its fifth printing.[9]
In the introduction, he describes how during his twenty years of

---

[5] Third revised and enlarged edition (London, 2003).

[6] Mark McNeilly, *Sun Tzu and the Art of Business* (New York, 1996), p. 6.

[7] See *Sunzi: The Art of War*, translated by Zhang Huimin, annotated by Major General Xie
Guoliang (Beijing, 1995), p. 37.

[8] Chin-ning Chu, *The Asian Mind Game: A Westerner's Survival Manual* (St Ives, NSW, 1996),
pp. 19 & 24-52. See also the same author's *Thick Face, Black Heart: thriving and succeeding in everyday
life and work using the ancient wisdom of the East* (St Leonards, NSW, 1992).

[9] Li Ling, *Bing yi zha li* (Beijing, 2006).

teaching the text, he has moved from an academic, text-based approach (his own background is in archaeology and philology), to a more wide-ranging exploration of the ideas underlying not only *The Art of War*, but also the *Book of Changes* and *The Way and Its Power*. His lectures are now standing-room only affairs, a reflection not only of the huge Chinese interest in this particular book, but also of the recent revival of interest in traditional Chinese culture in general.

A visit to one of the many websites devoted to the book (such as sonshi.com) offers a vivid, indeed startling, insight into the continuing and pervasive grip it has on the contemporary imagination. Phrases from the book feature prominently in Oliver Stone's movie *Wall Street*, in which the ruthless corporate raider Gordon Gecko comments: "I bet on sure things. Master Sun: 'Every battle is won before it is fought.' Think about it." The cult continues. So does the intellectual debate. The prominent French scholar of Chinese philosophy, François Jullien, has many challenging (and quite a few fanciful) things things to say about Master Sun in his *Traité de l'efficacité* (Paris, 1996). And most recently of all (2007), the American scholar David R. Cross has written an elegant and penetrating essay, "The aesthetics of command," in which he places the thought of Master Sun, and of the Taoist classic the *Daodejing*, in an enlightening post-modern transdisciplinary framework embracing philosophy, psychology, and Gregory Bateson's "ecology of mind," focussing above all on a discussion of the "deep structure of strategic action."[10]

But what sort of a book is it? And who wrote it? Neither of these questions is easy to answer. Indeed they may be the wrong questions. In many ways it is hardly a book at all. As the great scholar and translator of Chinese philosophy, Angus Graham, memorably put it: "Ancient Chinese thinkers did not write books. They jotted down sayings, verses, stories, thoughts and by the third century BC composed essays, on bamboo strips which were

---

[10] Unpublished essay, personal communication.

tied together in sheets and rolled up in scrolls."[11] Master Sun's *The Art of War* is certainly not a methodically organised, easily useable and applicable treatise on warfare. It is more like a series of gnomic utterances on the art of survival, and of interior (and exterior) methods of dealing with conflict and strategic decisions in general. By extension, it is a more generalised book of proverbial wisdom, an ancient book of life. As for the author, he may not even have existed. What "biographical" information we have about Master Sun as a person is fragmentary, colorful, and highly unreliable. The often quoted story from Sima Qian's *Historical Records* (Giles gives it in its entirety), shows him training the King of Wu's harem. It makes for wonderful reading (Sima Qian was a superb storyteller), but is almost certainly apocryphal.

Previous attempts (both Chinese and non-Chinese) to undermine the historicity of the text itself (some dating it several centuries into the Christian era) have however been conclusively proved false by recent archaeological discoveries. In the 1970s, copies on bamboo and wooden strips (just the sort of bundles Angus Graham was talking about) were unearthed in two widely separated sites (in Shandong to the East and Qinghai to the West), both dating to the Former Han dynasty (206BC-8AD), and one to a period as early as the second century BC. When the texts were deciphered they turned out to be very close to the traditional text handed down across the intervening two thousand years. Some scholars have argued from the lapidary style of the difficult classical Chinese in which the text is written, that is roughly contemporaneous with the even more famous and influential *Analects* 論語 of Confucius. In other words, stylistically it seems to date from the early part of the period known as the Warring States, or very roughly the fifth century BC. This was the time of the "killing fields" of early China, a time when the central authority of the Zhou dynasty was failing altogether and a varying number of peripheral states were engaged in an internecine struggle for

---

[11] *Chuang-tzu: The Seven Inner Chapters*, translated by A. C. Graham (London, 1981), p. 27.

survival and dominance (hegemony). Their leaders took (or refused to take) advice from peripatetic would-be philosopher-statesmen, such as Confucius and Master Sun.[12] Most probably this bundle-book was a collection of sayings put together at that time from a number of like-minded thinkers (somewhat like the *Analects*). It seems almost certainly to contain a number of old proverbial sayings, that have acquired (somewhat like their counterparts in *The Book of Changes*) a patina of "perennial" wisdom from frequent repetition. Examples of this can be found in chapter 4: "To lift an autumn hair is no sign of great strength; to see sun and moon is no sign of sharp sight; to hear the noise of thunder is no sign of a quick ear." At the same time, the frequent use of rhyme and half-rhyme (paralleled in the *Changes* and the *Way*) enhances the incantatory effect of much of the text.

Since its first advent as a "book" (a "product of a long process of sedimentation of strategic reflections, which eventually crystallized into the form of a manual"),[13] the text has been handed down through many generations of readers and commentators (many of whom were celebrated men of letters or generals or statesmen, or all three). By the beginning of the second millennium A.D., a standard text had come into existence, with a corpus of commentaries from eleven hands. It is this edition and its interpretations that have held sway ever since. Lionel Giles bases his translation on this tradition.

The book incorporates many interesting elements of early Chinese thinking, including much of the benign (if enigmatic) proto-Taoist life-philosophy of the *Changes*. It has always been thought to be an "empowering" book. This is part of its enduring attraction. Its fundamental and inspirational message of "harmony with the Tao" as a strategy for effective decision-making and living is one that has a greater appeal today than ever, and

---

[12] Thanks to the early Latin-using Jesuits, Kongfuzi or Master Kong-fu became Confucius, and Mengzi, or Master Meng, became Mencius. If Master Sun had shared their fate, he would have been Suncius.

[13] Jean Lévi, *Sun Tzu, L'art de la Guerre* (Paris, 2000), p. 16.

Master Sun elaborates it in an economical manner. In the fifth chapter, the title of which Giles translates as "Energy," much is made of this, of the importance of exploiting to the full the "energy" or "potential dynamic" of any given situation, of the circumambient environment in which one finds oneself, rather than fighting against the grain. This is a central notion in the book. It is the same principle found in many schools of Chinese Martial Arts, whereby one actually turns the momentum of one's enemy to one's own advantage, rather than struggling against it.

At other times, Master Sun's message is less palatable, more ruthless. Often it echoes the dark Fascist ideology and "amoral science of statecraft" of the so-called Legalists (thinkers like the fifth-century Shang Yang and the third-century Master Hanfei, whose ruthless and uncompromising ideas were put into such terrifyingly efficient practice by the notorious First Emperor of Qin and his Prime Minister Li Si). Master Sun at times preaches the calculated and cynical exploitation of one's fellow human beings: "The Way of War is a Way of Deception." In a celebrated dialogue the Confucian philosopher Xunzi (Master Xun, c.298-38 B.C.) argues for the importance of morality, protesting at the arguments of a Sun Tzŭ-like general from the southern state of Chu. "You prize plotting, scheming, the use of situation and advantage, sudden attacks and maneuvers, deception. These are the methods of the lesser rulers. The troops of the Benevolent Man cannot be fought with deception..."[14] As the good Father Amiot commented in the eighteenth century, "It is not necessary to say here that I disapprove of all the author has to say on this occasion about the use of artifice and ruse..." James Murdoch, the historian of Japan, complained that the book "expounded the dirtiest form of statecraft with unspeakable depths of duplicity..."[15] The modern writer Mark Edward Lewis has perceptively observed that "the stratagems and deceits by which the military philoso-

---

[14] *Xunzi xinzhu* (Peking, 1979), pp. 230-1.
[15] James Murdoch, *A History of Japan* (London, 1949), pp. 630-1.

phers promised to reduce violence wreaked even greater damage on the fabric of human society than any physical brutality."[16]

But this is not to deny the great fascination and power of the book, and its relevance to our times. Each reader must negotiate a way through it. As a Ming-dynasty writer urged, "Emerge from the mud untainted; understand cunning, but do not use it."

## Lionel Giles: Sinology, old and new

Lionel Giles in 1896. Courtesy of the Giles Pickford photographic collection, Menzies Library, Australian National University.

This translation by Lionel Giles, itself now almost a hundred years old, has stood the test of time very well. Lionel, like his more famous father Herbert (1845-1935), was a fine sinologist of the old school. He was born on the 29th of December 1875, at Sutton in Surrey, where his grandfather was Rector of the local church.[17] He was his father's fourth son by his first wife Catherine Fenn (the first two sons died in China in infancy), and died on 22nd January, 1958. He was educated privately in Belgium (Liège), Austria (Feldkirch), and Aberdeen,[18] and subsequently completed his education at Wadham College, Oxford University, where he studied Classics, obtaining his BA in 1899 (First Class Honors in Mods, Second Class in Greats). Lionel seems to have been a self-effacing individual. It is interesting to note

---

[16] Mark Edward Lewis, *Sanctioned Violence in Early China* (Albany, 1990), p. 135.

[17] Much of the family information is to be found in *Aegidiana, or Gleanings Among the Gileses*, printed for private circulation in 1910. I am much indebted to Giles Pickford, Lionel Giles' greatnephew, for pointing me in this direction, and to Darrell Dorrington for his help in locating this fascinating family chronicle. They were also both instrumental in allowing and facilitating the reproduction of the photograph of Lionel.

[18] As were all the other surviving sons—Bertram, Valentine, and Lancelot. Both Bertram (born 1874) and Lancelot (born 1878) entered the British China Consular Service, following in their father's footsteps. Valentine became a soldier and joined the Royal Engineers.

that Herbert Giles, in his Memoirs, confesses that his son Lionel acted as a "devil" for him in writing the substantial 1910 China entries for the new edition of the *Encyclopedia Britannica*.[19] His willingness to be a "backroom boy," to work quietly for others, seems to have characterised Lionel's life as a scholar.

During almost his entire professional career, he worked in the British Museum (which then incorporated what is now the British Library), entering it in 1900, and eventually rising to become Keeper of Oriental Printed Books and Manuscripts in 1936. There he worked with such distinguished "orientalists" as Laurence Binyon (1869-1943; worked in the Museum 1893-1933) and Arthur Waley (1889-1966; worked in the Museum 1913-1930). Lionel Giles retired officially in 1940, but continued to work informally in the Museum until a few years before his death. Unjustly neglected by today's students of China, he represents an era of sinology when a scrupulous respect for and familiarity with ancient texts was combined with a broad reading in several European languages, engagement with major intellectual issues and trends of the day, and a fluent English prose style. He produced a series of translations for the general reader of some of the great classics of Chinese philosophy—*The Sayings of Lao Tzu* (1904), *Musings of a Chinese Mystic: Selections from the Philosophy of Chuang Tzu* [selected and adapted from Herbert Giles' version] (1906), *The Sayings of Confucius* (1907), *Taoist Teachings from the Book of Lieh Tzu* (1912), *The Book of Mencius* (1942), *A Gallery of Chinese Immortals* (1948), all titles published in John Murray's excellent Wisdom of the East series, edited by Cranmer-Byng father and son. He also published a vast number of scholarly articles and shorter translations (many in the pages of the *Bulletin of the School of Oriental and African Studies*, the *Journal of the Royal Asiatic Society*, or *T'oung Pao*), and several valuable bibliographical studies including *An Al-*

---

[19] Charles Aylmer, "The Memoirs of H. A. Giles," *East Asian History*, 13/14 (June/December 1997), pp. 51-2.

*phabetical Index to the Chinese Encyclopedia*, which he finished in 1911 (the year after his *Art of War* translation). He quietly helped many other workers in the field, as when he undertook the huge task of proofreading W. E. Soothill (1861-1935) and Lewis Hodous's (b. 1872) *Dictionary of Chinese Buddhist Terms.*[20] Soothill, who was Professor of Chinese at Oxford, in his Preface dated 1934, gave thanks, hailing Lionel as the "illustrious son of an illustrious parent," and referring to his "ripe scholarship and experienced judgement." Soothill died shortly after writing the preface. Three years later (1937), his collaborator Hodous wrote a Preface, from Hartford, Connecticut, praising Lionel's work in glowing terms: "Dr. Giles…has had to assume a responsibility quite unexpected by himself and by us. For two to three years, with unfailing courtesy and patience, he has considered and corrected the very trying pages of the proofs, while the Dictionary was being printed. He gave chivalrously of his long knowledge both of Buddhism and of the Chinese literary characters."

In 1951, Lionel Giles was honored by King George VI who made him a C.B.E. "in recognition of his services to Sinology"—a most appropriate citation. In a fine obituary, printed in the Hong Kong University *Journal of Oriental Studies* in 1960, J. L. Cranmer-Byng writes of his friend as a "slight figure, a mild looking man with a rapt expression…Giles once confessed to me that he was a Taoist at heart, and I can well believe it, since he was fond of a quiet life, and was free of that extreme form of combative scholarship which seems to be the hall mark of most sinologists." He was "particularly fond of his home, The Knoll, in the village of Abbot's Langley near Watford. Here in summer weather he liked to sit in his small but well-grown garden and chat with a congenial friend or two." He was apparently a methodical and neat man. His manuscript of *A Gallery of Chinese Immortals* was "beautifully written in a neat hand with the footnotes added in

---

[20] Soothill, William Edward, and Lewis Hodous, *A Dictionary of Chinese Buddhist Terms, with Sanskrit and English equivalents and a Sanskrit-Pali index* (London, 1937).

red ink." Cranmer-Byng also alludes to Lionel Giles' important role as Secretary of the China Society (he took this on in 1911).

Lionel Giles wrote countless excellent book reviews for the *Bulletin of the School of Oriental and African Studies*. He was capable of being most generous in his appraisal of others (more so than his father). Of Lin Yutang's *The Wisdom of China* he wrote: "Brilliant and versatile as ever, he is able to give us a better insight into the hearts of his countrymen than any other writer."[21] On the subject of Pearl Buck's version of the novel *Shuihuzhuan*, he wrote: "One feels that the author of *The Good Earth*, with her broad and tolerant outlook on life, was the predestined translator of this work [*All Men Are Brothers*], instinct as it is with a warm, comprehensive humanity."[22] But he could also be severely, if politely, critical, as in his review of E. R. Hughes' *Chinese Philosophy in Classical Times*: "Though his fluency never deserts him, one cannot help feeling that it is being used not so much to fill the gaps in our knowledge as to conceal the deficiencies in his…We begin to wonder if the writer is fully competent to undertake a piece of work involving so much translation from the Chinese…"[23] In a lengthy review of Arthur Waley's *Catalogue of Paintings Recovered from Tun-huang,* he begins by singing his Museum colleague's praises: "It is…fortunate that the Catalogue has been prepared by a scholar of the calibre of Mr. Waley. Indeed, it is hardly too much to say that he is the one man in this country who combines sufficient knowledge of Buddhism, Oriental art, and the Chinese language to undertake such a task." But Giles goes on to devote fourteen pages to a list of polite but precise, fearless and judicious corrections, on occasions including the eminent French sinologue Pelliot: "Both Mr Waley and Professor Pelliot are wrong here…"[24] Contrast this with the earlier heated exchange in the pages of the *New China Review* between Waley

---

[21] *BSOAS* 13, 3 (1950), p. 798.
[22] *BSOAS* 7, 13 (1934), p. 631.
[23] *BSOAS* 11, 1 (1943), p. 236.
[24] *BSOAS* 7, 1 (1933), pp. 179-92.

and Giles père on the subject of translating Chinese poetry.[25]

From time to time, Lionel used the occasion of a book review to put forward a well-considered argument on some general matter, as when writing about Xiao Qian's *Etchings of a Tormented Age*: "He begins by telling how the collapse of the Manchu Empire led to a further revolution in the world of letters, in which the plain vernacular was universally adopted in place of the age-hallowed classical style. This is putting it too strongly. Chinese as it is actually spoken is too clumsy and diffuse to be suitable for most forms of literary expression, especially poetry; and although the old allusive, carefully balanced style of composition has been generally abandoned, it cannot be said that its place has been taken by the language of the market-place. There are many gradations between these two extremes, and even in journalism some compromise has been found necessary. Admittedly some change in the direction of greater simplicity was called for; but now that the first flush of revolutionary enthusiasm is over the reformers are beginning to realize how difficult it is for a nation to cut itself off from tradition and make an entirely fresh start. Our own great innovator, Wordsworth, found it impossible in the long run to use the language of common speech consistently for poetic purposes, and it may reasonably be doubted whether poems will ever be written in the vernacular to compare with those of the great T'ang masters. All the more must our sympathy go out to those ardent spirits who are struggling to solve so complex a problem, in order that Chinese literature may continue to prove not unworthy of its glorious past."[26]

He was sometimes highly critical of the missionary bias of the previous generation of translators, as in the Introduction to his own *Analects*, where he takes James Legge and others to task: "The truth is, though missionaries and other zealots have long attempted to obscure the fact, that the moral teaching of Confu-

---

[25] See, for example, Giles' "A Re-Translation", in *New China Review*, 2 (1920), pp. 319-40, and "Mr Waley and 'The Lute Girl's Song'" in *NCR*, 3 (1921), pp. 423-28.

[26] *BSOAS* 11, 1 (1943), pp. 238-9.

cius is absolutely the purest and least open to the charge of self-ishness of any in the world." He goes on to claim: "Confucianism really represents a more advanced stage of civilisation than bib-lical Christianity...His whole system is based on nothing more nor less than the knowledge of human nature."[27]

As a critic of translation, he could be firm: "M. Margouliès has a nice appreciation of Chinese literary composition which is re-markable in a foreigner; he can savour the fine points of style that distinguish authors of different dynasties and different schools; yet apparently he cannot see that a rigidly literal translation of these same authors must almost necessarily obliterate the style which is of their very essence, and reduce them all to a dead level devoid of inspiration...[And yet] good French prose, with its grace, flexibility, and lightness of touch, is precisely the medium which would appear best suited for the rendering of *ku-wen*."[28] Lionel proceeds to compare the French version unfavourably with his father's versions in *Gems of Chinese Literature*.[29]

During his long tenure at the British Museum, Lionel Giles worked on an exhaustive catalogue of the priceless collection of some seven thousand manuscripts dating between c.400 and 1000 A.D., which the explorer Aurel Stein had brought back from the oasis of Dunhuang after 1907. This life's work of his finally bore fruit in 1957, a year before his death, with the publication of the magnificently produced and impeccably researched descrip-tive *Catalogue of the Chinese Manuscripts from Tunhuang in the British Museum* (xxv + 333 pp).[30] 85% of the manuscripts were of Buddhist texts, 3% Taoist, 12% secular or non-religious. "It was no light task," he wrote in 1941, "even in a physical sense, for the total length of the sheets which had constantly to be unrolled and rolled up again must have amounted to something between

---

[27] *The Sayings of Confucius: A New Translation of the Greater Part of the Confucian Analects*, with Introduction and Notes by Lionel Giles (London, 1907), pp. 26-8.

[28] Review of Margouliès, *Le Kou-wen Chinois*, in *BSOAS*, 4, 3 (1927), pp. 640-643.

[29] Herbert A. Giles, *Gems of Chinese Literature: Prose*, second edition (Shanghai and London, 1922).

[30] "He devoted the greater part of his available time and energy to studying the manuscripts, con-tinuing this work as his health permitted after his retirement." E. G. Pulleyblank, *BSOAS*, 22, 2, p. 409.

ten and twenty miles." A simpler introduction to the subject is provided in his booklet for the China Society, *Six Centuries at Tunhuang* (1944), based on a lecture delivered in October 1941.

Lionel Giles was a fluent and elegant translator, with a wide repertoire of expressions. Take this passage from one of his earliest published works, *The Sayings of Lao Tzu*:

> All men are radiant with happiness, as if enjoying a great feast, as if mounted on a tower in spring. I alone am still, and give as yet no sign of joy. I am like an infant which has not yet smiled, forlorn as one who has nowhere to lay his head. Other men have plenty, while I alone seem to have lost all. I am a man foolish in heart, dull and confused. Other men are full of light; I alone seem to be in darkness. Other men are alert; I alone seem listless. I am unsettled as the ocean, drifting as though I had no stopping-place. All men have their usefulness; I alone am stupid and clownish.[31]

One of his finest translations was an eloquent rendering of the Tang-dynasty poet Wei Zhuang's (c.836-c.910) long ballad-poem about the devastating sack of the city of Chang'an by the brigand Huang Chao in 881. Lionel's somewhat old-fashioned and restrained style as a translator enhances the relentless detail of the terror, the rape, and pillage. The poem in translation reads almost like a present-day news report from a war-zone.

> *Every home now runs with bubbling fountains of blood,*
> *Every place rings with a victim's shrieks—*
> *shrieks that cause the very earth to quake.*
>
> *Our western neighbor had a daughter—verily, a fair maiden!*
> *Sidelong glances flashed from her large limpid eyes,*
> *And when her toilet was done, she reflected the spring in her mirror;*
> *Young in years, she knew naught of the world outside her door.*
> *A ruffian comes leaping up the steps of her abode;*
> *Pulling her robe from one bare shoulder, he attempts*
> *To do her violence,*

---

[31] *The Sayings of Lao Tzu*, translated from the Chinese, with an Introduction, by Lionel Giles, Assistant at the British Museum (London, 1904), p. 54.

*But though dragged by her clothes, she refuses to pass out of the ver-*
*milion portal,*
*And thus with rouge and fragrant unguents she meets her death un-*
*der the knife.*

Like so much of his work, this translation was published in
the pages of a learned journal (*T'oung Pao*, 1924). The poem itself had long been lost, and Giles re-discovered it among the
Dunhuang materials he was working on at the Museum. His account of this "most romantic discovery" is to be found on pp.
21-23 of *Six Centuries at Tunhuang*. As he writes: "Such things
are brought home to us with peculiar poignancy in these days of
air-raids and bombing."[32]

The Giles translation of *The Art of War* was first published
in 1910, by Luzac & Co., the old London Orientalist publishing
house. Lionel dedicated it to his younger brother, Capt. Valentine Giles, officer in the Royal Engineers, "in the hope that a
work 2400 years old may yet contain lessons worth consideration by the soldier of today." It is one of his most thorough and
scholarly works, and unlike his various popular translations,
contains not only the complete Chinese text, but also an extensive and excellent textual apparatus and commentary. It is quite
remarkable how deeply and thoroughly Giles enters into the
(often intractable) text, recognising the quality of the Chinese
writing (and even identifying the occasional rhyming jingle—
see XII:16). In some ways, and surprisingly, this is a superior si-
nological achievement to anything by his father, H. A. Giles, the
great Cambridge Professor. The care with which Lionel reads,
translates, and sometimes synthesises the often rambling and
contradictory commentaries, is remarkable. On top of all of this,
he enlivens the book with many stimulating, sometimes con-
troversial editorial asides, references to episodes in western history, to Maréchal Turenne (1611-1675), Napoleon, Wellington,
the Confederate General "Stonewall" Jackson (1824-1863) and

---

[32] His translation has recently been reprinted in a more widely read anthology. See Minford &
Lau, *Chinese Classical Literature: An Anthology of Translations* (New York, 2000), pp. 933-944.

Baden-Powell (1857-1941) and his *Aids to Scouting*. Giles (like Professor Li Ling today at Peking University) was constantly on the look-out for contemporary resonances ("lessons worthy of consideration"), as when he saw the link between Sun Tzǔ's thinking and the development of "scouting" as a branch of army training. It is also worth remembering the historical and personal context in which he was translating: a mere ten years earlier, the Boxer Uprising was at its height and the Western legations in Peking were under siege; one of Lionel's other brothers, Lancelot, was serving as a young Student Interpreter in Peking, where he was decorated for gallantry in the defence of the Legation.[33] In Chapter XI, section 13, Lionel comments that the commentators' injunction not to rape and loot "may well cause us to blush for the Christian armies that entered Peking in 1900 A.D."

The book has been reprinted many times, but often in truncated form. This is the first time it has been offered in its entirety complete with Chinese characters, transcribed now not according to the old Wade-Giles system (refined by Lionel's father), but according to the modern standard method of romanisation, known as *Hanyu pinyin* (literally, "Chinese Language Spelling"). The great advantage of the new system is that it is universally used both in China and internationally, whereas the old system was exclusive to the Anglophone world, and is anyway now hardly used. The one exception to this rule is the name Sun Tzǔ, which has been kept in its old familiar form.

With this new edition, readers of *The Art of War* are in safe hands. They are presented with a reliable and readable translation from a seasoned reader of literary Chinese, and (most importantly) as they read they are able to consult in English a rich selection of traditional Chinese readings and commentaries. Together these form a sound basis on which the reader can reach conclusions, as opposed to the ready-made (and often unques-

---

[33] See Lancelot Giles, *The siege of the Peking legations: a diary*, edited with introduction: "Chinese anti-foreignism and the Boxer uprising," by L.R. Marchant, foreword by Sir R. Scott (Nedlands, Western Australia, 1970).

tioning) interpretations and instructions that tend to emerge from the numerous more recent versions.

Some of us today are striving to bring back into Chinese Studies something of the depth (and excitement) of the best early sinology, to create a New Sinology, that transcends the narrow concerns of the prevalent Social Sciences-based model.[34] We recognise (as did Lionel Giles) the urgency of applying the past to the present, the pressing need to understand today's China, as the world's rising power. In so doing, we are deeply aware of the need to understand the historical roots of China's contemporary consciousness. For these purposes, this work is a model study, scholarly but at the same time alive both to enduring humanistic concerns and to concrete present-day issues. It exemplifies ideals similar to those announced by Lionel's contemporary, the great humanist, scholar, translator and promoter of the League of Nations, Gilbert Murray, when he wrote in 1918:

> The scholar's special duty is to turn the written signs in which old poetry or philosophy is now enshrined back into living thought or feeling. He must so understand as to re-live.[35]

To go a little further back in time, Giles' work continues the grand tradition of Thomas Arnold, father of Mathew, and reforming headmaster of Rugby School, of whom Rex Warner wrote:

> When he [Arnold] spoke of Thucydides or Livy his mind was directed to the present as well as the past… In his hands education became deliberately "education for life."[36]

These are the very goals, this is the very breadth, to which the New Sinology also aspires. And this little classic, so old, and yet

---

[34] I refer especially to the courageous work of my colleague Geremie Barmé, who together with others has over the past few years begun the rebuilding of a New Sinology.

[35] Gilbert Murray, "Religio Grammatici: The Religion of a Man of Letters," Presidential Address to the Classical Association, January 8, 1918, collected in *Humanist Essays* (London, 1964). Murray was born in Sydney, Australia, in 1866, and died in 1957 at Oxford, where he had been Professor of Greek for nearly thirty years (1908-1936).

[36] Rex Warner, *English Public Schools* (London, 1946).

so relevant and popular today, is an ideal text for the purpose. Which brings us to the next fundamental tenet. To read this book in the original, one needs to know literary (or classical) Chinese—now rarely taught in the world's universities. This basic ability, some degree of familiarity with the literary language in which the majority of China's heritage is expressed, is essential for anyone professing to "understand" China. David Hawkes made the point eloquently in his Inaugural Lecture at Oxford:

> To lack either one of these two languages [the Classical and the Colloquial] would not be a mere closing of certain doors; it would cripple the researcher and render his labours nugatory...Just as the study of Colloquial literature constantly involves the student in reading memoirs, biographies, commentaries, and criticisms in Classical Chinese, so the study of Chinese antiquity necessitates his perusal of learned works by modern Chinese scholars written in the Colloquial language...

For Hawkes, this insistence on a broad literacy in both kinds of Chinese (since they are so inextricably interwoven) is but part of a broader vision:

> The study of Chinese is not merely the study of a foreign language. It is the study of another culture, another world—"une autre Europe au bout de l'Asie," Michelet called it.[37] To go into this storehouse of dazzling riches and select from among the resplendent vessels of massive gold one small brass ashtray made in Birmingham – this would be to show a want of imagination, a lack of love, that would unfit us for university teaching of any kind.[38]

To return to the book in hand: to read *The Art of War* at all intelligently in translation, one needs to be familiar with its historical and philosophical context. And then its contemporary relevance becomes even clearer and even greater. Lionel Giles succeeds in providing the essential materials for this sort of informed reading. There exists no better representation of the old

---

[37] Jules Michelet, *Histoire de France*, vol. VIII, 'Réforme" (Paris, 1855), p. 488.
[38] David Hawkes, ed. Minford and Wong, *Chinese: Classical, Modern and Humane* (Hong Kong, 1989), pp. 18-9.

tradition of sinology at its most typical and at its best.

Giles occasionally made errors of judgement. For example, he misjudged the early French translation of Amiot, which he deemed "little better than an imposture." In fact Amiot was working (as did many Jesuits) from a Manchu paraphrase of the eighteenth century, which makes his "free" and discursive version all the more interesting. Giles' recurring and often ill-tempered broadsides against the unfortunate Captain Calthrop and his flawed 1908 translation (he almost seems to have been emulating his notoriously irascible and often petulant father) are the only feature that mars and dates an otherwise splendid book. This defect is not to be found in his other writings.

John Minford

# Further Reading

(My own 2002 translation contains a lengthy annotated Reading List.)

## Translations

Ames, Roger T., *Sun-tzu: The Art of Warfare* (New York, 1993)

Amiot, Jean-Joseph-Marie, *Les Treize Articles sur l'Art Militaire, ouvrage composé en Chinois par Sun-tse* (Paris, 1782)

Cleary, Thomas, *The Art of War: Sun-tzu* (Boston, 1988)

Griffith, Samuel B., *Sun Tzu: The Art of War* (Oxford, 1963)

Lau, D. C., and Roger T. Ames, *Sun Pin, The Art of Warfare* (New York, 1996)

Lévi, Jean, *Sun Tzu, L'art de la Guerre* (Paris, 2000)

Minford, John, *The Art of War* (New York, 2002).

Sawyer, Ralph D., *The Complete Art of War: Sun Tzu, Sun Pin* (Boulder, 1996)

Yuan Shibing, *Sun Tzu's Art of War: The Modern Chinese Interpretation by General Tao Hanzhang* (Kuala Lumpur, 1991; reprinted, Wordsworth Classics, 1998)

Zhang Huimin, *Sun Tzǔ: The Art of War with Commentaries* (Beijing, 1995)

## Studies

Chaliand, Gérard, ed., *The Art of War in World History* (Berkeley, 1994)

Cowan, Connell and Gail Parent, *The Art of War for Lovers* (New York, 1998)

Jullien, François, *Traité de l'Efficacité* (Paris, 1997)

Khoo Kheng-hor, *Sun Tzu & Management* (Selangor, 1992)

Lewis, Mark Edward, *Sanctioned Violence in Early China* (Albany, 1990)

McNeilly, Mark, *Sun Tzu and the Art of Business* (New York, 1996)

Needham, Joseph, Robin Yates, et al., *Science and Civilisation in China, vol 5, part VI: Military Technology* (Cambridge, 1994)

# PREFACE

The seventh volume of "Mémoires concernant l'histoire, les sciences, les arts, les mœurs, les usages, &c., des Chinois"[1] is devoted to the Art of War, and contains, amongst other treatises, "Les Treize Articles de Sun-tse," translated from the Chinese by a Jesuit Father, Joseph Amiot. Père Amiot appears to have enjoyed no small reputation as a Sinologue in his day, and the field of his labors was certainly extensive. But his so-called translation of Sun Tzŭ, if placed side by side with the original, is seen at once to be little better than an imposture. It contains a great deal that Sun Tzŭ did not write, and very little indeed of what he did. Here is a fair specimen, taken from the opening sentences of chapter 5:

> *De l'habileté dans le gouvernement des Troupes.* Sun-tse dit: Ayez les noms de tous les Officiers tant généraux que subalternes; inscrivez-les dans un catalogue à part, avec la note des talents & de la capacité de chacun d'eux, afin de pouvoir les employer avec avantage lorsque l'occasion en sera venue. Faites en sorte que tous ceux que vous devez commander soient persuadés que votre principale attention est de les preserver de tout dommage. Les troupes que vous ferez avancer contre l'ennemi doivent être comme des pierres que vous lanceriez contre des oeufs. De vous à l'ennemi il ne doit y avoir d'autre difference que celle du fort au foible, du vuide au plein. Attaquez à découvert, mais soyez vainqueur en secret. Voilà en peu de mots en quoi consiste l'habileté & toute la perfection même du gouvernement des troupes.

Throughout the nineteenth century, which saw a wonderful development in the study of Chinese literature, no translator ventured to tackle Sun Tzŭ, although his work was known to be

---

[1] Published at Paris in 1782

highly valued in China as by far the oldest and best compendium of military science. It was not until the year 1905 that the first English translation, by Capt. E. F. Calthrop, R.F.A., appeared at Tokyo under the title "Sonshi" (the Japanese form of Sun Tzŭ[2]). Unfortunately, it was evident that the translator's knowledge of Chinese was far too scanty to fit him to grapple with the manifold difficulties of Sun Tzŭ. He himself plainly acknowledges that without the aid of two Japanese gentlemen "the accompanying translation would have been impossible." We can only wonder, then, that with their help it should have been so excessively bad. It is not merely a question of downright blunders, from which none can hope to be wholly exempt. Omissions were frequent; hard passages were willfully distorted or slurred over. Such offences are less pardonable. They would not be tolerated in any edition of a Greek or Latin classic, and a similar standard of honesty ought to be insisted upon in translations from Chinese.

From blemishes of this nature, at least, I believe that the present translation is free. It was not undertaken out of any inflated estimate of my own powers; but I could not help feeling that Sun Tzŭ deserved a better fate than had befallen him, and I knew that, at any rate, I could hardly fail to improve on the work of my predecessors. Towards the end of 1908, a new and revised edition of Capt. Calthrop's translation was published in London, this time, however, without any allusion to his Japanese collaborators. My first three chapters were then already in the printer's hands, so that the criticisms of Capt. Calthrop therein contained must be understood as referring to his earlier edition. In the subsequent chapters I have of course transferred my attention to the second edition. This is on the whole an improvement on the other, though there remains much that cannot pass muster. Some of the grosser blunders have been rectified and lacunae filled up, but on the other hand a certain number of

---

[2] A rather distressing Japanese flavor pervades the work throughout. Thus, King He Lu masquerades as "Katsuryo," Wu and Yue become "Go" and "Etsu," etc. etc.

new mistakes appear. The very first sentence of the introduction is startlingly inaccurate; and later on, while mention is made of "an army of Japanese commentators" on Sun Tzǔ (who are these, by the way?), not a word is vouchsafed about the Chinese commentators, who nevertheless, I venture to assert, form a much more numerous and infinitely more important "army."

A few special features of the present volume may now be noticed. In the first place, the text has been cut up into numbered paragraphs, both in order to facilitate cross-reference and for the convenience of students generally. The division follows broadly that of Sun Xingyan's edition; but I have sometimes found it desirable to join two or more of his paragraphs into one. From the mass of native commentary my aim has been to extract the cream only, adding the Chinese text here and there when it seemed to present points of literary interest. Though constituting in itself an important branch of Chinese literature, very little commentary of this kind has hitherto been made directly accessible by translation.[3]

I may say in conclusion that, owing to the printing off of my sheets as they were completed, the work has not had the benefit of a final revision. On a review of the whole, without modifying the substance of my criticisms, I might have been inclined in a few instances to temper their asperity. Having chosen to wield a bludgeon, however, I shall not cry out if in return I am visited with more than a rap over the knuckles. Indeed, I have been at some pains to put a sword into the hands of future opponents by scrupulously giving either text or reference for every passage translated. A scathing review, even from the pen of the Shanghai critic who despises "mere translations," would not, I must confess, be altogether unwelcome. For, after all, the worst fate I shall have to dread is that which befell the ingenious paradoxes of George in *The Vicar of Wakefield*.

---

[3] A notable exception is to be found in Biot's translation of the *Zhou Li*.

# INTRODUCTION

## Sun Tzǔ and His Book

Sima Qian gives the following biography of Sun Tzǔ[1]:

Sun Tzǔ Wu 孫子武 was a native of the Qi State. His *Art of War* brought him to the notice of He Lu 闔盧, King of Wu 吳.[2] He Lu said to him: I have carefully perused your 13 chapters. May I submit your theory of managing soldiers to a slight test? Sun Tzǔ replied: You may. He Lu asked: May the test be applied to women? The answer was again in the affirmative, so arrangements were made to bring 180 ladies out of the Palace. Sun Tzǔ divided them into two companies, and placed one of the King's favorite concubines at the head of each. He then bade them all take spears in their hands, and addressed them thus: I presume you know the difference between front and back, right hand and left hand? The girls replied: Yes. Sun Tzǔ went on: When I say "Eyes front," you must look straight ahead. When I say, "Left turn," you must face towards your left hand. When I say, "Right turn," you must face towards your right hand. When I say "About turn," you must face round towards the back. Again the girls assented. The words of command having been thus explained, he set up the halberds and battles-axes in order to begin the drill. Then, to the sound of drums, he gave the order "Right turn." But the girls only burst out laughing. Sun Tzǔ said: If words of command are not clear and distinct, if orders are not thoroughly understood, then the general is to blame. So he started drilling them again, and this time gave the order "Left turn," whereupon the girls once more burst into fits of laughter. Sun Tzǔ said: If words of command are not clear and distinct, if orders are not thoroughly understood, the general is to blame. But if his orders *are* clear, and the soldiers nevertheless disobey, then it

---

[1] *Shiji juan*, 65.
[2] Also written He Lü 闔閭. He reigned from 514 to 496 B.C.

is the fault of their officers. So saying, he ordered the leaders of the two companies to be beheaded. Now the King of Wu was watching the scene from the top of a raised pavilion; and when he saw that his favorite concubines were about to be executed, he was greatly alarmed and hurriedly sent down the following message: We are now quite satisfied as to our general's ability to handle troops. If We are bereft of these two concubines, our meat and drink will lose their savor. It is our wish that they shall not be beheaded. Sun Tzŭ replied: Having once received His Majesty's commission to be general of his forces, there are certain commands of His Majesty which, acting in that capacity, I am unable to accept. Accordingly, he had the two leaders beheaded, and straightway installed the pair next in order as leaders in their place. When this had been done, the drum was sounded for the drill once more; and the girls went through all the evolutions, turning to the right or to the left, marching ahead or wheeling back, kneeling or standing, with perfect accuracy and precision, not venturing to utter a sound. Then Sun Tzŭ sent a messenger to the King saying: Your soldiers, Sire, are now properly drilled and disciplined, and ready for Your Majesty's inspection. They can be put to any use that their sovereign may desire; bid them go through fire and water, and they will not disobey. But the King replied: Let our general cease drilling and return to camp. As for us, We have no wish to come down and inspect the troops. Thereupon Sun Tzŭ said: The King is only fond of words, and cannot translate them into deeds. After that, He Lu saw that Sun Tzŭ was one who knew how to handle an army, and finally appointed him general. In the West, he defeated the Chu State and forced his way into Ying, the capital; to the north, he put fear into the States of Qi and Jin, and spread his fame abroad amongst the feudal princes. And Sun Tzŭ shared in the might of the King.

About Sun Tzŭ himself this is all that Sima Qian has to tell us in this chapter. But he proceeds to give a biography of his descendant, Sun Bin 孫臏, born about a hundred years after his famous ancestor's death, and also the outstanding military genius of his time. The historian speaks of him too as Sun Tzŭ, and in his preface we read: "Sun Tzŭ had his feet cut off and yet continued to discuss the art of war."[3] 孫子臏腳而論兵法 It seems likely, then, that "Pin" was a nickname bestowed on him after his mutilation, unless indeed the story was invented in order to account for the name. The crowning incident of his career, the crushing defeat of his treacherous rival Pang Juan, will be found briefly related on p. 91.

To return to the elder Sun Tzŭ. He is mentioned in two other passages of the *Shiji* :

> In the third year of his reign [512 B.C.] He Lu, King of Wu, took the field with Zixu 子胥 [i.e. Wu Yuan 伍員] and Bo Pei 伯嚭, and attacked Chu. He captured the town of Shu 舒 and slew the two prince's sons who had formerly been generals of Wu. He was then meditating a descent on Ying 郢 [the capital]; but the general Sun Wu said: "The army is exhausted.[4] It is not yet possible. We must wait"....[5][After further successful fighting,] "in the ninth year [506 B.C.], King He Lu of Wu addressed Wu Zixu and Sun Wu, saying: "Formerly, you declared that it was not yet possible for us to enter Ying. Is the time ripe now?" The two men replied: "Chu's general, Zichang 子常,[6] is grasping and covetous, and the princes of Tang 唐 and Cai 蔡 both have a grudge against him. If Your Majesty has resolved to make a grand attack, you must win over Tang and Cai, and then you may succeed." He Lu followed this advice, [beat Chu in five pitched battles and marched into Ying].[7]

This is the latest date at which anything is recorded of Sun Wu. He does not appear to have survived his patron, who died from the effects of a wound in 496.

In the chapter entitled 律書 (the earlier portion of which M. Chavannes believes to be a fragment of a treatise on Military Weapons), there occurs this passage[8]:

---

[3] *Shiji*, juan 130, f. 6 *r°*.

[4] I note that M. Chavannes translates 民勞 " le peuple est épuisé." But in Sun Tzŭ's own book (see especially VII §§ 24–26) the ordinary meaning of 民 is "army," and this, I think, is more suitable here.

[5] These words are given also in Wu Zixu's biography. Juan 66, fol. 3 *r°*.

[6] The appellation of Nang Wa 囊瓦.

[7] *Shiji*, juan 31, fol. 6 *r°*.

[8] *Ibid.* juan 25, fol. I *r°*.

From this time onward, a number of famous soldiers arose, one after the other: Gao-fan 咎犯,[9] who was employed by the Jin State; Wangzi, in the service of Qi; and Sun Wu, in the service of Wu. These men developed and threw light upon the principles of war 申明軍約).

It is obvious that Sima Qian at least[10] had no doubt about the reality of Sun Wu as an historical personage; and with one exception, to be noticed presently, he is by far the most important authority on the period in question. It will not be necessary, therefore, to say much of such a work as the *Wu Yue Chunqiu* 吳越春秋, which is supposed to have been written by Chao Ye 趙曄 of the 1st century A.D. The attribution is somewhat doubtful; but even if it were otherwise, his account would be of little value, based as it is on the *Shiji* and expanded with romantic details. The story of Sun Tzǔ will be found, for what it is worth, in chapter 2. The only new points in it worth noting are: 1) Sun Tzǔ was first recommended to He Lu by Wu Zixu. 2) He is called a native of Wu.[11] 3) He had previously lived a retired life, and his contemporaries were unaware of his ability.[12]

The following passage occurs in Huainanzi 淮南子: "When sovereign and ministers show perversity of mind, it is impossible even for a Sun Tzǔ to encounter the foe."[13] Assuming that this work is genuine (and hitherto no doubt has been cast upon it), we have here the earliest direct reference to Sun Tzǔ, for Huainanzi died in 122 B.C., many years before the *Shiji* was given to the world.

Liu Xiang 劉向 (B.C. 80-9) in his 新序 says: "The reason why Sun Wu at the head of 30,000 men beat Chu with 200,000 is that the latter were undisciplined."[14]

---

[9] The appellation of Hu Yan 狐偃, mentioned in juan 39 under the year 637.

[10] Wangzi Chengfu 王子城父, juan 32, year 607.

[11] The mistake is natural enough. Native critics refer to the 越絕書, work of the Han dynasty, which says (juan 2, fol. 3*v*° of my edition): "Ten *li* outside the *Wu* gate [of the city of 吳 Wu, now Suzhou in Jiangsu] there is a great mound, raised to commemorate the entertainment of Sun Wu of Ch'i, who excelled in the art of war, by the King of Wu,"... 巫門外大冢吳王客齊孫武冢也去縣十里善為兵法.

[12] 孫子者吳人也善為兵法辟幽居世人莫知其能.

[13] 君臣乖心則孫子不能以應敵.

Deng Mingshi 鄧名世 in his 姓名辨證書 (completed in 1134) informs us that the surname 孫 was bestowed on Sun Wu's grandfather by Duke Jing 景公 of Qi [547-490 B.C.]. Sun Wu's father Sun Ping 馮, rose to be a Minister of State in Qi, and Sun Wu himself, whose style was Changqing 長卿, fled to Wu on account of the rebellion which was being fomented by the kindred of Tian Bao 田鮑. He had three sons, of whom the second, named Ming 明, was the father of Sun Pin. According to this account, then, Bin was the grandson of Wu,[15] which, considering that Sun Bin's victory over Wei 魏 was gained in 341 B.C., may be dismissed as chronologically impossible. Whence these data were obtained by Deng Mingshi I do not know, but of course no reliance whatever can be placed in them.

An interesting document which has survived from the close of the Han period is the short preface written by the great Cao Cao 曹操, or Wei Wudi 魏武帝, for his edition of Sun Tzŭ. I shall give it in full:

I have heard that the ancients used bows and arrows to their advantage.[16] The *Lunyu* says: "There must be a sufficiency of military strength."[17] The *Shu Jing* mentions "the army" among the "eight objects of government."[18] The *Yijing* says: "師 'army' indicates firmness and justice; the experienced leader will have good fortune."[19]

The *Shi Jing* says: "The King rose majestic in his wrath, and he marshaled his troops."[20] The Yellow Emperor, Tang the Completer and Wu Wang all used spears and battle-axes in order to succor their generation. The *Sima Fa* says: "If one man slay another of set

---

[14] 孫武以三萬破楚二十萬者楚無法故也.

[15] The *Shiji*, on the other hand, says: 臏亦孫武之後世子孫也. I may remark in passing that the name 武 for one who was a great warrior is just as suspicious as 臏 for a man who had his feet cut off.

[16] An allusion to 易經, 繫辭, II. 2: "They attached strings to wood to make bows, and sharpened wood to make arrows. The use of bows and arrows is to keep the Empire in awe." 弦木為弧剡木為矢弧矢之利以威天下.

[17] 論語 XII. 7.

[18] 書經 V. iv. 7.

[19] 易經, 7th diagram (師).

[20] 詩經 III. I. vii. 5.

purpose, he himself may rightfully be slain."[21] He who relies solely on warlike measures shall be exterminated; he who relies solely on peaceful measures shall perish. Instances of this are Fu Chai[22] on the one hand and Yan Wang[23] on the other. In military matters, the Sage's rule is normally to keep the peace, and to move his forces only when occasion requires. He will not use armed force unless driven to it by necessity.[24]

Many books have I read on the subject of war and fighting; but the work composed by Sun Wu is the profoundest of them all. [Sun Tzŭ was a native of the Qi state, his personal name was Wu. He wrote the *Art of War* in 13 chapters for He Lü, King of Wu. Its principles were tested on women, and he was subsequently made a general. He led an army westwards, crushed the Chu State and entered Ying the capital. In the north, he kept Qi and Jin in awe. A hundred years and more after his time, Sun Bin lived. He was a descendant of Wu.][25] In his treatment of deliberation and planning, the importance of rapidity in taking the field,[26] clearness of conception, and depth of design, Sun Tzŭ stands beyond the reach of carping criticism. My contemporaries, however, have failed to grasp the full meaning of his instructions, and while putting into practice the smaller details in which his work abounds, they have overlooked its essential purport. That is the motive that has led me to outline a rough explanation of the whole.[27]

---

[21] 司馬法 juan I (仁本) *ad init.* The text of the passage in the *Tu Shu* 圖書 (戎政典, juan 85) is: 是故殺人安人殺之可也.

[22] The son and successor of He Lu. He was finally defeated and overthrown by Gou Jian 勾踐, King of Yue, in 473 B.C. See *post*.

[23] King Yan of Xu 徐, a fabulous being, of whom Sun Xingyan says in his preface: 仁而敗 "His humanity brought him to destruction." See *Shiji*, juan 5 f. I v (°). And M. Chavannes' note, *Mémoires Historiques*, tom. II, p. 8.

[24] *Tu Shu, ibid.* juan 90: 操聞上古有弧矢之利論語曰足兵尚書八政曰師易曰師貞丈人吉 詩曰王赫斯怒爰征其旅黃帝湯　武咸用干戚以　濟世也司馬法曰人故殺人殺之可也恃武 者滅恃文者亡夫差偃王是也聖人之用兵在戢而時動不得已而用之.

[25] The passage I have put in brackets is omitted in the *Tu Shu*, and may be an interpolation. It was known, however, to Zhang Shoujie 張守節 of the Tang dynasty, and appears in the *Taiping Yulan*.

[26] Cao Gong seems to be thinking of the first part of chap. II, perhaps especially of § 8.

[27] 吾觀兵書戰策多矣孫武所著深矣孫子者齊人也名武為吳王闔閭作兵法一十三篇 試之婦人卒以為將西破強楚入郢北威齊晉後百威餘　有孫　臏是武之後也審計重舉明畫 深圖不可相誣而但世人未之深亮訓說文煩富行於世者失其旨要故撰為略解焉.

One thing to be noticed in the above is the explicit statement that the 13 chapters were specially composed for King He Lu. This is supported by the internal evidence of I, § 15, in which it seems clear that some ruler is addressed.

In the bibliographical section of the *Han Shu*,[28] there is an entry which has given rise to much discussion: "The works of Sun Tzŭ of Wu in 82 *pian* (or chapters) 吳孫子八十二篇圖九卷, with diagrams in 9 *juan*." It is evident that this cannot be merely the 13 chapters known to Sima Qian, or those we possess today. Zhang Shoujie in his 史記正義 refers to an edition of Sun Tzŭ's 兵法 of which the "13 chapters" formed the first *juan*, adding that there were two other *juan* besides.[29] This has brought forth a theory, that the bulk of these 82 chapters consisted of other writings of Sun Tzŭ—we should call them apocryphal—similar to the *Wen Da* 問答, of which a specimen dealing with the Nine Situations[30] is preserved in the *Tongdian* 通典, and another in Heshi's commentary. It is suggested that before his interview with He Lu, Sun Tzŭ had only written the 13 chapters, but afterwards composed a sort of exegesis in the form of question and answer between himself and the King. Bi Yixun 畢以珣, author of the *Sunzi xulu* 孫子敘錄, backs this up with a quotation from the *Wu Yue Chunqiu*: "The King of Wu summoned Sun Tzŭ, and asked him questions about the art of war. Each time he set forth a chapter of his work, the King could not find words enough to praise him."[31] As he points out, if the whole work was expounded on the same scale as in the above-mentioned fragments, the total number of chapters could not fail to be considerable.[32] Then the numerous other treatises attributed to Sun Tzŭ[33] might also be included. The fact that the *Han Zhih* mentions no work of Sun

---

[28] 漢書藝文志、兵權謀.

[29] The 宋藝文志 mentions two editions of Sun Tzŭ in 3 *juan,* namely 孫武孫子 and 朱服校定孫子.

[30] See chap. XI.

[31] 吳王召孫子問以兵法每陳一篇王不知口之稱善.

[32] 按此皆釋九地篇義辭意甚詳故其篇帙不能不多也.

Tzŭ except the 82 *pian*, whereas the Sui and Tang bibliographies give the titles of others in addition to the "13 chapters," is good proof, Bi Yixun thinks, that all of these were contained in the 82 *pian*. Without pinning our faith to the accuracy of details supplied by the *Wu Yue Chunqiu*, or admitting the genuineness of any of the treatises cited by Bi Yixun, we may see in this theory a probable solution of the mystery. Between Sima Qian and Ban Gu there was plenty of time for a luxuriant crop of forgeries to have grown up under the magic name of Sun Tzŭ, and the 82 *pian* may very well represent a collected edition of these lumped together with the original work. It is also possible, though less likely, that some of them existed in the time of the earlier historian and were purposely ignored by him.[34]

Du Mu, after Cao Gong the most important commentator on Sun Tzŭ, composed the preface to his edition[35] about the middle of the ninth century. After a somewhat lengthy defense of the military art,[36] he comes at last to Sun Tzŭ himself, and makes one or two very startling assertions:"The writings of Sun Wu," he says, "originally comprised several hundred thousand words, but Cao Cao, the Emperor Wu Wei, pruned away all redundancies and wrote out the essence of the whole, so as to form a single book in 13 chapters."[37] He goes on to remark that Cao Cao's commentary on Sun Tzŭ leaves a certain proportion of difficulties unexplained. This, in Du Mu's opinion, does not necessarily imply that he was unable to furnish a complete commentary.[38] According to the *Wei Zhi*, Cao himself wrote a book on war in something over 100,000 words, known as the 新書. It appears to

---

[33] Such as the 八陣圖, quoted in Zheng Xuan's 鄭玄 commentary on the *Zhou Li*, the 戰鬬大甲兵法 and 兵法雜占, mentioned in the *Sui Zhi* 隋志, and the 三十二壘經, in the *Xin Tang Zhi*.

[34] On the other hand, it is noteworthy that *Wuzi* 吳子, which is now in 6 chapters, has 48 assigned to it in the *Han Zhi*. Likewise, the *Zhong Yong* 中庸 is credited with 49 chapters, though now in one only. In the case of such very short works, one is tempted to think that 篇 might simply mean "Leaves."

[35] See *Tu Shu*, 經籍典, juan 442, 彙考 2.

[36] An extract will be found on p. lx.

[37] 武所著書凡數十萬言曹魏武帝削其繁剩筆其精切凡十三篇成為一編.

[38] 其所為注解十不釋一此蓋非曹不能盡注解也.

have been of such exceptional merit that he suspects Cao to have used for it the surplus material which he had found in Sun Tzŭ. He concludes, however, by saying: "The *Xin Shu* is now lost, so that the truth cannot be known for certain."[39]

Du Mu's conjecture seems to be based on a passage in the 漢官解詁 "Wei Wudi strung together Sun Wu's Art of War,"[40] which in turn may have resulted from a misunderstanding of the final words of Cao Gong's preface: 故撰為略解焉. This, as Sun Xingyan points out,[41] is only a modest way of saying that he made an explanatory paraphrase,[42] or in other words, wrote a commentary on it. On the whole, the theory has met with very little acceptance. Thus, the 四庫全書[43] says: "The mention of the 13 chapters in the *Shiji* shows that they were in existence before the *Han Zhi*, and that later accretions are not to be considered part of the original work. Du Mu's assertion can certainly not be taken as proof."[44]

There is every reason to suppose, then, that the 13 chapters existed in the time of Sima Qian practically as we have them now. That the work was then well known he tells us in so many words: "Sun Tzŭ's 13 Chapters and Wu Qi's Art of War are the two books that people commonly refer to on the subject of military matters. Both of them are widely distributed, so I will not discuss them here."[45] But as we go further back, serious difficulties begin to arise. The salient fact which has to be faced is that the *Zuozhuan*, the great contemporary record, makes no mention whatever of Sun Wu, either as a general or as a writer. It is natural, in view of this awkward circumstance, that many scholars should not only

---

[39] 予尋魏志見曹自作兵書十餘萬言諸將征戰皆以新書從事從令者克捷違教者負敗意曹自於新書中馳驟其說自成一家事業不欲隨孫武後盡解其書不然者曹其不能耶今新書已亡不可復知.

[40] 魏氏瑣連孫武之法.

[41] See 孫子兵法序.

[42] 謙言解其觕略.

[43] Juan 99, fol. 5 r°.

[44] 然史記稱十三篇在漢志之前不得以後來附益者為本書牧之言固未可以為據也.

[45] *Shiji*, juan 65 *ad fin*: 世俗所稱師旅皆道孫子十三篇吳起兵法世多有故弗論.

cast doubt on the story of Sun Wu as given in the *Shiji*, but even show themselves frankly skeptical as to the existence of the man at all. The most powerful presentment of this side of the case is to be found in the following disquisition by Ye Shuixin 葉水心[46]:

It is stated in Sima Qian's history that Sun Wu was a native of the Qi State, and employed by Wu and that in the reign of He Lü he crushed Chu, entered Ying, and was a great general. But in Zuo's Commentary no Sun Wu appears at all. It is true that Zuo's Commentary need not contain absolutely everything that other histories contain. But Zuo has not omitted to mention vulgar plebeians and hireling ruffians such as Ying Kaoshu,[47] Cao Gui,[48] Zhu Zhiwa[49] and Zhuan Shezhu.[50] In the case of Sun Wu, whose fame and achievements were so brilliant, the omission is much more glaring. Again, details are given, in their due order, about his contemporaries Wu Yuan and the Minister Pei.[51] Is it credible that Sun Wu alone should have been passed over?[52]

In point of literary style, Sun Tzŭ's work belongs to the same school as *Guanzi*,[53] the *Liu Tao*,[54] and the *Yue Yu*,[55] and may have been the production of some private scholar living towards the end of the "Spring and Autumn" or the beginning of the "Warring States" period.[56] The story that his precepts were actually applied by the Wu State, is merely the outcome of big talk on the part of his followers.[57]

From the flourishing period of the Zhou dynasty[58] down to the

---

[46] Yeh Shi 葉適 of the Song dynasty [1151-1223]. See 文獻通考, juan 221, ff. 7,8.

[47] See *Zuozhuan*, 隱公, I.3 *ad init*. He hardly deserves to be bracketed with assassins.

[48] See notes to VII. 27 and XI. 28.

[49] See *Zuozhuan*, 僖公, XXX. 5.

[50] See XI. 28. Zhuan Zhu is the abbreviated form of his name.

[51] *I. e.* Bo Pei. See *ante*.

[52] 遷載孫武齊人而用於吳在闔閭時破楚入郢為大將按左氏無孫武他書所有左氏不必盡有然顧考叔曹劌燭之武鱄設諸之流微賤暴用事左氏未嘗遺而武功名章灼如此乃更闕又同時伍員豁一一銓次乃獨不及武邪.

[53] The nucleus of this work is probably genuine, though large additions have been made by later hands. Guan Zhong died in 645 B.C.

[54] See *Bibliography*.

[55] I do not know what work this is, unless it be the last chapter of the 國語. Why that chapter should be singled out, however, is not clear.

[56] About 480 B.C.

[57] 詳味孫子與管子六韜越語相出入春秋末戰國初山林處士所為其言得用於吳者其徒夸大之說也.

[58] That is, I suppose, the age of Wu Wang and Zhou Gong.

time of the "Spring and Autumn," all military commanders were statesmen as well, and the class of professional generals, for conducting external campaigns, did not then exist. It was not until the period of the "Six States"[59] that this custom changed. Now although Wu was an uncivilized State, is it conceivable that Zuo should have left unrecorded the fact that Sun Wu was a great general and yet held no civil office? What we are told, therefore, about Rangju[60] and Sun Wu, is not authentic matter, but the reckless fabrication of theorizing pundits. The story of He Lü's experiment on the women, in particular, is utterly preposterous and incredible.[61]

Ye Shuixin represents Sima Qian as having said that Sun Wu crushed Chu and entered Ying. This is not quite correct. No doubt the impression left on the reader's mind is that he at least shared in these exploits; but the actual subject of the verbs 破, 入, 威 and 顯 is certainly 闔廬, as is shown by the next words: 孫子與有力焉.[62] The fact may or may not be significant; but it is nowhere explicitly stated in the *Shiji* either that Sun Tzǔ was general on the occasion of the taking of Ying, or that he even went there at all. Moreover, as we know that Wu Yuan and Bo Pei both took part in the expedition, and also that its success was largely due to the dash and enterprise of Fu Gai 夫槩, He Lu's younger brother, it is not easy to see how yet another general could have played a very prominent part in the same campaign.

Chen Zhensun 陳振孫 of the Song dynasty has the note[63]:

> Military writers look upon Sun Wu as the father of their art. But the fact that he does not appear in the *Zuozhuan*, although he is said to have served under He Lü King of Wu, makes it uncertain what period he really belonged to.[64]

---

[59] In the 3rd century B.C.

[60] Sima Rangju, whose family name was Tian 田, lived in the latter half of the 6th century B.C., and is also believed to have written a work on war. See *Shiji*, juan 64.

[61] 自周之盛至春秋凡將兵者必與聞國政未有特將於外者六國時此制始改吳雖蠻夷而孫武為大將乃不為命卿而左氏無傳焉可乎故凡謂穰苴孫武者皆辯士妄相標指非事實其言闔閭試以婦人尤為奇險不足信.

[62] See the end of the passage quoted from the *Shiji* on p. xii.

[63] In the 書錄解題, a classified catalog of his family library.

He also says:

The works of Sun Wu and Wu Qi may be of genuine antiquity.[65]

It is noticeable that both Ye Shuixin and Chen Zhensun, while rejecting the personality of Sun Wu as he figures in Sima Qian's history, are inclined to accept the date traditionally assigned to the work which passes under his name. The author of the *Xu Lu* fails to appreciate this distinction, and consequently his bitter attack on Chen Zhensun really misses its mark. He makes one or two points, however, which certainly tell in favor of the high antiquity of our "13 chapters." "Sun Tzŭ," he says, "must have lived in the age of Jing Wang [519-476], because he is frequently plagiarized in subsequent works of the Zhou, Qin, and Han dynasties."[66] The two most shameless offenders in this respect are Wu Qi and Huainanzi, both of them important historical personages in their day. The former lived only a century after the alleged date of Sun Tzŭ, and his death is known to have taken place in 381 B.C. It was to him, according to Liu Xiang, that Zeng Shen 曾申 delivered the *Zuozhuan*, which had been entrusted to him by its author.[67] Now the fact that quotations from the *Art of War*, acknowledged or otherwise, are to be found in so many authors of different epochs, establishes a very strong probability that there was some common source anterior to them all—in other words, that Sun Tzŭ's treatise was already in existence towards the end of the 5th century B.C. Further proof of Sun Tzŭ's

---

[64] See *Wen Hsine Tongkao*, juan 221, f 9rº: 世之言兵者祖孫武然孫武事與闔閭而不見於左傳不知果何時人也.

[65] See *Hsü Lu*, f. 14 rº: 孫吳或是古書.

[66] 按孫子生於敬王之代故周秦兩漢諸書皆襲用其文. Here is a list of the passages in Sun Tzŭ from which either the substance or the actual words have been appropriated by early authors: VII. 9; IX. 17; I. 24 (戰國策). IX. 23; IX. 1, 3, 7; V. 1; III. 18; XI. 58; VII. 31; VII. 24; VII26; IX. 4 *(bis)* (吳子). III. 8; IV 7 (尉繚子) VII. 19; V. 14; III 2 (鶡冠子). III. 8; XI. 2; I. 19; XI. 58; X.10 & VI. 1 (史記. Two of the above are given as quotations). V. 13; IV. 2 (呂氏春秋). IX 11, 12; XI. 30; I. 13; VII. 19 & IV. 7; VII. 32; VII. 25; IV. 20 & V. 23; IX. 43; V. 15; VII. 26; V. 4 & XII. 39; VIII. 11; VI. 4 (淮南子). V.4 (太元經). II. 20; X. 14 (潛夫論).

[67] See Legge's Classics, vol. V, prolegomena p. 27. Legge thinks that the *Zuozhuan* must have been written in the 5th century, but not before 424 B.C.

antiquity is furnished by the archaic or wholly obsolete meanings attaching to a number of the words he uses. A list of these, which might perhaps be extended, is given in the *Xu Lu*; and though some of the interpretations are doubtful, the main argument is hardly affected thereby.[68] Again, it must not be forgotten that Ye Shuixin, a scholar and critic of the first rank, deliberately pronounces the style of the 13 chapters to belong to the early part of the fifth century. Seeing that he is actually engaged in an attempt to disprove the existence of Sun Wu himself, we may be sure that he would not have hesitated to assign the work to a later date had he not honestly believed the contrary. And it is precisely on such a point that the judgment of an educated Chinaman will carry most weight. Other internal evidence is not far to seek. Thus, in XIII. § 1, there is an unmistakable allusion to the ancient system of land-tenure which had already passed away by the time of Mencius, who was anxious to see it revived in a modified form.[69] The only warfare Sun Tzŭ knows is that carried on between the various feudal princes (諸侯), in which armored chariots play a large part. Their use seems to have entirely died out before the end of the Zhou dynasty. He speaks as a man of Wu, a state that ceased to exist as early as 473 B.C. On this I shall touch presently.

But once refer the work to the 5th century or earlier, and the chances of its being other than a *bona fide* production are sensibly diminished. The great age of forgeries did not come until long after. That it should have been forged in the period immediately following 473 is particularly unlikely, for no one, as a rule, hastens to identify himself with a lost cause. As for Ye Shuixin's theory, that the author was a literary recluse,[70] that seems to me

---

[68] The instances quoted are: III. 14, 15: 同 is said to be equivalent to 冒; II. 15: 箕 = 其; VII. 28: 歸 = 息; XI 60: 詳 = 佯; XI. 24: the use of 鬥 instead of 鬭 (the later form); XI. 64: 誅 = 治; IX. 3: 絕 = 越; III.11: 周 and 隙 antithetically opposed in the sense of 無缺 and 有缺; XI. 56: 犯 = 動; XI. 31: 方 = 縛.

[69] See *Mencius* III. 1 iii. 13-20.

[70] 山林處士 need not be pressed to mean an actual dweller in the mountains. I think it simply denotes a person living a retired life and standing aloof from public affairs.

quite untenable. If one thing is more apparent than another after reading the maxims of Sun Tzŭ, it is that their essence has been distilled from a large store of personal observation and experience. They reflect the mind not only of a born strategist, gifted with a rare faculty of generalization, but also of a practical soldier closely acquainted with the military conditions of his time. To say nothing of the fact that these sayings have been accepted and endorsed by all the greatest captains of Chinese history, they offer a combination of freshness and sincerity, acuteness and common sense, which quite excludes the idea that they were artificially concocted in the study. If we admit, then, that the 13 chapters were the genuine production of a military man living towards the end of the "Chunqiu" period, are we not bound, in spite of the silence of the *Zuozhuan*, to accept Sima Qian's account in its entirety? In view of his high repute as a sober historian, must we not hesitate to assume that the records he drew upon for Sun Wu's biography were false and untrustworthy? The answer, I fear, must be in the negative. There is still one grave, if not fatal, objection to the chronology involved in the story as told in the *Shiji*, which, so far as I am aware, nobody has yet pointed out. There are two passages in Sun Tzŭ in which he alludes to contemporary affairs. The first is in VI. § 21:

> Though according to my estimate the soldiers of Yue exceed our own in number, that shall advantage them nothing in the matter of victory. I say then that victory can be achieved.

The other is in XI. § 30:

> Asked if an army can be made to imitate the shuairan, I should answer, Yes. For the men of Wu and the men of Yue are enemies; yet if they are crossing a river in the same boat and are caught by a storm, they will come to each other's assistance just as the left hand helps the right.

These two paragraphs are extremely valuable as evidence of the date of composition. They assign the work to the period of the struggle between Wu and Yue. So much has been observed by Bi Yixun. But what has hitherto escaped notice is that they also seriously impair the credibility of Sima Qian's narrative. As we have seen above, the first positive date given in connection with Sun Wu is 512 B.C. He is then spoken of as a general, acting as confidential adviser to He Lu, so that his alleged introduction to that monarch had already taken place, and of course the 13 chapters must have been written earlier still. But at that time, and for several years after, down to the capture of Ying in 506, Chu 楚, and not Yue, was the great hereditary enemy of Wu. The two states, Chu and Wu, had been constantly at war for over half a century,[71] whereas the first war between Wu and Yue was waged only in 510,[72] and even then was no more than a short interlude sandwiched in the midst of the fierce struggle with Chu. Now Chu is not mentioned in the 13 chapters at all. The natural inference is that they were written at a time when Yue had become the prime antagonist of Wu, that is, after Chu had suffered the great humiliation of 506. At this point, a table of dates may be found useful.

| B.C. | |
|---|---|
| 514 | Accession of He Lu. |
| 512 | He Lu attacks Chu, but is dissuaded from entering Ying 郢, the capital. *Shiji* mentions Sun Wu as general. |
| 511 | Another attack on Chu. |
| 510 | Wu makes a successful attack on Yue. This is the first war between the two states. |
| 509 or 508 | Chu invades Wu, but is signally defeated at Yuzhang 豫章. |
| 506 | He Lu attacks Chu with the aid of Tang and Cai. Decisive battle of Boju 柏舉, and capture of Ying. Last mention of Sun Wu in *Shiji*. |

---

[71] When Wu first appears in the *Chun Qiu* in 584, it is already at variance with its powerful neighbour. The *Chun Qiu* first mentions Yue in 537, the *Zuozhuan* in 601.

[72] This is explicitly stated in the *Zuozhuan*, 昭公 XXXII, 2: 夏吳伐越始用師於越也.

| B.C. | |
|---|---|
| 505 | Yue makes a raid on Wu in the absence of its army. Wu is beaten by Qin and evacuates Ying. |
| 504 | He Lu sends Fu Chai 夫差 to attack Chu. |
| 497 | Gou Jian 勾踐 becomes King of Yue. |
| 496 | Wu attacks Yue, but is defeated by Gou Jian at Zuili 檇李. He Lu is killed. |
| 494 | Fu Chai defeats Gou Jian in the great battle of Fujiao 夫椒, and enters the capital of Yue. |
| 485 or 484 | Gou Jian renders homage to Wu. Death of Wu Zixu. |
| 482 | Gou Jian invades Wu in the absence of Fu Chai. |
| 478 or 476 | Further attacks by Yue on Wu. |
| 475 | Gou Jian lays siege to the capital of Wu. |
| 473 | Final defeat and extinction of Wu. |

The sentence quoted above from VI. § 21 hardly strikes me as one that could have been written in the full flush of victory. It seems rather to imply that, for the moment at least, the tide had turned against Wu, and that she was getting the worst of the struggle. Hence we may conclude that our treatise was not in existence in 505, before which date Yue does not appear to have scored any notable success against Wu. He Lu died in 496, so that if the book was written for him, it must have been during the period 505-496, when there was a lull in the hostilities, Wu having presumably been exhausted by its supreme effort against Chu. On the other hand, if we choose to disregard the tradition connecting Sun Wu's name with He Lu, it might equally well have seen the light between 490 and 494, or possibly in the period 482-473, when Yue was once again becoming a very serious menace.[73] We may feel fairly certain that the author, whoever

---

[73] There is this to be said for the later period, that the feud would tend to grow more bitter after each encounter, and thus more fully justify the language used in XI. § 30.

he may have been, was not a man of any great eminence in his own day. On this point the negative testimony of the *Zuozhuan* far outweighs any shred of authority still attaching to the *Shiji*, if once its other facts are discredited. Sun Xingyan, however, makes a feeble attempt to explain the omission of his name from the great commentary. It was Wu Zixu, he says, who got all the credit of Sun Wu's exploits, because the latter (being an alien) was not rewarded with an office in the State.[74]

How then did the Sun Tzǔ legend originate? It may be that the growing celebrity of the book imparted by degrees a kind of factitious renown to its author. It was felt to be only right and proper that one so well versed in the science of war should have solid achievements to his credit as well. Now the capture of Ying was undoubtedly the greatest feat of arms in He Lu's reign; it made a deep and lasting impression on all the surrounding states, and raised Wu to the shorted-lived zenith of her power. Hence, what more natural, as time went on, than that the acknowledged master of strategy, Sun Wu, should be popularly identified with that campaign, at first perhaps only in the sense that his brain conceived and planned it; afterwards, that it was actually carried out by him in conjunction with Wu Yuan, Bo Pei, and Fu Gai?

It is obvious that any attempt to reconstruct even the outline of Sun Tzǔ's life must be based almost wholly on conjecture. With this necessary proviso, I should say that he probably entered the service of Wu about the time of He Lu's accession, and gathered experience, though only in the capacity of a subordinate officer, during the intense military activity which marked the first half of that prince's reign.[76] If he rose to be a general at all, he certainly was never on an equal footing with the three above mentioned. He was doubtless present at the investment

---

[74] See his preface to Sun Tzǔ: 入郢威齊晉之功歸之子胥故春秋傳不載其名蓋功成不受官.

[75] With Wu Yuan himself the case is just the reverse: — a spurious treatise on war has been fathered on him simply because he was a great general. Here we have an obvious inducement to forgery. Sun Wu, on the other hand, cannot have been widely known to fame in the 5th century.

[76] See *Zuozhuan*, 定公, 4th year (506), § 14: 自昭王即位無歲不有吳師 "From the date of King Zhao's accession [515] there was no year in which Chu was not attacked by Wu."

and occupation of Ying, and witnessed Wu's sudden collapse in the following year. Yue's attack at this critical juncture, when her rival was embarrassed on every side, seems to have convinced him that this upstart kingdom was the great enemy against whom every effort would henceforth have to be directed. Sun Wu was thus a well-seasoned warrior when he sat down to write his famous book, which according to my reckoning must have appeared towards the end, rather that the beginning, of He Lu's reign. The story of the women may possibly have grown out of some real incident occurring about the same time. As we hear no more of Sun Wu after this from any source, he is hardly likely to have survived his patron or to have take part in the death-struggle with Yue, which began with the disaster at Zuili.

If these inferences are approximately correct, there is a certain irony in the fate that decreed that China's most illustrious man of peace should be contemporary with her greatest writer on war.

## The Text of Sun Tzŭ

I have found it difficult to glean much about the history of Sun Tzŭ's text. The quotations that occur in early authors go to show that the "13 chapters" of which Sima Qian speaks were essentially the same as those now extant. We have his word for it that they were widely circulated in his day, and can only regret that he refrained from discussing them on that account.[77] Sun Xingyan says in his preface:

> During the Qin and Han dynasties Sun Tzŭ's *Art of War* was in general use amongst military commanders, but they seem to have treated it as a work of mysterious import, and were unwilling to expound it for the benefit of posterity. Thus it came about that Wei Wu was the first to write a commentary on it.[78]

---

[77] See *supra*, p. xxxviii.
[78] 秦漢已來用兵皆用其法而或祕其書不肯注以傳世魏武始為之注.

As we have already seen, there is no reasonable ground to suppose that Cao Gong tampered with the text. But the text itself is often so obscure, and the number of editions which appeared from that time onward so great, especially during the Tang and Song dynasties, that it would be surprising if numerous corruptions had not managed to creep in. Towards the middle of the Song period, by which time all the chief commentaries on Sun Tzŭ were in existence, a certain Ji Tianbao 吉天保 published a work in 15 *juan* entitled "Sun Tzŭ with the collected commentaries of ten writers" 十家孫子會注.[79] There was another text, with variant readings put forward by Zhu Fu of Daxing 大興,[80] which also had supporters among the scholars of that period; but in the Ming editions, Sun Xingyan tells us, these readings were for some reason or other no longer put into circulation.[81] Thus, until the end of the 18th century, the text in sole possession of the field was one derived from Ji Tianbao's edition, although no actual copy of that important work was known to have survived. That, therefore, is the text of Sun Tzŭ which appears in the War section of the great Imperial encyclopedia printed in 1726, the *Gujin tushu jicheng* 古今圖書集成. Another copy at my disposal of what is practically the same text, with slight variations, is that contained in the "Eleven philosophers of the Zhou and Qin dynasties" 周秦十一子 [1758]. And the Chinese printed in Capt. Calthrop's first edition is evidently a similar version that has filtered through Japanese channels. So things remained until Sun Xingyan 孫星衍 [1752-1818], a distinguished antiquarian and classical scholar,[82] who claimed to be an actual descendant of Sun Wu,[83] accidentally discovered a copy of Ji Tianbao's long-lost

---

[79] See 宋藝文志.

[80] Alluded to in note 29 above.

[81] *Loc. cit.*: 蓋宋人又從大興朱氏處見明人刻本餘則世無傳者.

[82] A good biographical notice, with a list of his works, will be found in the 國朝詩人徵略, juan 48 fol. 18 *sqq.*

[83] Preface *ad fin.*: 吾家出樂安眞孫子之後媿余徒讀祖書考証文字不通方略亦享承平之福者久也 "My family comes from Le'an, and we are really descended from Sun Tzŭ. I am ashamed to say that I only read my ancestor's work from a literary point of view, without comprehending the military technique. So long have we been enjoying the blessings of peace!"

work, when on a visit to the library of the Huayin 華陰 temple.[84]
Appended to it was the *Yishuo* 遺說 of Zheng Youxian 鄭友賢,
mentioned in the *Tongzhi*, and also believed to have perished.[85]
This is what Sun Xingyan designates as the "original edition (or
text)" 古本 or 原本—a rather misleading name, for it cannot by
any means claim to set before us the text of Sun Tzŭ in its pristine purity. Ji Tianbao was a careless compiler,[86] and appears to
have been content to reproduce the somewhat debased version
current in his day, without troubling to collate it with the earliest editions then available. Fortunately, two versions of Sun Tzŭ,
even older than the newly discovered work, were still extant, one
buried in the *Tongdian*, Du You's great treatise on the Constitution, the other similarly enshrined in the *Taiping Yulan* encyclopedia. In both the complete text is to be found, though split
up into fragments, intermixed with other matter, and scattered
piecemeal over a number of different sections. Considering that
the *Yulan* takes us back to the year 983, and the *Tongdian* about
200 years further still, to the middle of the Tang dynasty, the
value of these early transcripts of Sun Tzŭ can hardly be overes-
timated. Yet the idea of utilizing them does not seem to have occurred to anyone until Sun Xingyan, acting under Government
instructions, undertook a thorough recension of the text. This is
his own account:

> Because of the numerous mistakes in the text of Sun Tzŭ which
> his editors had handed down, the Government ordered that the
> ancient edition [of Ji Tianbao] should be used, and that the text
> should be revised and corrected throughout. It happened that Wu
> Nianhu, the Governor Bi Gua, and Xi, a graduate of the second de-

---

[84] Huayin is about 14 miles from Tongguan 潼關 on the eastern border of Shaanxi. The temple
in question is still visited by those about to make the ascent of the 華山 or Western Sacred Mountain.
It is mentioned in the 大明一統志 [A.D. 1416], juan 32, f. 22, as the 西嶽廟: — 在華陰縣東五里
廟有唐玄宗所製華山碑 "Situated five *li* east of the district city of Huayin. The temple contains the
Huashan tablet inscribed by the Tang Emperor Xuanzong [713-755]."

[85] 曩予游關中讀華陰嶽廟道藏見有此書後有鄭友賢遺說一卷.

[86] Cf. Sun Xingyan's remark *à propos* of his mistakes in the names and order of the commentators: 吉天保之不深究此書可知.

gree, had all devoted themselves to this study, probably surpassing me therein. Accordingly, I have had the whole work cut on blocks as a textbook of military men.[87]

The three individuals here referred to had evidently been occupied on the text of Sun Tzŭ prior to Sun Xingyan's commission, but we are left in doubt as to the work they really accomplished. At any rate, the new edition, when ultimately produced, appeared in the names of Sun Xingyan and only one co-editor, Wu Renji 吳人驥. They took the "original text" as their basis, and by careful comparison with the older versions, as well as the extant commentaries and other sources of information such as the *Yishuo*, succeeded in restoring a very large number of doubtful passages, and turned out, on the whole, what must be accepted as the closet approximation we are ever likely to get to Sun Tzŭ's original work. This is what will hereafter be denominated the "standard text."

The copy that I have used belongs to a re-issue dated 1877. It is in 6 *ben*, forming part of a well-printed set of 23 early philosophical works in 83 *ben*.[88] It opens with a preface by Sun Xingyan (largely quoted in this introduction), vindicating the traditional view of Sun Tzŭ's life and performances, and summing up in remarkably concise fashion the evidence in its favor. This is followed by Cao Gong's preface to his edition, and the biography of Sun Tzŭ from the *Shiji*, both translated above. Then come, firstly, Zheng Youxian's *Yishuo*,[89] with author's preface, and next, a short miscellany of historical and bibliographical information entitled *Sunzi xulu* 孫子敘錄, compiled by Bi Yixun 畢以珣. As regards the body of the work, each separate sentence is followed by a note on the text, if required, and then by the various com-

---

[87] 國家令甲以孫子校士所傳本或多錯謬當用古本是正其文適吳念湖太守畢恬溪孝廉皆為此學所得或過于予遂刊一編以課武士.

[88] *See* my "Catalogue of Chinese Books" (Luzac & Co., 1908), no. 40.

[89] This is a discussion of 29 difficult passages in Sun Tzŭ, namely: I. 2; 26; 16; II. 9 & 10; III. 3; III &VIII; III. 17; IV. 4; 6; V. 3; 10 & 11; 14; the headings of the 13 chapters, with special reference to chap. VII; VII. 5; 15 & 16; 27; 33, &c.; VIII. 1-6; IX. 11; X. 1-20; XI. 23; 31; 19; 43; VII. 12-14 & XI. 52; XI.56; XIII. 15 & 16; XIII in general.

mentaries appertaining to it, arranged in chronological order. These we shall now proceed to discuss briefly, one by one.

# The Commentators

Sun Tzŭ can boast an exceptionally long and distinguished roll of commentators, which would do honor to any classic. Ouyang Xiu 歐陽修 remarks on this fact, though he wrote before the tale was complete, and rather ingeniously explains it by saying that the artifices of war, being inexhaustible, must therefore be susceptible of treatment in a great variety of way.[90]

1. **Cao Cao** 曹操 or Cao Gong 曹公, afterwards known as Wei Wudi 魏武帝 [A.D. 155-220]. There is hardly any room for doubt that the earliest commentary on Sun Tzŭ actually came from the pen of this extraordinary man, whose biography in the *Sanguozhi* reads like a romance.[91] One of the greatest military geniuses that the world has seen, and Napoleonic in the scale of his operation, he was especially famed for the marvelous rapidity of his marches, which has found expression in the line "Talk of Cao Cao, and Cao Cao will appear." 說曹操曹操就到. Ouyang Xiu says of him that he was a great captain who "measured his strength against Dong Zhuo, Lü Bu, and the two Yuan, father and son, and vanquished them all; whereupon he divided the Empire of Han with Wu and Shu, and made himself king. It is recorded that wherever a council of war was held by Wei on the eve of a far-reaching campaign, he had all his calculations ready; those generals who made use of them did not lose one battle in ten; those who ran counter to them in any particular saw their armies incontinently beaten and put to flight."[92] Cao Gong's notes on Sun Tzŭ, models of austere brevity, are so thor-

---

[90] Preface to Mei Yaochen's edition: 孫子注者尤多武之書本於兵兵之術非一而以不窮為奇宜其說者之多也.

[91] See 魏書, juan 1.

[92] *Loc. cit.*: 然前世言善用兵稱曹公曹公嘗與董呂諸袁角其力而勝之遂與吳蜀分漢而王傳言魏之將出兵千里每坐計勝敗授其成算諸將用之十不失一一有違者兵輒敗北.

oughly characteristic of the stern commander known to history that it is hard indeed to conceive of them as the work of a mere *littérateur*. Sometimes, indeed, owning to extreme compression, they are scarcely intelligible and stand no less in need of a commentary than the text itself.[93] As we have seen, Cao Gong is the reputed author of the 新書, a book on war in 100,000 old words, now lost, but mentioned in the 魏志.[94]

2. **Mengshi** 孟氏. The commentary that has come down to us under this name is comparatively meager, and nothing about the author is known. Even his personal name has not been recorded. Ji Tianbao's edition places him after Jia Lin, and Chao Gongwu 晁公武 also assigns him to the Tang dynasty,[95] but this is obviously a mistake, as his work is mentioned in the 隋書經籍志. In Sun Xingyan's preface, he appears as Mengshi of the Liang dynasty [502-557]. Others would identify him with Meng Kang 孟康 of the 3rd century. In the 宋史藝文志,[96] he is named last of the "Five Commentators," 五家 the others being Wei Wudi, Du Mu, Chen Hao, and Jia Lin.

3. **Li Quan** 李筌 of the 8th century was a well-known writer on military tactics. His 太白陰經 has been in constant use down to the present day. The 通志 mentions 閫外春秋 (lives of famous generals from the Zhou to the Tang dynasty) as written by him.[97] He is also generally supposed to be the real author of the popular Taoist tract, the 陰符經. According to Chao Gongwu and the *Tianyige* catalog,[98] he followed the 太乙遁甲 text of Sun Tzŭ, which differs considerably from those now extant. His notes are mostly short and to the point, and he frequently illustrates his remarks by anecdotes from Chinese history.

---

[93] Cf. 天一閣藏書總目 Catalogue of the library of the Fan 范 family at Ningbo, 子部, fol. 12 v°: 其註多隱辭引而不發 "His commentary is frequently obscure; it furnishes a clue, but does not fully develop the meaning."

[94] See 玉海, juan 141 *ad init.*

[95] *Wenxian tongkao*, juan 221, f. 9 v°.

[96] Juan 207, f. 5 r°

[97] It is interesting to note that M. Pelliot has recently discovered chapters 1, 4 and 5 of this lost work in the "Grottos of the Thousand Buddhas." *See* B. E. F. E. O, t. VII, nos. 3-4, p. 525.

[98] *Loc. Cit.*

4. **Du You** 杜佑 (died 812) did not publish a separate commentary on Sun Tzŭ, his notes being taken from the *Tongdian*, the encyclopedic treatise on the Constitution which was his life work. They are largely repetitions of Cao Gong and Mengshi, besides which it is believed that he drew on the ancient commentaries of Wang Ling 王凌 and others. Owing to the peculiar arrangement of the *Tongdian*, he has to explain each passage on its merits, apart from the context, and sometimes his own explanation does not agree with that of Cao Gong, whom he always quotes first. Though not strictly to be reckoned as one of the "Ten Commentators," he was added to their number by Ji Tianbao, being wrongly placed after his grandson Du Mu.

5. **Du Mu** 杜牧 (803-852) is perhaps best known as a poet—a bright star even in the glorious galaxy of the Tang period. We learn from Chao Gongwu that although he had no practical experience of war, he was extremely fond of discussing the subject, and was moreover well read in the military history of the *Chunqiu* and *Zhanguo* eras.[99] His notes, therefore, are well worth attention. They are very copious, and replete with historical parallels. The gist of Sun Tzŭ's work is thus summarized by him: "Practice benevolence and justice, but on the other hand make full use of artifice and measures of expediency."[100] He further declared that all the military triumph and disasters of the thousand years which had elapsed since Sun Wu's death would, upon examination, be found to uphold and corroborate, in every particular, the maxims contained in his book.[101] Du Mu's somewhat spiteful charge against Cao Gong has already been considered elsewhere.

6. **Chen Hao** 陳皞 appears to have been a contemporary of Du Mu. Chao Gongwu says that he was impelled to write a new commentary on Sun Tzŭ because Cao Gong's on the one hand was too obscure and subtle, and that of Du Mu on the other too

---

[99] *Wenxian tongkao*, juan 221, f. 9: 世謂牧慨然最喜論兵欲試而不得者其學能道春秋戰國時事甚博而詳知兵者有取焉.

[100] Preface to his commentary (*Tu Shu*, 經籍典, juan 442): 武之所論大約用仁義使機權也.

[101] *Ibid.*: 自武死後凡千歲將兵者有成者有敗者勘其事跡皆與武所著書一一相抵當.

long-winded and diffuse.[102] Ouyang Xiu, writing in the middle of the 11th century, calls Cao Gong, Du Mu, and Chen Hao the three chief commentators on Sun Tzŭ (三家), and observes that Chen Hao is continually attacking Du Mu's shortcomings. His commentary, though not lacking in merit, must rank below those of his predecessors.

7. **Jia Lin** 賈林 is known to have lived under the Tang dynasty, for his commentary on Sun Tzŭ is mentioned in the 唐書 and was afterwards republished by Ji Xie 紀燮 of the same dynasty together with those of Mengshi and Du You.[103] It is of somewhat scanty texture, and in point of quality, too, perhaps the least valuable of the eleven.

8. **Mei Yaochen** 梅堯臣 (1002-1060), commonly known by his "style" as Mei Shengyu 聖兪, was, like Du Mu, a poet of distinction. His commentary was published with a laudatory preface by the great Ouyang Xiu, from which we may cull the following:

> Later scholars have misread Sun Tzŭ, distorting his words and trying to make them square with their own one-sided views. Thus, though commentators have not been lacking, only a few have proved equal to the task. My friend Shengyu has not fallen into this mistake. In attempting to provide a critical commentary for Sun Tzŭ's work, he does not lose sight of the fact that these sayings were intended for states engaged in internecine warfare; that the author is not concerned with the military conditions prevailing under the sovereigns of the three ancient dynasties,[104] nor with the nine punitive measures prescribed to the Minister of War.[105] Again, Sun Wu loved brevity of diction, but his meaning is always deep. Whether the subject be marching an army, or handling soldiers, or estimating the enemy, or controlling the forces of victory, it is always systematically treated; the sayings are bound together

---

[102] *Tongkao, loc.* cit.: 嶭以曹公注隱微杜牧注闊疎重為之注云.

[103] *Ibid.*

[104] The Xia, the Shang and the Zhou. Although the last-named was nominally existent in Sun Tzŭ's day, it retained hardly a vestige of power, and the old military organization had practically gone by the board. I can suggest no other explanation of the passage.

[105] See *Zhou Li*, XXXIX. 6-10.

in strict logical sequence, though this has been obscured by commentators who have probably failed to grasp their meaning. In this own commentary, Mei Shengyu has brushed aside all the obstinate prejudices of these critics, and has tried to bring out the true meaning of Sun Tzǔ himself. In this way, the clouds of confusion have been dispersed and the sayings made clear. I am convinced that the present work deserves to be handed down side by side with the three great commentaries; and for a great deal that they find in the sayings, coming generations will have constant reason to thank my friend Shengyu.[106]

Making some allowance for the exuberance of friendship, I am inclined to endorse this favorable judgment, and would certainly place him above Chen Hao in order of merit.

9. **Wang Xi** 王晳, also of the Song dynasty, is decidedly original in some of his interpretations, but much less judicious than Mei Yaochen, and on the whole not a very trustworthy guide. He is fond of comparing his own commentary with that of Cao Gong, but the comparison is not often flattering to him. We learn from Chao Gongwu that Wang Xi revised the ancient text of Sun Tzǔ, filling up lacunae and correcting mistakes.[107]

10. **He Yanxi** 何延錫 of the Song dynasty. The personal name of this commentator is given as above by Zheng Qiao 鄭樵 in the *Tongzhi*, written about the middle of the twelfth century, but he appears simply as Heshi 何氏 in the *Yuhai*, and Ma Duanlin quotes Chao Gongwu as saying that his personal name is unknown. There seems to be no reason to doubt Zheng Qiao's statement, otherwise I should have been inclined to hazard a guess and identify him with one He Qufei 何去非, the author of a short treatise on war entitled 備論, who lived in the latter part

---

[106] See *Tu Shu*, 戎政典, juan 90, f. 2 v°: 後之學者徒見其書又各牽於己見是以注者雖多而少當也獨吾友聖俞不然嘗評武之書曰此戰國相傾之說也三代王者之師司馬九伐之法武不及也然亦愛其文略而意深其行師用兵料敵制勝亦皆有法其言甚有序次而注者汩之或失其意乃自為注凡膠于偏見者皆抉去傳以己意而發之然後武之說不汩而明吾知此書當與三家並傳而後世取其說者往往于吾聖俞多焉.

[107] *Tongkao*, juan 221. f. 11 r°: 晳以古本校正闕誤.

of the 11th century.[108] Heshi's commentary, in the words of the *Tianyige* catalog, "contains helpful additions" 有所裨益 here and there, but is chiefly remarkable for the copious extracts taken, in adapted form, from the dynastic histories and other sources.

11. **Zhang Yu** 張預. The list closes with a commentator of no great originality perhaps, but gifted with admirable powers of lucid exposition. His commentary is based on that of Cao Gong, whose terse sentences he contrives to expand and develop in masterly fashion. Without Zhang Yu, it is safe to say that much of Cao Gong's commentary would have remained cloaked in its pristine obscurity and therefore valueless. His work is not mentioned in the Song history, the *Tongkao*, or the *Yuhai*, but it finds a niche in the *Tongzhi*, which also names him as the author of the "Lives of Famous Generals" 百將傳.[109]

It is rather remarkable that the last-named four should all have flourished within so short a space of time. Chao Gongwu accounts for it by saying: "During the early years of the Song dynasty the Empire enjoyed a long spell of peace, and men ceased to practice the art of war. But when [Zhao] Yuanhao's rebellion came [1038-42] and the frontier generals were defeated time after time, the Court made strenuous enquiry for men skilled in war, and military topics became the vogue amongst all the high officials. Hence it is that the commentators of Sun Tzŭ in our dynasty belong mainly to that period."[110]

Besides these eleven commentators, there are several others whose work has not come down to us. The *Sui Shu* mentions four, namely Wang Ling 王凌 (often quoted by Du You as 王子); Zhang Zishang 張子尚; Jia Xu 賈詡 of Wei 魏;[111] and Shen You 沈友 of Wu 吳. The *Tang Shu* adds Sun Hao 孫鎬, and the *Tongzhi* Hsiao Chi 蕭吉, while the *Tu Shu* mentions a Ming

---

[108] See 四庫全書, juan 99, f. 16 *v°*.

[109] This appears to be still extant. See Wylie's "Notes," p. 91 (new edition).

[110] *Tongkao, loc. cit.*: 仁廟時天下久承平人不習兵元昊既叛邊將數敗朝廷頗訪知兵者士大夫人人言兵矣故本朝注解孫武書者大抵皆其時人也.

[111] A notable person in his day. His biography is given in the *San Guo Zhi*, juan 10.

commentator, Huang Runyu 黃潤玉. It is possible that some of these may have been merely collectors and editors of other commentaries, like Ji Tianbao and Ji Xie, mentioned above. Certainly in the case of the latter, the entry 紀燮注孫子 in the *Tongkao*, without the following note, would give one to understand that he had written an independent commentary of his own.

There are two works, described in the *Siku Quanshu*[112] and no doubt extremely rare, which I should much like to have seen. One is entitled 孫子參同 Xin, in 5 *juan*. It gives selections from four new commentators, probably of the Ming dynasty, as well as from the eleven known to us. The names of the four are Xie Yuan 解元; Zhang Ao 張鰲; Li Cai 李材; and Huang Zhizheng 黃治徵. The other work is 孫子彙徵 in 4 juan, compiled by Zheng Duan 鄭瑞 of the present dynasty. It is a compendium of information on ancient warfare, with special reference to Sun Tzŭ's 13 chapters.

## Appreciations of Sun Tzŭ

Sun Tzŭ has exercised a potent fascination over the minds of some of China's greatest men. Among the famous generals who are known to have studied his pages with enthusiasm may be mentioned Han Xin 韓信 (*d.* B.C. 196),[113] Feng Yi 馮異 (*d.* A.D. 34),[114] Lü Meng 呂蒙 (*d.* 219),[115] and Yue Fei 岳飛 (1103-1141).[116] The opinion of Cao Gong, who disputes with Han Xin the highest place in Chinese military annals, has already been recorded.[117] Still more remarkable, in one way, is the testimony of purely literary men, such as Su Xun 蘇洵 (the father

---

[112] Juan 100, ff. 2, 3.

[113] *See* p. XXX.

[114] *Hou Han Shu,* juan 17 *ad init.*

[115] *San Guo Zhi,* juan 54, f. 10 *v°*.

[116] *Song Shi,* juan 365 *ad init.*

[117] The few Europeans who have yet an opportunity of acquainting themselves with Sun Tzŭ are not behindhand in their praise. In this connection, I may perhaps be excused for quoting from a letter from Lord Roberts, to whom the sheets of the present work were submitted previous to publication: "Many of Sun Wu's maxims are perfectly applicable to the present day, and no. 11 on page 77 [33] [Chapter VIII] is one that the people of this country would do well to take to heart."

of Su Dongpo), who wrote several essays on military topics, all of which owe their chief inspiration to Sun Tzǔ. The following short passage by him is preserved in the *Yuhai*:[118]

> Sun Wu's saying, that in war one cannot make certain of conquering,[119] is very different indeed from what other books tell us.[120] Wu Qi was a man of the same stamp as Sun Wu: they both wrote books on war, and they are linked together in popular speech as "Sun and Wu." But Wu Qi's remarks on war are less weighty, his rules are rougher and more crudely stated, and there is not the same unity of plan as in Sun Tzǔ's work, where the style is terse, but the meaning fully brought out.[121]

The 性理彙要, chap. 17, contains the following extract from the 藝圃折衷 "Impartial Judgments in the Garden of Literature" by Zheng Hou 鄭厚:

> Sun Tzǔ's 13 chapters are not only the staple and base of all military men's training, but also compel the most careful attention of scholars and men of letters. His sayings are terse yet elegant, simple yet profound, perspicuous and eminently practical. Such works as the *Lunyu*, the *Yijing* and the great Commentary,[122] as well as the writings of Mencius, Xun Kuang and Yang Zhu, all fall below the level of Sun Tzǔ.[123]

Zhu Xi, commenting on this, fully admits the first part of the criticism, although he dislikes the audacious comparison with the venerated classical works. Language of this sort, he says, "encourages a ruler's bent towards unrelenting warfare and reckless militarism."[124]

---

[118] Juan 140, f. 13 *r°*.

[119] *See* IV. § 3.

[120] The allusion may be to Mencius VI. 2 ix. 2: 戰必克.

[121] 武用兵不能必克與書所言遠甚吳起與武一體之人皆著書言兵世稱之曰孫吳然而起之言兵也輕法制草略無所統紀不若武之書詞約而義盡.

[122] The *Zuozhuan*.

[123] 孫子十三篇不惟武人之根本文士亦當盡心焉其詞約而緯易而深暢而可用論語易大傳之流孟荀楊著書皆不及也.

[124] 是啟人君窮兵黷武之心.

# Apologies for War

Accustomed as we are to think of China as the greatest peace-loving nation on earth, we are in some danger of forgetting that her experience of war in all its phases has also been such as no modern State can parallel. Her long military annals stretch back to a point at which they are lost in the mists of time. She had built the Great Wall and was maintaining a huge standing army along her frontier centuries before the first Roman legionary was seen on the Danube. What with the perpetual collisions of the ancient feudal States, the grim conflicts with Huns, Turks, and other invaders after the centralization of government, the terrific upheavals which accompanied the overthrow of so many dynasties, besides the countless rebellions and minor disturbances that have flamed up and flickered out again one by one, it is hardly too much to say that the clash of arms has never ceased to resound in one portion or another of the Empire.

No less remarkable is the succession of illustrious captains to whom China can point with pride. As in all countries, the greatest are found emerging at the most fateful crises of her history. Thus, Bo Qi stands out conspicuous in the period when Qin was entering upon her final struggle with the remaining independent states. The stormy years that followed the break-up of the Qin dynasty are illumined by the transcendent genius of Han Xin. When the House of Han in turn is tottering to its fall, the great and baleful figure of Cao Cao dominates the scene. And in the establishment of the Tang dynasty, one of the mightiest tasks achieved by man, the superhuman energy of Li Shimin (afterwards the Emperor Taizong) was seconded by the brilliant strategy of Li Jing. None of these generals need fear comparison with the greatest names in the military history of Europe.

In spite of all this, the great body of Chinese sentiment, from Laozi downwards, and especially as reflected in the standard literature of Confucianism, has been consistently pacific and intensely opposed to militarism in any form. It is such an uncommon thing to find any of the literati defending warfare on principle, that I have thought it worthwhile to collect and translate a few passages in which the unorthodox view is upheld. The following, by Sima Qian, shows that for all his ardent admiration of Confucius, he was yet no advocate of peace at any price:

> Military weapons are the means used by the Sage to punish violence and cruelty, to give peace to troublous times, to remove difficulties and dangers, and to succor those who are in peril. Every animal with blood in its veins and horns on its head will fight when it is attacked. How much more so will man, who carries in his breast the faculties of love and hatred, joy and anger! When he is pleased, a feeling of affection springs up within him; when angry, his poisoned sting is brought into play. That is the natural law that governs his being....What then shall be said of those scholars of our time, blind to all great issues, and without any appreciation of relative values, who can only bark out their stale formulas about "virtue" and "civilization," condemning the use of military weapons? They will surely bring our country to impotence and dishonor and the loss of her rightful heritage; or, at the very least, they will bring about invasion and rebellion, sacrifice of territory and general enfeeblement. Yet they obstinately refuse to modify the position they have taken up. The truth is that, just as in the family the teacher must not spare the rod, and punishments cannot be dispensed with in the State, so military chastisement can never be allowed to fall into abeyance in the Empire. All one can say is that among those who bear arms some will be loyal and others rebellious.[125]

The next piece is taken from Du Mu's preface to his commentary on Sun Tzǔ:

> War may be defined as punishment, which is one of the functions of government. It was the profession of Zhong You and Ran Qiu, both disciples of Confucius. Nowadays, the holding of trials and

---

[125] *Shiji*, juan 25, fol. I: 兵者聖人所以討彊暴平亂世夷險阻救危殆自含血戴角之獸見犯則校而況於人懷好惡喜怒之氣喜則愛心生怒則毒螫加情性之理也...豈與世儒闇於大較不權輕重猥云德化不當用兵大至窘辱失守小乃侵犯削弱遂執不移等哉故教笞不可廢於家刑罰不可捐於國誅伐不可偃於天下用之有巧拙行之有逆順耳.

hearing of litigation, the imprisonment of offenders and their execution by flogging in the marketplace, are all done by officials. But
the wielding of huge armies, the throwing down of fortified cities,
the haling of women and children into captivity, and the behead-
ing of traitors—this is also work which is done by officials. The objects of the rack[126] and of military weapons are essentially the same.
There is no intrinsic difference between the punishment of flogging
and cutting off heads in war. For the lesser infractions of law, which
are easily dealt with, only a small amount of force need be employed: hence the institution of torture and flogging. For more serious outbreaks of lawlessness, which are hard to suppress, a greater
amount of force is necessary: hence the use of military weapons
and wholesale decapitation. In both cases, however, the end in view
is to get rid of wicked people, and to give comfort and relief to the
good....[127] Ji Sun asked Ran You, saying: "Have you, Sir, acquired
your military aptitude by study or is it innate?" Ran You replied:
"It has been acquired by study."[128] "How can that be so," said Ji Sun,
"seeing that you are a disciple of Confucius?" "It is a fact," replied
Ran You; "I was taught by Confucius. It is fitting that the great Sage
should exercise both civil and military functions, though to be sure
my instruction in the art of fighting has not yet gone very far."

Now, who the author was of this rigid distinction between the
"civil" and the "military," and the limitation of each to a separate
sphere of action, or in what year of which dynasty it was first in-
troduced, is more than I can say. But, at any rate, it has come about
that the members of the governing class are quite afraid of enlarg-
ing on military topics, or do so only in a shamefaced manner. If any
are bold enough to discuss the subject, they are at once set down
as eccentric individuals of coarse and brutal propensities. This is
an extraordinary instance of the way in which though sheer lack of
reasoning, men unhappily lose sight of fundamental principles.[129]

---

[126] The first instances of 木索 given in the *Peiwen Yunfu* is from Sima Qian's letter to Ren An 任
安 (see 文選, juan 41, f. 9 r°), where M. Chavannes translates it "la cangue et la chaîne." But in the
present passage it seems rather to indicate some single instrument of torture.

[127] 兵者刑也刑者政事也為夫子之徒實由冉求之事也今者據案聽訟械繫罪人笞死
于市者吏之所為也驅兵數萬撅其城郭纍其妻子斬其罪人亦束之所為也木索兵刃無異意
也笞之與斬無異刑也小而易制用力少者木索笞也大而難治用力多者兵刃斬也俱期於除
去惡民安活善民.

[128] Cf. *Shiji*, juan 47, f. 11 v°.

When the Duke of Zhou was minister under Cheng Wang, he regulated ceremonies and made music, and venerated the arts of scholarship and learning; yet when the barbarians of the River Huai revolted,[130] he sallied forth and chastised them. When Confucius held office under the Duke of Lu, and a meeting was convened at Jiagu,[131] he said: "If pacific negotiations are in progress, warlike preparations should have been made beforehand." He rebuked and shamed the Marquis of Qi, who cowered under him and dared not proceed to violence. How can it be said that these two great Sages had no knowledge of military matters?[132]

We have seen that the great Zhu Xi held Sun Tzŭ in high esteem. He also appeals to the authority of the Classics:

Our Master Confucius, answering Duke Ling of Wei, said: "I have never studied matters connected with armies and battalions."[133] Replying to Kong Wenzi, he said: "I have not been instructed about buff-coats and weapons."[134] But if we turn to the meeting at Jiagu,[135] we find that he used armed force against the men of Lai,[136] so that the Marquis of Qi was overawed. Again, when the inhabitants of Bi revolted, he ordered his officers to attack them, whereupon they were defeated and fled in confusion.[137] He once uttered the words: "If I fight, I conquer."[138] And Ran You also said: "The Sage exercises both civil and military functions."[139] Can it be a fact that Confucius never studied or received instruction in the art of war? We can only

---

[129] 季孫問于冉有曰子之戰學之乎性達之乎對曰學之季孫曰事孔子惡乎學冉有曰即學之於孔子者大聖兼該文武並用適聞其戰法實未之詳也夫不知自何代何年何人分為二道曰文曰文離而俱行因使縉紳之士不敢言兵甚或恥言之苟有言者世以為麤暴異人人不比數嗚呼此失根本斯為最甚。

[130] See *Shujing*, preface § 55.

[131] See *Zuozhuan*, 定公 X. 2; *Shiji*, juan 47, i. 4 *r°*.

[132] 周公相成王制禮作樂尊大儒術有淮夷叛則出征之夫子相魯公會于夾谷曰有文事者必有武備叱辱齊侯伏不敢動是二大聖人豈不知兵乎.

[133] *Lunyu*, XV. 1.

[134] *Zuozhuan*, 哀公, XI. 7.

[135] See *supra*.

[136] *Zuozhuan*, 定公, X. 2.

[137] *Ibid*. XII. 5; *Jiayu*, juan 1 *ad fin*.

[138] I have failed to trace this utterance. See note 120.

[139] See *supra*.

say that he did not specially choose matters connected with armies and fighting to be the subject of his teaching.[140]

Sun Xingyan, the editor of Sun Tzǔ, writes in similar strain:

Confucius said: "I am unversed in military matters." He also said: "If I fight, I conquer."[141] Confucius ordered ceremonies and regulated music. Now war constitutes one of the five classes of State ceremonial,[142] and must not be treated as an independent branch of study. Hence, the words "I am unversed in" must be taken to mean that there are things that even an inspired Teacher does not know. Those who have to lead an army and devise stratagems, must learn the art of war. But if one can command the services of a good general like Sun Tzǔ, who was employed by Wu Zixu, there is no need to learn it oneself. Hence the remark added by Confucius: "If I fight, I conquer."[143]

The men of the present day, however, willfully interpret these words of Confucius in their narrowest sense, as though he meant that books on the art of war were not worth reading. With blind persistency, they adduce the example of Zhao Gua, who pored over his father's books to no purpose,[144] as a proof that all military is useless. Again seeing that books on war have to do with such things as opportunism in designing plans, and the conversion of spies, they hold that the art is immoral and unworthy of a sage. These people ignore the fact that the studies of our scholars and the civil administration of our officials also require steady application and practice before efficiency is reached. The ancients were particularly chary of allowing mere novices to botch their work.[145] Weapons are

---

[140] 性理彙要, *loc. cit.*: 昔吾夫子對衛靈公以軍旅之事未之學答孔文子以甲兵之事未之聞及觀夾谷之會則以兵加萊人而齊侯懼費人之亂則命將士以伐之而費人北嘗曰我戰則克而冉有亦曰聖人文武並用孔子豈有眞未學未聞哉特以軍旅甲兵之事非所以為訓也.

[141] See *supra*.

[142] *Viz*, 軍禮, the other four being 吉, 凶, 賓 and 嘉 "worship, mourning, entertainment of guests and festive rites." See *Shujing*, II. I. iii. 8, and *Zhou Li*, IX. fol. 49.

[143] Preface to Sun Tzǔ: 孔子曰軍旅之事未之學又曰我戰則克孔子定禮正樂兵則五禮之一不必以為專門之學故云未學所為聖人有所不知或行軍好謀則學之或善將將如伍子胥之用孫子又何必自學之故又曰我戰則克也,.

[144] See chapter XIII, section II, note.

[145] This is a rather obscure allusion to *Zuozhuan*, 襄公, XXXI. 4, where Zichan says: "If you have a piece of beautiful brocade, you will not employ a mere learner to make it up" 子有美錦不使人學製焉.

baneful[146] and fighting perilous; and unless a general is in constant practice, he ought not to hazard other men's lives in battle.[147] Hence it is essential that Sun Tzǔ's 13 chapters should be studied.[148]

Xiang Liang used to instruct his nephew Ji[149] in the art of war. Ji got a rough idea of the art in its general bearings, but would not pursue his studies to their proper outcome, the consequence being that he was finally defeated and overthrown. He did not realize that the tricks and artifices of war are beyond verbal computation. Duke Xiang of Song[150] and King Yan of Xu[151] were brought to destruction by their misplaced humanity. The treacherous and underhand nature of war necessitates the use of guile and stratagem suited to the occasion. There is a case on record of Confucius himself having violated an extorted oath,[152] and also of his having left the Song State in disguise.[153] Can we then recklessly arraign Sun Tzǔ for disregarding truth and honesty?[154]

# Bibliography

The following are the oldest Chinese treatises on war, after Sun Tzǔ. The notes on each have been drawn principally from the *Siku quanshu jianming mulu* 四庫全書簡明目錄, ch. 9, fol. 22 *sqq.*

1. **Wuzi** 吳子, in I *Juan* or 6 chapters 篇. By Wu Qi 吳起 (*d.* B.C. 381). A genuine work. See *Shiji*, ch. 65.

2. **Sima Fa** 司馬法, in I *juan* or 5 chapters. Wrongly attributed to Sima Ranju 司馬穰苴 of the 6th century B.C. Its dates, how-

---

[146] Cf. *Daodejing*, chapter 31: 兵者不祥之器.

[147] Sun Xingyan might have quoted Confucius again. See *Lunyu*, XIII. 29, 30.

[148] 今世泥孔子之言以為兵書不足觀又泥趙括徒能讀父書之言以為成法不足用又見兵書有權謀有反間以為非聖人之法皆不知吾儒之學者吏之治事可習而能然古人猶有學製之懼兵凶戰危將不素習未可以人命為嘗試則十三篇之不可不觀也.

[149] Better known as Xiang Yu 羽 (B.C. 233-202).

[150] The third among the 五伯 (or 霸) enumerated in chapter XI, section 53, note. For the incident referred to, see *Zuozhuan*, 僖公, XXII. 4.

[151] See *supra*, note 23.

[152] *Shiji*, juan 47, f. 7 *r°*.

[153] *Ibid.*, juan 38, f. 8 *v°*.

[154] 項梁教籍兵法籍略知其意不肯竟學卒以傾覆不知兵法之弊可勝言哉宋襄徐偃仁而敗兵者危機當用權謀孔子猶有要盟勿信微服過宋之時安得妄責孫子以言之不純哉.

ever, must be early, as the customs of the three ancient dynasties are constantly to be met with in its pages.[155] See *Shiji*, ch. 64.

The *Siku quanshu* (ch. 99, f. 1) remarks that the oldest three treatises on war, *Sun Tzŭ, Wuzi* and the *Sima Fa*, are, generally speaking, only concerned with things strictly military—the art of producing, collecting, training and drilling troops, and the correct theory with regard to measures of expediency, laying plans, transport of goods and the handling of soldiers[156]—in strong contrast to later works, in which the science of war is usually blended with metaphysics, divination and magical arts in general.

3. **Liu Tao** 六韜, in 6 *juan* or 60 chapters. Attributed to Lü Wang 呂望 (or Lü Shang 尚, also known as Tai Gong 太公) of the 12th century B.C.[157] But its style does not belong to the era of the Three Dynasties.[158] Lu Deming 陸德明 (550-625 A.D.) mentions the work, and enumerates the headings of the six sections, 文, 武, 虎, 豹, 龍 and 犬, so that the forgery cannot have been later than the Sui dynasty.

4. **Weiliaozi** 尉繚子, in 5 *juan*. Attributed to Wei Liao (4th cent. B.C.), who studied under the famous Guiguzi 鬼谷子. The 漢志, under 兵家, mentions a book of Wei Liao in 31 chapters, whereas the text we posses contains only 24. Its matter is sound enough in the main, though the strategical devices differ considerably from those of the Warring States period.[159] It has been furnished with a commentary by the well-known Sung philosopher Chang Zai 張載.

5. **San Lüe** 三略, in 3 *juan*. Attributed to Huangshi Gong 黃石公, a legendary personage who is said to have bestowed it on

---

[155] 其時去古未遠三代遺規往往於此書見之.

[156] 其最古者當以孫子吳子司馬法為本大抵生聚訓練之術權謀運用之宜而已.

[157] See p. 187. Further details on Tai Gong will be found in the *Shiji*, juan 32 *ad init*. Besides the tradition which makes him a former minister of Zhou Xin, two other accounts of him are there given, according to which he would appear to have been first raised from a humble private station by Wen Wang.

[158] 其文義不類三代.

[159] 其言多近於正與戰國權謀頗殊.

Zhang Liang (*d.* B.C. 187) in an interview on a bridge.[160] But here again, the style is not that of works dating from the Qin or Han period. The Han Emperor Guang Wu (A.D. 25-57) apparently quotes from it in one of his proclamations; but the passage in question may have been inserted later on, in order to prove the genuineness of work. We shall not be far out if we refer it to the Northern Song period (420-478 A.D.), or somewhat earlier.[161]

6. **Li Wei Gong wendui** 李衛公問對, in 3 sections. Written in the form of a dialogue between Taizong and his great general Li Jing 李靖, it is usually ascribed to the latter. Competent authorities consider it a forgery, though the author was evidently well versed in the art of war.[162]

7. **Li Jing Bingfa** 李靖兵法 (not to be confounded with the foregoing) is a short treatise in 8 chapters, preserved in the *Tongdian,* but not published separately. This fact explains its omission from the *Siku quanshu.*

8. **Wu Qi Jing** 握奇經,[163] in 1 *juan.* Attributed to the legendary minister Fêng Hou 風后, with exegetical notes by Gongsun Hong 公孫宏 of the Han dynasty (*d.* B.C. 121), and said to have been eulogized by the celebrated general Ma Long 馬隆 (*d.* A.D. 300). Yet the earliest mention of it is in the 宋志. Although a forgery, the work is well put together.[164]

Considering the high popular estimation in which Zhuge Liang 諸葛亮 has always been held, it is not surprising to find

---

[160] See *Han Shu,* 張良傳, juan 40. The work is there called 太公兵法. Hence it has been confused with the *Liu Tao.* The *Tu Shu* attributes both the *Liu Tao* and the *San Lüe* to Tai Gong.

[161] 其文不纇秦漢間書漢光武帝詔雖嘗引之安知非反撼詔中所引二語以證實其書謂之北宋以前舊本則可矣. Another work said to have been written by Huangshi Gong, and also included in the military section of the Imperial Catalogue, is the *Su Shu* 素書 in 1 *juan.* A short ethical treatise of Taoist savour, having no reference whatever to war, it is pronounced a forgery from the hand of Zhang Shangying 張商英 (*d.* 1121), who edited it with commentary. Correct Wylie's "Notes," new edition, p. 90, and Courant's "Catalogue des Lives Chinois," no. 5056.

[162] 其書雖偽亦出於有學識謀略者之手也. We are told in the 讀書志 that the above six works, together with Sun Tzŭ, were those prescribed for military training in the 元豐 period (1078-85). See *Yü Hai,* juan 140 f. rº.

[163] Also written 握機經 and *Wu Ji Jing* 幄機經.

[164] 其言具有條理.

more than one work on war ascribed to his pen. Such are (1) the **Shiliu ce** 十六策 (1 *juan*), preserved in the *Yongle dadian* 永樂大典; (2) **Jiang Yuan** 蔣苑 (1 *juan*); and (3) **Xin Shu** 心書 (1 *juan*), which steals wholesale from Sun Tzŭ. None of these has the slightest claim to be considered genuine.

Most of the large Chinese encyclopedias contain extensive sections devoted to the literature of war. The following references may be found useful:

**Tongdian** 通典 ( *circa* 800 A.D.), ch. 148-162.
**Taiping Yulan** 太平御覽 (983), ch. 270-359.
**Wenxian Tongkao** 文獻通考 (13th cent.), ch. 221.
**Yuhai** 玉海 (13th cent.), ch. 140, 141.
**Sancai Tuhui** 三才圖會 (16th cent.), 人事 ch. 7,8.
**Guang bowu zhi** 廣博物志 (1607), ch. 31, 32.
**Qianque Leishu** 潛確類書 (1632), ch. 75.
**Yuanjian Leihan** 淵鑑類函 (1710), ch. 206-229.
**Gujin tushu jicheng** 古今圖書集成 (1726), section XXX, *esp*. ch. 81-90.
**Xu Wenxian Tongkao** 續文獻通考 (1784), ch. 121-134.
**Huangchao jingshi wenbian** 皇朝經世文編 (1826), ch. 76, 77.

The bibliographical sections of certain historical works also deserve mention:

**Qian Han Shu** 前漢書, ch. 30.
**Sui Shu** 隋書, ch. 32-35.
**Jiu Tang Shu** 舊唐書, ch. 46, 47.
**Xin Tang Shu** 新唐書, ch. 57-60.
**Song Shi** 宋史, ch. 202-209.
**Tongzhi** 通志 (*circa* 1150), ch. 68.

To these of course must be added the great Catalogue of the Imperial Library:

**Siku quanshu zongmu tiyao** 四庫全書總目提要 (1790), ch. 99, 100.

## Part One

# 孫 子 兵 法
# The Art of War

### Complete Chinese Text

### and

### English Translation

# CHAPTER 1

# Laying Plans[1]
# 計篇第一

1. 孫子曰：兵者，國之大事。
2. 死生之地，存亡之道，不可不察也。
3. 故經之以五，校之以計，而索其情。

1.   Sun Tzŭ said: The art of war is of vital importance to the State.

2.   It is a matter of life and death, a road either to safety or to ruin. Hence it is a subject of inquiry that can on no account be neglected.

3.   The art of war, then, is governed by five constant factors, to be taken into account in one's deliberations, when seeking to determine the conditions obtaining in the field.[2]

4. 一曰道，二曰天，三曰地，四曰將，五曰法。
5. 道者，令民與上同意也。
6. 故可與之死，可與之生，而民不畏危。
7. 天者，陰陽、寒暑、時制也。
8. 地者，遠近、險易、廣狹、死生也。

4.   These are: (1) The Moral Law; (2) Heaven; (3) Earth; (4) The Commander; (5) Method and discipline.[3]

5, 6. *The Moral Law* causes the people to be in complete accord with their ruler, so that they will follow him regardless of their lives, undismayed by any danger.[4]

7.   *Heaven* signifies night and day, cold and heat, times and seasons.[5]

8.   *Earth* comprises distances, great and small; danger and security; open ground and narrow passes; the chances of life and death.[6]

9. 將者, 智、信、仁、勇、嚴也。
10. 法者, 曲制、官道、主用也。
11. 凡此五者, 將莫不聞, 知之者勝, 不知之者不勝。
12. 故校之以計, 而索其情。

9. *The Commander* stands for the virtues of wisdom, sincerity, benevolence, courage, and strictness.[7]

10. By *Method and discipline* are to be understood the marshalling of the army in its proper subdivisions, the gradations of rank among the officers, the maintenance of roads by which supplies may reach the army, and the control of military expenditure.[8]

11. These five heads should be familiar to every general: he who knows them will be victorious; he who knows them not will fail.

12. Therefore, in your deliberations, when seeking to determine the military conditions, let them be made the basis of a comparison, in this wise:[9]

13. 曰：主孰有道？將孰有能？天地孰得？法令孰行？兵眾
   孰強？士卒孰練？賞罰孰明？
14. 吾以此知勝負矣。

13. (1) Which of the two sovereigns is imbued with the Moral law?[10] (2) Which of the two generals has most ability? (3) With whom lie the advantages derived from Heaven and Earth?[11] (4) On which side is discipline most rigorously enforced?[12] (5) Which army is the stronger?[13] (6) On which side are officers and men more highly trained?[14] (7) In which army is there the greater constancy both in reward and punishment?[15]

14. By means of these seven considerations I can forecast victory or defeat.

15. 將聽吾計, 用之必勝, 留之；將不聽吾計, 用之必敗,
   去之。
16. 計利以聽, 乃為之勢, 以佐其外。

17. 勢者, 因利而制權也。

15. The general that hearkens to my counsel and acts upon it, will conquer: let such a one be retained in command! The general that hearkens not to my counsel nor acts upon it, will suffer defeat: let such a one be dismissed![16]

16. While heeding the profit of my counsel, avail yourself also of any helpful circumstance over and beyond the ordinary rules.[17]

17. According as circumstances are favorable, one should modify one's plans.[18]

18. 兵者, 詭道也。
19. 故能而示之不能, 用而示之不用, 近而示之遠, 遠而示之近。
20. 利而誘之, 亂而取之。
21. 實而備之, 強而避之。
22. 怒而撓之, 卑而驕之。

18. All warfare is based on deception.[19]

19. Hence, when able to attack, we must seem unable; when using our forces, we must seem inactive; when we are near, we must make the enemy believe we are far away; when far away, we must make him believe we are near.

20. Hold out baits to entice the enemy. Feign disorder, and crush him.[20]

21. If he is secure at all points, be prepared for him. If he is in superior strength, evade him.[21]

22. If your opponent is of choleric temper, seek to irritate him. Pretend to be weak, that he may grow arrogant.[22]

23. 佚而勞之, 親而離之。
24. 攻其無備, 出其不意。
25. 此兵家之勝, 不可先傳也。

26. 夫未戰而廟算勝者, 得算多也; 未戰而廟算不勝者, 得算少也。多算勝, 少算不勝, 而況無算乎!吾以此觀之, 勝負見矣。

23. If he is taking his ease, give him no rest.[23] If his forces are united, separate them.[24]

24. Attack him where he is unprepared, appear where you are not expected.

25. These military devices, leading to victory, must not be divulged beforehand.[25]

26. Now the general who wins a battle makes many calculations in his temple ere the battle is fought.[26] The general who loses a battle makes but few calculations beforehand. Thus do many calculations lead to victory, and few calculations to defeat: how much more no calculation at all! It is by attention to this point that I can foresee who is likely to win or lose.

# CHAPTER 2

# Waging War[1]
## 作戰篇第二

1. 孫子曰：凡用兵之法, 馳車千駟, 革車千乘, 帶甲十萬, 千里饋糧, 則內外之費, 賓客之用, 膠漆之材, 車甲之奉, 日費千金, 然後十萬之師舉矣。

1. Sun Tzŭ said: In the operations of war, where there are in the field a thousand swift chariots, as many heavy chariots, and a hundred thousand mail-clad soldiers,[2] with provisions enough to carry them a thousand *li*,[3] the expenditure at home and at the front, including entertainment of guests, small items such as glue and paint, and sums spent on chariots and armor, will reach the total of a thousand ounces of silver per day.[4] Such is the cost of raising an army of 100,000 men.[5]

2. 其用戰也勝久則鈍兵挫銳, 攻城則力屈。
3. 久暴師則國用不足。

2. When you engage in actual fighting, if victory is long in coming, the men's weapons will grow dull and their ardor will be damped.[6] If you lay siege to a town, you will exhaust your strength.[7]

3. Again, if the campaign is protracted, the resources of the State will not be equal to the strain.[8]

4. 夫鈍兵挫銳, 屈力殫貨, 則諸侯乘其弊而起, 雖有智者, 不能善其後矣。
5. 故兵聞拙速, 未睹巧之久也。

4.   Now, when your weapons are dulled, your ardor damped, your strength exhausted and your treasure spent, other chieftains will spring up to take advantage of your extremity. Then no man, however wise, will be able to avert the consequences that must ensue.[9]

5.   Thus, though we have heard of stupid haste in war, cleverness has never been seen associated with long delays.[10]

6.   夫兵久而國利者, 未之有也。
7.   故不盡知用兵之害者, 則不能盡知用兵之利也。
8.   善用兵者, 役不再籍, 糧不三載。
9.   取用於國, 因糧於敵, 故軍食可足也。

6.   There is no instance of a country having benefited from prolonged warfare.[11]

7.   It is only one who is thoroughly acquainted with the evils of war that can thoroughly understand the profitable way of carrying it on.[12]

8.   The skillful soldier does not raise a second levy, neither are his supply-wagons loaded more than twice.[13]

9.   Bring war material with you from home, but forage on the enemy. Thus the army will have food enough for its needs.[14]

10.  國之貧於師者遠輸, 遠輸則百姓貧。
11.  近於師者貴賣, 貴賣則百姓財竭。
12.  財竭則急於丘役。

10.  Poverty of the State exchequer causes an army to be maintained by contributions from a distance. Contributing to maintain an army at a distance causes the people to be impoverished.[15]

11.  On the other hand, the proximity of an army causes prices to go up; and high prices cause the people's substance to be drained away.[16]

12.  When their substance is drained away, the peasantry will be afflicted by heavy exactions.[17]

13. 力屈、財殫, 中原內虛於家。百姓之費, 十去其七;
14. 公家之費:破軍罷馬, 甲冑矢弩, 戟楯蔽櫓, 丘牛大車, 十去其六。

13, 14. With this loss of substance and exhaustion of strength, the homes of the people will be stripped bare, and three-tenths of their income will be dissipated;[18] while Government expenses for broken chariots, worn-out horses, breast-plates and helmets, bows and arrows, spears and shields, protective mantlets, draught-oxen and heavy wagons, will amount to four-tenths of its total revenue.[19]

15. 故智將務食于敵。食敵一鐘, 當吾二十鐘;蒝秆一石, 當吾二十石。
16. 故殺敵者, 怒也;取敵之利者, 貨也。
17. 故車戰, 得車十乘已上, 賞其先得者, 而更其旌旗, 車雜而乘之, 卒善而養之。

15. Hence a wise general makes a point of foraging on the enemy. One cartload of the enemy's provisions is equivalent to twenty of one's own, and likewise a single picul of his provender is equivalent to twenty from one's own store.[20]

16. Now in order to kill the enemy, our men must be roused to anger; that there may be advantage from defeating the enemy, they must have their rewards.[21]

17. Therefore in chariot fighting, when ten or more chariots have been taken, those should be rewarded who took the first.[22] Our own flags should be submitted for those of the enemy, and the chariots mingled and used in conjunction with ours. The captured soldiers should be kindly treated and kept.

18. 是謂勝敵而益強。
19. 故兵貴勝, 不貴久。
20. 故知兵之將, 民之司命, 國家安危之主也。

18. This is called, using the conquered foe to augment one's own strength.

19. In war, then, let your great object be victory, not lengthy campaigns.[23]

20. Thus it may be known that the leader of armies is the arbiter of the people's fate. The man on whom it depends whether the nation shall be in peace or in peril.[24]

# CHAPTER 3

# Attack By Strategem
## 謀攻篇第三

1. 孫子曰：凡用兵之法，全國為上，破國次之；全軍為上，破軍次之。全旅為上，破旅次之；全卒為上，破卒次之；全伍為上，破伍次之。
2. 是故百戰百勝，非善之善者也；不戰而屈人之兵，善之善者也。
3. 故上兵伐謀，其次伐交，其次伐兵，下政攻城。

1.　Sun Tzŭ said: In the practical art of war, the best thing of all is to take the enemy's country whole and intact; to shatter and destroy it is not so good. So, too, it is better to capture an army entire than to destroy it, to capture a regiment, a detachment, or a company entire than to destroy them.[1]

2.　Hence to fight and conquer in all your battles is not supreme excellence; supreme excellence consists in breaking the enemy's resistance without fighting.[2]

3.　Thus the highest form of generalship is to baulk the enemy's plans;[3] the next best is to prevent the junction of the enemy's forces;[4] and the worst policy of all is to besiege walled cities.[5]

4. 攻城之法為不得已。修櫓轒輼、具器械、三月而後成，距闉，又三月而後已。

4.　The rule is, not to besiege walled cities if it can possibly be avoided.[6] The preparation of mantlets, movable shelters, and various implements of war, will take up three whole months;[7] And the piling up of mounds over against the walls will take three months more.[8]

5.　將不勝其忿, 而蟻附之, 殺士三分之一, 而城不拔者,
　　此攻之災也。
6.　故善用兵者, 屈人之兵而非戰也。拔人之城而非攻也,
　　毀人之國而非久也。

5.　The general, unable to control his irritation, will launch his men to the assault like swarming ants,[9] with the result that one-third of his men are slain, while the town still remains untaken. Such are the disastrous effects of a siege.[10]

6.　Therefore the skillful leader subdues the enemy's troops without any fighting; he captures their cities without laying siege to them; he overthrows their kingdom without lengthy operations in the field.[11]

7.　必以全爭于天下, 故兵不頓, 而利可全, 此謀攻之法也。
8.　故用兵之法, 十則圍之, 五則攻之, 倍則分之。

7.　With his forces intact he will dispute the mastery of the Empire, and thus, without losing a man, his triumph will be complete.[12] This is the method of attacking by stratagem.

8.　It is the rule in war, if our forces are ten to the enemy's one, to surround him; if five to one, to attack him;[13] if twice as numerous, to divide our army into two.[14]

9.　敵則能戰之, 少則能逃之, 不若則能避之。
10.　故小敵之堅, 大敵之擒也。
11.　夫將者, 國之輔也。輔周則國必強, 輔隙則國必弱。
12.　故君之所以患于軍者三：

9.　If equally matched, we can offer battle;[15] if slightly inferior in numbers, we can avoid the enemy;[16] if quite unequal in every way, we can flee from him.

10.　Hence, though an obstinate fight may be made by a small force, in the end it must be captured by the larger force.[17]

11.　Now the general is the bulwark of the State: if the bulwark is complete at all points, the State will be strong; if the bulwark is defective, the State will be weak.[18]

12. There are three ways in which a ruler can bring misfortune upon his army:

13. 不知軍之不可以進而謂之進, 不知軍之不可以退而
謂之退, 是為縻軍;
14. 不知三軍之事, 而同三軍之政者, 則軍士惑矣;

13. (1) By commanding the army to advance or to retreat, being ignorant of the fact that it cannot obey. This is called hobbling the army.[19]

14. (2) By attempting to govern an army in the same way as he administers a kingdom, being ignorant of the conditions that obtain in an army. This causes restlessness in the soldier's mind.[20]

15. 不知三軍之權, 而同三軍之任, 則軍士疑矣。
16. 三軍既惑且疑, 則諸侯之難至矣, 是謂亂軍引勝。
17. 故知勝有五：知可以戰與不可以戰者勝, 識眾寡之用
者勝, 上下同欲者勝, 以虞待不虞者勝, 將能而君不
御者勝。此五者, 知勝之道也。

15. (3) By employing the officers of this army without discrimination,[21] through ignorance of the military principle of adaptation to circumstances. This shakes the confidence of the soldiers.[22]

16. But when the army is restless and distrustful, trouble is sure to come from the other feudal princes. This is simply bringing anarchy into the army, and flinging victory away.[23]

17. Thus we may know that there are five essentials for victory: (1) He will win who knows when to fight and when not to fight.[24] (2) He will win who knows how to handle both superior and inferior forces.[25] (3) He will win whose army is animated by the same spirit throughout all its ranks.[26] (4) He will win who, prepared himself, waits to take the enemy unprepared. (5) He will

win who has military capacity and is not interfered with by the sovereign.[27] Victory lies in the knowledge of these five points.[28]

18. 故曰：知己知彼, 百戰不殆；不知彼而知己, 一勝一負；不知彼不知己, 每戰必殆。

18. Hence the saying: If you know the enemy and know yourself, you need not fear the result of a hundred battles. If you know yourself but not the enemy, for every victory gained you will also suffer a defeat.[29] If you know neither the enemy nor yourself, you will succumb in every battle.[30]

# CHAPTER 4

# Tactical Dispositions[1]
# 形篇第四

1. 孫子曰：昔之善戰者，先為不可勝，以待敵之可勝。
2. 不可勝在己，可勝在敵。

1. Sun Tzǔ said: The good fighters of old first put themselves beyond the possibility of defeat, and then waited for an opportunity of defeating the enemy.

2. To secure ourselves against defeat lies in our own hands, but the opportunity of defeating the enemy is provided by the enemy himself.[2]

3. 故善戰者，能為不可勝，不能使敵必可勝。
4. 故曰：勝可知，而不可為。
5. 不可勝者，守也：可勝者，攻也。
6. 守則不足，攻則有餘。
7. 善守者，藏于九地之下：善攻者，動于九天之上。故能自保而全勝也。

3. The good fighter is able to secure himself against defeat,[3] but cannot make certain of defeating the enemy.[4]

4. Hence the saying: One may *know* how to conquer without being able to *do* it.[5]

5. Security against defeat implies defensive tactics; ability to defeat the enemy means taking the offensive.[6]

6. Standing on the defensive indicates insufficient strength: attacking, a superabundance of strength.

7. The general who is skilled in defense hides in the most secret recesses of the earth;[7] he who is skilled in attack flash-

es forth from the topmost heights of heaven.[8] Thus on the one hand we have ability to protect ourselves, on the other, a victory that is complete.[9]

8. 見勝不過眾人之所知, 非善之善者也。
9. 戰勝而天下曰善, 非善之善者也。

8. To see victory only when it is within the ken of the common herd is not the acme of excellence.[10]

9. Neither is it the acme of excellence if you fight and conquer and the whole empire says, "Well done!"[11]

10. 故舉秋毫不為多力, 見日月不為明目, 聞雷霆不為聰耳。
11. 古之所謂善戰者, 勝勝易勝者也。
12. 故善戰之勝也, 無智名, 無勇功。

10. To lift an autumn hair is no sign of great strength;[12] to see sun and moon is no sign of sharp sight; to hear the noise of thunder is no sign of quick ear.[13]

11. What the ancients called a clever fighter is one who not only wins, but excels in winning with ease.[14]

12. Hence his victories bring him neither reputation for wisdom nor credit for courage.[15]

13. 故其戰勝不忒。不忒者, 其所措必勝, 勝已敗者也。
14. 故善戰者, 立於不敗之地, 而不失敵之敗也。
15. 是故勝兵先勝而後求戰, 敗兵先戰而後求勝。

13. He wins his battle by making no mistakes.[16] Making no mistakes is what establishes the certainty of victory, for it means conquering an enemy that is already defeated.[17]

14. Hence the skilful fighter puts himself to a position that makes defeat impossible, and does not miss the moment for defeating the enemy.[18]

15. Thus it is that in war the victorious strategist only seeks

battle after the victory has been won, whereas he who is destined to defeat first fights and afterwards looks for victory. [19]

16. 善用兵者, 修道而保法, 故能為勝敗之政。
17. 兵法：一曰度, 二曰量, 三曰數, 四曰稱, 五曰勝。
18. 地生度, 度生量, 量生數, 數生稱, 稱生勝。

16. The consummate leader cultivates the moral law, and strictly adheres to method and discipline;[20] thus it is in his power to control success.

17. In respect of military method, we have, firstly, Measurement; secondly, Estimation of quantity; thirdly, Calculation; fourthly, Balancing of chances; fifthly, Victory.

18. Measurement owes its existence to Earth; Estimation of quantity to Measurement; Calculation to Estimation of quantity; Balancing of chances to Calculation; and Victory to Balancing of chances.[21]

19. 故勝兵若以鎰稱銖, 敗兵若以銖稱鎰。
20. 勝者之戰民也, 若決積水於千仞之谿者, 形也。

19. A victorious army opposed to a routed one, is as a pound's weight placed in the scale against grain.[22]

20. The onrush of a conquering force is like the bursting of pent-up waters into a chasm a thousand fathoms deep. So much for tactical dispositions.[23]

# CHAPTER 5

# Energy[1]
# 埶篇第五

1. 孫子曰：凡治眾如治寡，分數是也。
2. 鬥眾如鬥寡，形名是也。

1.   Sun Tzŭ said: The control of a large force is the same in principle as the control of a few men: it is merely a question of dividing up their numbers.[2]
2.   Fighting with a large army under your command is nowise different from fighting with a small one: it is merely a question of instituting signs and signals.[3]

3. 三軍之眾，可使必受敵而無敗者，奇正是也；

3.   To ensure that your whole host may withstand the brunt of an enemy's attack and remain unshaken—this is effected by maneuvers direct and indirect.[4]

4. 兵之所加，如以碬投卵者，虛實是也。
5. 凡戰者，以正合，以奇勝。

4.   That the impact of your army may be like a grindstone dashed against an egg—this is effected by the science of weak points and strong.[5]
5.   In all fighting, the direct method may be used for joining battle, but indirect methods will be needed in order to secure victory.[6]

6. 故善出奇者, 無窮如天地, 不竭如江河。終而復始,
   日月是也。死而復生, 四時是也。

7. 聲不過五, 五聲之變, 不可勝聽也。

8. 色不過五, 五色之變, 不可勝觀也。

9. 味不過五, 五味之變, 不可勝嘗也。

6. Indirect tactics, efficiently applied, are inexhaustible as Heaven and Earth, unending as the flow of rivers and streams;[7] like the sun and moon, they end but to begin anew; like the four seasons, they pass away but to return once more.[8]

7. There are not more than five musical notes, yet the combinations of these five give rise to more melodies than can ever be heard.[9]

8. There are not more than five primary colors,[10] yet in combination they produce more hues than can ever be seen.

9. There are not more than five cardinal tastes,[11] yet combinations of them yield more flavors than can ever be tasted.

10. 戰勢不過奇正, 奇正之變, 不可勝窮也。

11. 奇正相生, 如循環之無端, 孰能窮之？

12. 激水之疾, 至於漂石者, 勢也。

13. 鷙鳥之疾, 至於毀拆者, 節也。

10. In battle, there are not more than two methods of attack—the direct and the indirect; yet these two in combination gives rise to an unending series of maneuvers.

11. The direct and the indirect lead on to each other in turn. It is like moving in a circle—you never come to an end. Who can exhaust the possibilities of their combination?[12]

12. The onset of troops is like the rush of a torrent, which will even roll stones along in its course.

13. The quality of decision is like the well-timed swoop of a falcon, which enables it to strike and destroy its victim.[13]

14. 是故善戰者, 其勢險, 其節短。
15. 勢如彍弩, 節如發機。
16. 紛紛紜紜, 鬥亂而不可亂也。渾渾沌沌, 形圓而不可敗也。

14. Therefore the good fighter will be terrible in his onset, and prompt in his decision.[14]

15. Energy may be linked to the bending of a crossbow; decision, to the releasing of the trigger.[15]

16. Amid the turmoil and tumult of battle, there may be seeming disorder and yet no real disorder at all; amid confusion and chaos, your array may be without head or tail, yet it will be proof against defeat.[16]

17. 亂生于治, 怯生于勇, 弱生于強。
18. 治亂, 數也; 勇怯勢也; 強弱, 形也。

17. Simulated disorder postulates perfect discipline; simulated fear postulates courage; simulated weakness postulates strength.[17]

18. Hiding order beneath the cloak of disorder is simply a question of subdivision;[18] concealing courage under a show of timidity presupposes a fund of latent energy; masking strength with weakness is to be effected by tactical dispositions.[19]

19. 故善動敵者, 形之, 敵必從之; 予之, 敵必取之。
20. 以利動之, 以卒待之。

19. Thus one who is skillful at keeping the enemy on the move maintains deceitful appearances, according to which the enemy will act.[20] He sacrifices something, that the enemy may snatch at it.[21]

20. By holding out baits, he keeps him on the march; then with a body of picked men he lies in wait for him.[22]

21. 故善戰者, 求之於勢, 不責於人, 故能擇人而任勢。
22. 任勢者, 其戰人也, 如轉木石。木石之性, 安則靜, 危則動, 方則止, 圓則行。
23. 故善戰人之勢, 如轉圓石於千仞之山者, 勢也。

21. The clever combatant looks to the effect of combined energy, and does not require too much from individuals.[23] Hence his ability to pick out the right men and to utilize combined energy.[24]

22. When he utilizes combined energy, his fighting men become as it were like unto rolling logs or stones. For it is the nature of a log or stone to remain motionless on level ground, and to move when on a slope; if four-cornered, to come to a standstill, but if round- shape, to go rolling down.[25]

23. Thus the energy developed by good fighting men is as the momentum of a round stone rolled down a mountain thousands of feet in height. So much on the subject of energy.[26]

# CHAPTER 6

# Weak Points And Strong[1]
## 虛實篇第六

1. 孫子曰：凡先處戰地而待敵者佚，後處戰地而趨戰者勞。
2. 故善戰者，致人而不致於人。

1. Sun Tzŭ said: Whoever is first in the field and awaits the coming of the enemy, will be fresh for the fight; whoever is second in the field and has to hasten to battle, will arrive exhausted.[2]

2. Therefore the clever combatant imposes his will on the enemy, but does not allow the enemy's to be imposed on him.[3]

3. 能使敵人自至者，利之也；能使敵人不得至者，害之也。
4. 故敵佚能勞之，飽能飢之，安能動之。
5. 出其所不趨，趨其所不意。
6. 行千里而不勞者，行於無人之地也。

3. By holding out advantages to him, he can cause the enemy to approach of his own accord; or, by inflicting damage, he can make it impossible for the enemy to draw near.[4]

4. If the enemy is taking his ease, he can harass him;[5] if well supplied with food, he can starve him out;[6] if quietly encamped, he can force him to move.

5. Appear at points which the enemy must hasten to defend; march swiftly to places where you are not expected.[7]

6. An army may march great distances without distress, if it marches through country where the enemy is not.[8]

7. 攻而必取者，攻其所不守也。守而必固者，守其所不攻也。

8. 故善攻者，敵不知其所守。善守者，敵不知其所攻。

7. You can be sure of succeeding in your attack if you only attack places that are undefended.[9] You can ensure the safety of your defense if you only hold positions that cannot be attacked.[10]

8. Hence that general is skilful in attack whose opponent does not know what to defend, and he is skilful in defense whose opponent does not know what to attack.[11]

9. 微乎微乎，至於無形，神乎神乎，至於無聲，故能為敵之司命。

10. 進而不可禦者，衝其虛也；退而不可追者，速而不可及也。

11. 故我欲戰，敵雖高壘深溝，不得不與我戰者，攻其所必救也。

9. O divine art of subtlety and secrecy! Through you we learn to be invisible, through you inaudible[12] and hence we can hold the enemy's fate in our hands.[13]

10. You may advance and be absolutely irresistible, if you make for the enemy's weak points; you may retire and be safe from pursuit if your movements are more rapid than those of the enemy.[14]

11. If we wish to fight, the enemy can be forced to an engagement even though he be sheltered behind a high rampart and a deep ditch. All we need do is to attack some other place that he will be obliged to relieve.[15]

12. 我不欲戰，畫地而守之，敵不得與我戰者，乖其所之也。

13. 故形人而我無形，則我專而敵分。

12. If we do not wish to fight, we can prevent the enemy from engaging us even though the lines of our encampment be merely traced out on the ground. All we need do is to throw something odd and unaccountable in his way.[16]

13. By discovering the enemy's dispositions and remaining invisible ourselves, we can keep our forces concentrated, while the enemy's must be divided.[17]

14. 我專為一, 敵分為十, 是以十攻其一也, 則我眾而敵寡;
15. 能以眾擊寡者, 則吾之所與戰者, 約矣。
16. 吾所與戰之地不可知, 不可知, 則敵所備者多, 敵所備者多, 則吾之所戰者, 寡矣。

14. We can form a single united body, while the enemy must split into fractions. Hence there will be a whole pitted against separate parts of a whole.[18]

15. And if we are able thus to attack an inferior force with a superior one, our opponents will be in dire straits.[19]

16. The spot where we intend to fight must not be made known; for then the enemy will have to prepare against a possible attack at several different points;[20] and his forces being thus disturbed in many directions, the numbers we shall have to face at any given point will be proportionately few.

17. 故備前則後寡, 備後則前寡, 備左則右寡, 備右則左寡, 無所不備, 則無所不寡。
18. 寡者備人者也, 眾者使人備己者也。
19. 故知戰之地, 知戰之日, 則可千里而會戰。

17. For should the enemy strengthen his van, he will weaken his rear; should he strengthen his rear, he will weaken his van; should he strengthen his left, he will weaken his right; should he strengthen his right, he will weaken his left. If he sends reinforcements everywhere, he will everywhere be weak.[21]

18. Numerical weakness comes from having to prepare against possible attacks; numerical strength, from compelling our adversary to make these preparations against us.[22]

19. Knowing the place and the time of the coming battle, we may concentrate from the greatest distances in order to fight.[23]

20. 不知戰地, 不知戰日, 則左不能救右, 右不能救左, 前不能救後, 後不能救前, 而況遠者數十里, 近者數里乎?

21. 以吾度之, 越人之兵雖多, 亦奚益於勝敗哉。故曰：勝可為也。

20. But if neither time nor place be known, then the left wing will be impotent to succor the right, the right equally impotent to succor the left, the van unable to relieve the rear, or the rear to support the van. How much more so if the furthest portions of the army are anything under a hundred *li* apart, and even the nearest are separated by several *li*![24]

21. Though according to my estimate the soldiers of Yue exceed our own in number, that shall advantage them nothing in the matter of victory.[25] I say then that victory can be achieved.[26]

22. 敵雖眾, 可使無鬥。故策之而知得失之計。

23. 作之而知動靜之理, 形之而知死生之地。

22. Though the enemy be stronger in numbers, we may prevent him from fighting.[27] Scheme so as to discover his plans and the likelihood of their success.

23. Rouse him, and learn the principle of his activity or inactivity.[28]

Force him to reveal himself, so as to find out his vulnerable spots.[29]

24. 角之而知有餘不足之處。
25. 故形兵之極, 至於無形; 無形, 則深間不能窺, 知者不
    能謀。

24. Carefully compare the opposing army with your own,[30] so that you may know where strength is superabundant and where it is deficient.[31]

25. In making tactical dispositions, the highest pitch you can attain is to conceal them;[32] conceal your dispositions, and you will be safe from the prying of the subtlest spies, from the machinations of the wisest brains.[33]

26. 因形而錯勝于眾, 眾不能知。
27. 人皆知我所以勝之形, 而莫知吾所以制勝之形。
28. 故其戰勝不復, 而應形於無窮。

26. How victory may be produced for them out of the enemy's own tactics—that is what the multitude cannot comprehend.[34]

27. All men can see the tactics whereby I conquer, but what none can see is the strategy out of which victory is evolved.[35]

28. Do not repeat the tactics that have gained you one victory, but let your methods be regulated by the infinite variety of circumstances.[36]

29. 夫兵形象水, 水之形避高而趨下。
30. 兵之形, 避實而擊虛。
31. 水因地而制流, 兵應敵而制勝。
32. 故兵無常勢, 水無常形。
33. 能因敵變化而取勝者, 謂之神。
34. 故五行無常勝, 四時無常位, 日有短長, 月有死生。

29. Military tactics are like unto water; for water in its natural course runs away from high places and hastens downwards.[37]

30. So in war, the way is to avoid what is strong and to strike at what is weak.[38]

31. Water shapes its course according to the nature of the ground over which it flows:[39] The soldier works out his victory in relation to the foe whom he is facing.

32. Therefore, just as water retains no constant shape, so in warfare there are no constant conditions.

33. He who can modify his tactics in relation to his opponent and thereby succeed in winning, may be called a heaven-born captain.

34. The five elements[40] are not always equally prominent;[41] the four seasons make way for each other in turn.[42] There are short days and long; the moon has its periods of waning and waxing.[43]

# CHAPTER 7

# Maneuvering[1]
## 軍爭篇第七

1. 孫子曰：凡用兵之法，將受命于君，
2. 合軍聚眾，交和而舍，

1. Sun Tzŭ said: In war, the general receives his commands from the sovereign.[2]

2. Having collected an army and concentrated his forces, he must blend and harmonize the different elements thereof before pitching his camp.[3]

3. 莫難於軍爭。軍爭之難者，以迂為直，以患為利。

3. After that, comes tactical maneuvering, than which there is nothing more difficult.[4] The difficulty of tactical maneuvering consists in turning the devious into the direct, and misfortune into gain.[5]

4. 故迂其途，而誘之以利，後人發，先人至，此知迂直之計者也。

4. Thus to take a long and circuitous route; after enticing the enemy out of the way, and though starting after him, to contrive to reach the goal before him, shows knowledge of the artifice of *deviation*.[6]

5. 故軍爭為利，眾爭為危。
6. 舉軍而爭利，則不及；委軍而爭利，則輜重捐。
7. 是故卷甲而趨，日夜不處，倍道兼行，百里而爭利，則擒三將軍。

5.   Maneuvering with an army is advantageous; with an undisciplined multitude, most dangerous.[7]

6.   If you set a fully equipped army in march in order to snatch an advantage, the chances are that you will be too late.[8] On the other hand, to detach a flying column for the purpose involves the sacrifice of its baggage and stores.[9]

7.   Thus, if you order your men to roll up their buff-coats, and make forced[10] marches without halting day or night, covering double the usual distance at a stretch,[11] doing a hundred *li* in order to wrest an advantage, the leaders of all your three divisions will fall into the hands of the enemy.

8.   勁者先, 罷者後, 其法十一而至。
9.   五十里而爭利, 則蹶上將軍, 其法半至。
10.  三十里而爭利, 則三分之二至。

8.   The stronger men will be in front, the jaded ones will fall behind, and on this plan only one-tenth of your army will reach its destination.[12]

9.   If you march fifty *li* in order to outmaneuver the enemy, you will lose the leader of your first division, and only half your force will reach the goal.[13]

10.  If you march thirty *li* with the same object, two-thirds of your army will arrive.[14]

11.  是故軍無輜重則亡, 無糧食則亡, 無委積則亡。
12.  故不知諸侯之謀者, 不能豫交。
13.  不知山林、險阻、沮澤之形者, 不能行軍。
14.  不用鄉導者, 不能得地利。

11.  We may take it then that an army without its baggage-train is lost; without provisions it is lost; without bases of supply it is lost.[15]

12.  We cannot enter into alliances until we are acquainted with the designs of our neighbors.[16]

13. We are not fit to lead an army on the march unless we are familiar with the face of the country—its mountains and forests, its pitfalls[17] and precipices,[18] its marshes[19] and swamps.[20]

14. We shall be unable to turn natural advantages to account unless we make use of local guides.[21]

15. 故兵以詐立, 以利動。
16. 以分和為變者也。
17. 故其疾如風, 其徐如林。
18. 侵掠如火, 不動如山。

15. In war, practice dissimulation and you will succeed.[22] Move only if there is a real advantage to be gained.[23]

16. Whether to concentrate or to divide your troops, must be decided by circumstances.

17. Let your rapidity be that of the wind,[24] your compactness that of the forest.[25]

18. In raiding and plundering be like fire,[26] in immovability like a mountain.[27]

19. 難知如陰, 動如雷震。
20. 掠鄉分眾, 廓地分利。

19. Let your plans be dark and impenetrable as night, and when you move, fall like a thunderbolt.[28]

20. When you plunder a countryside, let the spoil be divided amongst your men;[29] when you capture new territory, cut it up into allotments for the benefit of the soldiery.[30]

21. 懸權而動。
22. 先知迂直之計者勝, 此軍爭之法也。
23. 軍政曰:「言不相聞, 故為今鼓;視而不見, 故為旌旗。

21. Ponder and deliberate[31] before you make a move.[32]
22. He will conquer who has learnt the artifice of deviation.[33]

Such is the art of maneuvering.[34]

23. The Book of Army Management says:[35] On the field of battle,[36] the spoken word does not carry far enough: hence the institution of gongs and drums.[37]

24. 夫金鼓旌旗者, 所以一民之耳目也。

25. 民既專一, 則勇者不得獨進, 怯者不得獨退, 此用眾之法也。

24. Gongs and drums, banners and flags, are means whereby the ears and eyes of the eyes of the host[38] may be focused on one particular point.[39]

25. The host thus forming a single united body, it is impossible either for the brave to advance alone, or for the cowardly to retreat alone.[40] This is the art of handling large masses of men.

26. 故夜戰多火鼓, 晝戰多旌旗, 所以變民之耳目也。

27. 故三軍可奪氣, 將軍可奪心。

26. In night fighting, then, make much use of signal-fires and drums, and in fighting by day, of flags and banners, as a means of influencing the ears and eyes of your army.[41]

27. A whole army may be robbed of its spirit;[42] a commander-in-chief may be robbed of his presence of mind.[43]

28. 是故朝氣銳, 晝氣惰, 暮氣歸。

29. 故善用兵者, 避其銳氣, 擊其惰歸, 此治氣者也。

28. Now a soldier's spirit is keenest in the morning;[44] by noonday it has begun to flag; and in the evening, his mind is bent only on returning to camp.

29. A clever general, therefore[45] avoids an army when its spirit is keen, but attacks it when it is sluggish and inclined to return. This is the art of studying moods.[46]

30. 以治待亂, 以靜待譁, 此治心者也。
31. 以近待遠, 以佚待勞, 以飽待飢, 此治力者也。
32. 無邀正正之旗, 無擊堂堂之陣, 此治變者也。

30. Disciplined and calm, to await the appearance of disorder and hubbub amongst the enemy: this is the art of retaining self-possession.

31. To be near the goal while the enemy is still far from it, to wait at ease[47] while the enemy is toiling and struggling, to be well fed while the enemy is famished: this is that art of husbanding one's strength.

32. To refrain from intercepting[48] an enemy whose banners are in perfect order, to refrain from attacking an army drawn up in calm and confident array:[49] this is the art of studying circumstances.[50]

33. 故用兵之法, 高陵勿向, 背邱勿逆,
34. 佯北勿從, 銳卒勿攻。
35. 餌兵勿食, 歸師勿遏。

33. It is a military axiom not to advance uphill against the enemy, not to oppose him when he comes downhill.

34. Do not pursue an enemy who stimulates flight; do not attack soldiers whose temper is keen.

35. Do not swallow a bait offered by the enemy.[51] Do not interfere with an army that is returning home.[52]

36. 圍師遺闕, 窮寇勿迫。

36. When you surround an army, leave an outlet free.[53] Do not press a desperate foe too hard.[54]

37. 此用兵之法也。

37. Such is the art of warfare.[55]

# CHAPTER 8

# Variation Of Tactics[1]
## 九變篇第八

1. 孫子曰：凡用兵之法，將受命于君，合軍聚眾。
2. 圮地無舍，衢地合交，絕地勿留，圍地則謀，死地則戰。

1. Sun Tzŭ said: In war, the general receives his commands from the sovereign, collects his army and concentrates his force.[2]
2. When in difficult country, do not encamp.[3] In the country where high roads intersect, join hands with your allies.[4] Do not linger in dangerous isolated positions.[5] In hemmed-in situations, you must resort to stratagem.[6] In a desperate position, you must fight.[7]

3. 塗有所不由，軍有所不擊，城有所不攻，地有所不爭，君命有所不受。

3. There are roads that must not be followed,[8] armies that must not be attacked,[9] towns[10] that must not be besieged,[11] positions that must not be contested, commands of the sovereign that must not be obeyed.[12]

4. 故將通于九變之利者，知用兵矣。
5. 將不通于九變之利者，雖知地形，不能得地之利矣。
6. 治兵不知九變之術，雖知五利，不能得人之用矣。

4. The general who thoroughly understands the advantages that accompany variation of tactics knows how to handle his troops.[13]
5. The general who does not understand these, may be well

acquainted with the configuration of the country, yet he will not be able to turn his knowledge to practical account.[14]

6.   So, the student of war who is unversed in the art of varying his plans, even though he is acquainted with the Five Advantages, will fail to make the best use of his men.[15]

7.　是故智者之慮, 必雜于利害。
8.　雜于利, 而務可信也;
9.　雜于害, 而患可解也。

7.   Hence in the wise leader's plans, considerations of advantage and of disadvantage will be blended together.[16]

8.   If our expectation of advantage be tempered in this way, we may succeed in accomplishing the essential part of our schemes.[17]

9.   If, on the other hand, in the midst of difficulties we are always ready to seize an advantage , we may extricate ourselves from misfortune.[18]

10.　是故屈諸侯者以害, 役諸侯者以業, 趨諸侯者以利。

10.   Reduce the hostile chiefs by inflicting damage on them;[19] make trouble for them,[20] and keep them constantly engaged;[21] hold out specious allurements, and make them rush to any given point.[22]

11.　故用兵之法, 無恃其不來, 恃吾有以待也;無恃其不攻, 恃吾有所不可攻也。
12.　故將有五危:必死, 可殺也;必生, 可虜也;忿速, 可侮也;廉潔, 可辱也;愛民, 可煩也。

11.   The art of war teaches us to rely not on the likelihood of the enemy's not coming, but on our own readiness to receive him;[23] not on the chance of his not attacking, but rather on the facts that have made our position unassailable.[24]

12. There are five dangerous faults that may affect a general: (1) Recklessness, which leads to destruction;[25] (2) cowardice, which leads to capture;[26] (3) a nasty temper, which can be provoked by insults;[27] (4) a delicacy of honor that is sensitive to shame;[28] (5) over solicitude for his men, which exposes him to worry and trouble.[29]

13. 凡此五者, 將之過也, 用兵之災也。
14. 覆軍殺將, 必以五危, 不可不察也。

13. These are the five besetting sins of the general, ruinous to the conduct or war.

14. When an army is overthrown and its leader slain, the cause will surely be found among these five dangerous faults. Let them be a subject of meditation.

# CHAPTER 9

# The Army On The March[1]
# 行軍篇第九

1. 孫子曰：凡處軍、相敵, 絕山依谷。

1. Sun Tzŭ said: We come now to the question of encamping the army, and observing signs of the enemy.[2] Pass quickly over mountains,[3] and keep in the neighborhood of valleys.

2. 視生處高, 戰隆無登, 此處山之軍也。
3. 絕水必遠水。
4. 客絕水而來, 勿迎之於水內, 令半濟而擊之, 利。

2. Camp in high places,[4] facing the sun.[5] Do not climb heights in order to fight.[6] So much for mountain warfare.[7]

3. After crossing a river, you should get far away from it.[8]

4. When an invading force crosses a river in its onward march, do not advance to meet it in mid-stream. It will be best to let half the army get across, and then deliver your attack.[9]

5. 欲戰者, 無附於水而迎客。
6. 視生處高, 無迎水流, 此處水上之軍也。

5. If you are anxious to fight, you should not go to meet the invader near a river that he has to cross.[10]

6. Moor your craft higher up than the enemy, and facing the sun.[11] Do not move upstream to meet the enemy.[12] So much for river warfare.

7. 絕斥澤, 惟亟去無留。

8. 若交軍於斥澤之中, 必依水草, 而背眾樹, 此處斥澤之軍也。

9. 平陸處易, 而右背高, 前死後生, 此處平陸之軍也。

7. In crossing salt marches, your sole concern should be to get over them quickly, without any delay.[13]

8. If forced to fight in a salt marsh, you should have water and grass near you, and get your back to a clump of trees.[14] So much for operations in salt marshes.

9. In dry, level country, take up an easily accessible position[15] with rising ground to your right and on your rear,[16] so that the danger may be in front, and safety lie behind.[17] So much for campaigning in flat country.

10. 凡此四軍之利, 黃帝之所以勝四帝也。

11. 凡軍喜高而惡下, 貴陽而賤陰。

12. 養生而處實, 軍無百疾, 是謂必勝。

10. These are the four useful branches of military knowledge,[18] which enabled the Yellow Emperor to vanquish four several sovereigns.[19]

11. All armies prefer high ground to low,[20] and sunny places to dark.

12. If you are careful of your men,[21] and camp on hard ground,[22] the army will be free from disease of every kind,[23] and this will spell victory.

13. 邱陵隄防, 必處其陽, 而右背之。此兵之利, 地之助也。

14. 上雨, 水沫至, 欲涉者, 待其定也。

15. 凡地有絕澗、天井、天牢、天羅、天陷、天隙, 必亟去之, 勿近也。

13. When you come to a hill or a bank, occupy the sunny side, with the slope on your right rear. Thus you will at once act

for the benefit of your soldiers and utilize the natural advantages of the ground.

14. When, in consequence of heavy rains up-country, a river that you wish to ford is swollen and flecked with foam, you must wait until it subsides.[24]

15. Country in which there are precipitous cliffs with torrents running between,[25] deep natural hollows,[26] confined places,[27] tangled thickets,[28] quagmires,[29] and crevasses,[30] should be left with all possible speed and not approached.

16. 吾遠之，敵近之；吾迎之，敵背之。
17. 軍旁有險阻、蔣潢井生、葭葦、小林、蘙薈，必謹覆索之，此伏姦之所處也。

16. While we keep away from such places, we should get the enemy to approach them; while we face them, we should let the enemy have them on his rear.

17. If in the neighborhood of your camp[31] there should be any hilly country,[32] ponds surrounded by aquatic grass, hollow basins filled with reeds,[33] or woods with thick undergrowth,[34] they must be carefully routed out and searched; for these are places where men in ambush or insidious spies are likely to be lurking.

18. 敵近而靜者，恃其險也。

18. When the enemy is close at hand and remains quiet, he is relying on the natural strength of his position.[35]

19. 遠而挑戰者，欲人之進也。
20. 其所居易者，利也。
21. 眾樹動者，來也；眾草多障者，疑也。

19. When he keeps aloof and tries to provoke a battle, he is anxious for the other side to advance.[36]

20.  If his place of encampment is easy of access, he is tendering a bait.[37]

21.  Movement amongst the trees of a forest shows that the enemy is advancing.[38] The appearance of a number of screens in the midst of thick grass means that the enemy wants to make us suspicious.[39]

22. 鳥起者, 伏也;獸駭者, 覆也。
23. 塵高而銳者, 車來也;卑而廣者, 徒來也;散而條達者, 樵採也;少而往來者, 營軍也。

22.  The rising of birds in their flight is the sign of an ambuscade.[40] Startled beasts indicate that a sudden attack is coming.[41]

23.  When there is dust rising in a high column, it is the sign of chariots advancing; when the dust is low, but spread over a wide area, it betokens the approach of infantry.[42] When it branches out in different directions, it shows that parties have been sent to collect firewood.[43] A few clouds of dust moving to and fro signify that the army is encamping.[44]

24. 辭卑而益備者, 進也;辭強而進驅者, 退也。

24.  Humble words and increased preparations are signs that the enemy is about to advance.[45] Violent language and driving forward as if to the attack are signs that he will retreat.[46]

25. 輕車先出其側者, 陣也。
26. 無約而請和者, 謀也。

25.  When the light chariots[47] come out first and take up a position on the wings, it is a sign that the enemy is forming for battle.[48]

26.  Peace proposals unaccompanied by a sworn covenant indicate a plot.[49]

27. 奔走而陳兵者, 期也。
28. 半進半退者, 誘也。
29. 倚杖而立者, 飢也。
30. 汲而先飲者, 渴也。

27. When there is much running about[50] and the soldiers fall into rank,[51] it means that the critical moment has come.[52]

28. When some are seen advancing and some retreating, it is a lure.[53]

29. When the soldiers stand leaning on their spears, they are faint from want of food.[54]

30. If those who are sent to draw water begin by drinking themselves, the army is suffering from thirst.[55]

31. 見利而不進者, 勞也。
32. 鳥集者, 虛也; 夜呼者, 恐也。
33. 軍擾者, 將不重也; 旌旗動者, 亂也; 吏怒者, 倦也。
34. 粟馬肉食, 軍無懸甀而不返其舍者, 窮寇也。

31. If the enemy sees an advantage to be gained[56] and makes no effort to secure it, the soldiers are exhausted.

32. If birds gather on any spot, it is unoccupied.[57] Clamor by night betokens nervousness.[58]

33. If there is disturbance in the camp, the general's authority is weak. If the banners and flags are shifted about, sedition is afoot.[59] If the officers are angry, it means that the men are weary.[60]

34. When an army feeds its horses with grain and kills its cattle for food,[61] and when the men do not hang their cooking-pots[62] over the camp-fires, showing that they will not return to their tents,[63] you may know that they are determined to fight to the death.[64]

35. 諄諄翕翕, 徐言入入者, 失眾也。

35. The sight of men whispering together[65] in small knots or

speaking in subdued tones[66] points to disaffection amongst the rank and file.

36. 數賞者, 窘也; 數罰者, 困也。
37. 先暴而後畏其眾者, 不精之至也。
38. 來委謝者, 欲休息也。

36. Too frequent rewards signify that the enemy is at the end of his resources;[67] too many punishments betray a condition of dire distress.[68]

37. To begin by bluster, but afterwards to take fright at the enemy's numbers, shows a supreme lack of intelligence.[69]

38. When envoys are sent with compliments in their mouths, it is a sign that the enemy wishes for a truce.[70]

39. 兵怒而相迎, 久而不合, 又不相去, 必謹察之。
40. 兵非益多也, 惟無武進, 足以併力、料敵、取人而已。

39. If the enemy's troops march up angrily and remain facing ours for a long time without either joining battle or taking themselves off again, the situation is one that demands great vigilance and circumspection.[71]

40. If our troops are no more in number than the enemy, that is amply sufficient;[72] it only means that no direct attack can be made.[73] What we can do is simply to concentrate all our available strength, keep a close watch on the enemy, and obtain reinforcements.[74]

41. 夫惟無慮而易敵者, 必擒於人。
42. 卒未親附而罰之, 則不服, 不服則難用也。卒已親附而罰不行, 則不可用也。

41. He who exercises no forethought but makes light of his opponents is sure to be captured by them.[75]

42. If soldier are punished before they have grown attached

to you, they will not prove submissive; and, unless submissive, they will be practically useless. If, when the soldiers have become attached to you, punishments are not enforced, they will still be useless.[76]

43. 故令之以文, 齊之以武, 是謂必取。
44. 令素行以教其民。則民服;令不素行以教其民;則民不服。
45. 令素信著者, 與眾相得也。

43. Therefore soldiers must be treated in the first instance with humanity, but kept under control by means of iron discipline.[77] This is a certain road to victory.

44. If in training soldiers commands are habitually enforced, the army will be well disciplined; if not, its discipline will be bad.[78]

45. If a general shows confidence in his men but always insists on his orders being obeyed,[79] the gain will be mutual.[80]

# CHAPTER 10

# Terrain[1]
## 地行篇第十

1. 孫子曰：地形有通者、有挂者、有支者、有隘者、有險
者、有遠者。

1. Sun Tzǔ said: We may distinguish six kinds of terrain to
wit: (1) Accessible ground;[2] (2) entangling ground;[3] (3) temporizing ground;[4] (4) narrow passes (5) precipitous heights;[5] (6)
positions at a great distance from the enemy.[6]

2. 我可以往，彼可以來，曰通。
3. 通形者，先居高陽，利糧道，以戰則利。

2. Ground that can be freely traversed by both sides is
called *accessible*.[7]
3. With regard to ground of this nature,[8] be before the enemy
in occupying the raised and sunny spots,[9] and carefully guard your
line of supplies.[10] Then you be able to fight with advantage.[11]

4. 可以往，難以返，曰挂。
5. 挂形者，敵無備，出而不勝之，敵若有備，出而不勝，
則難以返，不利。
6. 我出而不利，彼出而不利，曰支。
7. 支形者，敵雖利我，我無出也，引而去之，令敵半出而
擊之，利。

4. Ground that can be abandoned but is hard to re-occupy
is called *entangling*.[12]
5. From a position of this sort, if the enemy is unprepared,

you may sally forth and defeat him. But if the enemy is prepared for your coming, and you fail to defeat him, then, return being impossible, disaster will ensue.[13]

6. When the position is such that neither side will gain by making the first move, it is called *temporizing* ground.[14]

7. In a position of this sort, even though the enemy should offer us an attractive bait,[15] it will be advisable not to stir forth, but rather to retreat, thus enticing the enemy in his turn; then, when part of his army has come out, we may deliver our attack with advantage.

8. 隘形者, 我先居之, 必盈之以待敵。
9. 若敵先居之, 盈而勿從, 不盈而從之。
10. 險形者, 我先居之, 必居高陽以待敵;

8. With regard to *narrow passes*, if you can occupy them first,[16] let them be strongly garrisoned and await the advent of the enemy.

9. Should the enemy forestall you in occupying a pass, do not go after him if the pass is fully garrisoned, but only if it is weakly garrisoned.

10. With regard to *precipitous heights*, if you are beforehand with your adversary, you should occupy the raised and sunny spots, and there wait for him to come up.[17]

11. 若敵先居之, 引而去之, 勿從也。
12. 遠形者, 勢均, 難以挑戰, 戰而不利。
13. 凡此六者, 地之道也, 將之至任, 不可不察也。

11. If the enemy has occupied them before you, do not follow him, but retreat and try to entice him away.[18]

12. If you are situated at a great distance from the enemy, and the strength of the two armies is equal,[19] it is not easy to provoke a battle,[20] and fighting will be to your disadvantage.

13. These six are the principles connected with Earth.[21] The

general who has attained a responsible post must be careful to study them.[22]

14. 故兵有走者、有弛者、有陷者、有崩者、有亂者、有北者。凡此六者, 非天之災, 將之過也。
15. 夫勢均, 以一擊十, 曰走。
16. 卒強吏弱, 曰弛。吏強卒弱, 曰陷。

14. Now an army is exposed to six several calamities, not arising from natural causes,[23] but from faults for which the general is responsible. These are: (1) Flight; (2) insubordination; (3) collapse; (4) ruin; (5) disorganization; (6) rout.[24]

15. Other conditions being equal, if one force is hurled against another ten times its size, the result will be the *flight* of the former.[25]

16. When the common soldiers are too strong and their officers too weak, the result is *insubordination*.[26] When the officers are too strong and the common soldiers too weak, the result is *collapse*.[27]

17. 大吏怒而不服, 遇敵懟而自戰, 將不知其能, 曰崩。

17. When the higher officers[28] are angry and insubordinate, and on meeting the enemy give battle on their own account from a feeling of resentment, before the commander-in-chief can tell whether or not he is in a position to fight, the result is *ruin*.[29]

18. 將弱不嚴, 教道不明, 吏卒無常, 陳兵縱橫, 曰亂。
19. 將不能料敵, 以少合眾, 以弱擊強, 兵無選鋒, 曰北。

18. When the general is weak and without authority; when his orders are not clear and distinct;[30] when there are no fixed duties assigned to officers and men,[31] and the ranks are formed in a slovenly haphazard manner, the result is utter *disorganization*.

19. When a general, unable to estimate the enemy's strength, allows an inferior force to engage a larger one, or hurls a weak detachment against a powerful one, and neglects to place picked

soldiers in the front rank, the result must be a *rout*.[32]

20. 凡此六者, 敗之道也, 將之至任, 不可不察也。
21. 夫地形者, 兵之助也。料敵制勝, 計險阨遠近, 上將
    之道也。

20. These are six ways of courting defeat,[33] which must be carefully noted by the general who has attained a responsible post.[34]

21. The natural formation of the country is the soldier's best ally;[35] but a power of estimating the adversary,[36] of controlling the forces of victory,[37] and of shrewdly calculating difficulties, dangers and distances,[38] constitutes the test of a great general.[39]

22. 知此而用戰者必勝;不知此而用戰者比敗。
23. 故戰道必勝, 主曰無戰, 必戰可也;戰道不勝, 主曰必
    戰, 無戰可也。

22. He who knows these things, and in fighting puts his knowledge into practice, will win his battles. He who knows them not, nor practices them, will surely be defeated.

23. If fighting is sure to result in victory, then you must fight, even though the ruler forbid it; if fighting will not result in victory, then you must not fight even at the ruler's bidding.[40]

24. 故進不求名, 退不避罪, 唯民是保, 而利合於主, 國之
    寶也。
25. 視卒如嬰兒, 故可與之赴深谿;視卒如愛子, 故可與
    之俱死。

24. The general who advances without coveting fame and retreats without fearing disgrace,[41] whose only thought is to protect his country and do good service for his sovereign,[42] is the jewel of the kingdom.[43]

25. Regard your soldiers as your children, and they will fol-

low you into the deepest valleys; look on them as your own be-
loved sons, and they will stand by you even unto death.[44]

26. 厚而不能使, 愛而不能令, 亂而不能治, 譬如驕子,
不可用也。
27. 知吾卒之可以擊, 而不知敵之不可擊, 勝之半也。

26. If, however, you are indulgent, but unable to make your
authority felt; kind-hearted, but unable to enforce your commands; and incapable, moreover, of quelling disorder:[45] then
your soldiers must be likened to spoilt children; they are useless
for any practical purpose.[46]

27. If we know that our own men are in a condition to attack,
but are unaware that the enemy is not open to attack, we have
gone only halfway towards victory.[47]

28. 知敵之可擊, 而不知吾卒之不可以擊, 勝之半也。
29. 知敵之可擊, 知吾卒之可以擊, 而不知地形之不可以
戰, 勝之半也。
30. 故知兵者, 動而不迷, 舉而不窮。
31. 故曰:知己知彼, 勝乃不殆;知天知地, 勝乃可全。

28. If we know that the enemy is open to attack, but are unaware that our men are not in a condition to attack, we have gone
only halfway towards victory.[48]

29. If we know that the enemy is open to attack, and also
know that our men are in a condition to attack, but are unaware
that the nature of the ground makes fighting impracticable, we
have still gone only halfway towards victory.[49]

30. Hence the experienced soldier, once in motion, is never
bewildered; once he has broken camp, he is never at a loss.[50]

31. Hence the saying: If you know the enemy and know yourself, your victory will not stand in doubt;[51] if you know Heaven
and know Earth,[52] you may make your victory complete.

# CHAPTER 11

# The Nine Situations[1]
## 九地篇第十一

1. 孫子曰:用兵之法, 有散地, 有輕地, 有爭地, 有交地, 有衢地, 有重地, 有圮地, 有圍地, 有死地。
2. 諸侯自戰其地者, 為散地。

1.  Sun Tzŭ said: The art of war recognizes nine varieties of ground: (1) Dispersive ground; (2) facile ground; (3) contentious ground; (4) open ground; (5) ground of intersecting highways; (6) serious ground; (7) difficult ground; (8) hemmed-in ground; (9) desperate ground.

2.  When a chieftain is fighting in his own territory, it is dispersive ground.[2]

3. 入人之地而不深者, 為輕地。
4. 我得則利, 彼得亦利者, 為爭地。

3.  When he has penetrated into hostile territory, but to no great distance, it is facile ground.[3]

4.  Ground the possession of which imports great advantage to either side, is contentious ground.[4]

5. 我可以住, 彼可以來者, 為交地。
6. 諸侯之地三屬, 先至而得天下之眾者, 為衢地。

5.  Ground on which each side has liberty of movement is open ground.[5]

6.  Ground that forms the keys to three contiguous states,[6]

so that he who occupies it first has most of the Empire at his command,[7] is ground of intersecting highways.[8]

7. 入人之地深, 背城邑多者, 為重地。
8. 山林、險阻、沮澤, 凡難行之道者, 為圮地。
9. 所由入者隘, 所從歸者迂, 彼寡可以擊吾之眾者, 為圍地。
10. 疾戰則存, 不疾戰則亡者, 為死地。

7.　When an army has penetrated into the heart of a hostile country, leaving a number of fortified cities in its rear,[9] it is serious ground.

8.　Mountain forests,[10] rugged steeps, marches and fens—all country that is hard to traverse: this is difficult ground.[11]

9.　Ground which is reached through narrow gorges, and from which we can only retire by tortuous paths, so that a small number of the enemy would suffice to crush a large body of our men: this is hemmed-in ground.

10.　Ground on which we can only be saved from destruction by fighting without delay, is desperate ground.[12]

11. 是故散地則無戰, 輕地則無止, 爭地則無攻。

11.　On dispersive ground, therefore, fight not. On facile ground, halt not. On contentious ground, attack not.[13]

12. 交地則無絕, 衢地則合交。
13. 重地則掠, 圮地則行。

12.　On open ground, do not try to block the enemy's way.[14] On ground of intersecting highways, join hands with your allies.[15]

13.　On serious ground, gather in plunder.[16] In difficult ground, keep steadily on the march.[17]

14. 圍地則謀, 死地則戰。

15. 所謂古之善用兵者, 能使敵人前後不相及, 眾寡不相恃, 貴賤不相救, 上下不相扶。

14. On hemmed-in ground, resort to stratagem.[18] On desperate ground, fight.[19]

15. Those who were called skilful leaders of old[20] knew how to drive a wedge between the enemy's front and rear;[21] to prevent co-operation between his large and small divisions; to hinder the good troops from rescuing the bad,[22] the officers from rallying their men.[23]

16. 卒離而不集, 兵合而不齊。
17. 合於利而動, 不合於利而止。
18. 敢問:"敵眾整而將來, 待之若何?"曰:"先奪其所愛, 則聽矣。"

16. When the enemy's men were scattered, they prevented them from concentrating;[24] even when their forces were united, they managed to keep them in disorder.[25]

17. When it was to their advantage, they made a forward move; when otherwise, they stopped still.[26]

18. If asked how to cope with a great host of the enemy in orderly array and on the point of marching to the attack,[27] I should say: "Begin by seizing something which your opponent holds dear; then he will be amenable to your will."[28]

19. 兵之情主速, 乘人之不及, 由不虞之道, 攻其所不戒也。

19. Rapidity is the essence of war:[29] take advantage of the enemy's unreadiness, make your way by unexpected routes, and attack unguarded spots.

20. 凡為客之道:深入則專, 主人不克。
21. 掠於饒野, 三軍足食。
22. 謹養而勿勞, 併氣積力, 運兵計謀, 為不可測。

20. The following are the principles to be observed by an invading force: The further you penetrate into a country, the greater will be the solidarity of your troops, and thus the defenders will not prevail against you.

21. Make forays in fertile country in order to supply your army with food.[30]

22. Carefully study the wellbeing of your men,[31] and do not overtax them. Concentrate your energy and hoard your strength.[32] Keep your army continually on the move,[33] and devise unfathomable plans.[34]

23. 投之無所往, 死且不北。死焉不得, 士人盡力。

24. 兵士甚陷則不懼, 無所往則固, 深入則拘, 不得已則鬥。

23. Throw your soldiers into positions whence there is no escape, and they will prefer death to flight.[35] If they will face death, there is nothing they may not achieve.[36] Officers and men alike will put forth their uttermost strength.[37]

24. Soldiers when in desperate straits lose the sense of fear. If there is no place of refuge, they will stand firm. If they are in the heart of a hostile country, they will show a stubborn front.[38] If there is no help for it, they will fight hard.

25. 是故其兵不修而戒, 不求而得, 不約而親, 不令而信。

26. 禁祥去疑, 至死無所災。

25. Thus, without waiting to be marshaled, the soldiers will be constantly on the *qui vive*;[39] without waiting to be asked, they will do your will;[40] without restrictions, they will be faithful;[41] without giving orders, they can be trusted.[42]

26. Prohibit the taking of omens, and do away with superstitious doubts.[43] Then, until death itself comes, no calamity need be feared.[44]

27. 吾士無餘財, 非惡貨也; 無餘命, 非惡壽也。

28. 令發之日, 士卒坐者涕沾襟, 偃臥者淚交頤。投之無所
往者, 諸、劌之勇也。

27. If our soldiers are not overburdened with money, it is not because they have a distaste for riches; if their lives are not unduly long, it is not because they are disinclined to longevity.[45]

28. On the day they are ordered out to battle, your soldiers may weep,[46] those sitting up bedewing their garments, and those lying down letting the tears run down their cheeks.[47] But let them once be brought to bay, and they will display the courage of a Chu or a Kuei.[48]

29. 故善用兵者, 譬如率然。率然者, 常山之蛇也。擊其首
則尾至, 擊其尾則首至, 擊其中則首尾俱至。

29. The skilful tactician may be likened to the *shuairan*. Now the *shuairan* is a snake that is found in the Ch'ang mountains.[49] Strike at its head, and you will be attacked by its tail; strike at its tail, and you will be attacked by its head; strike at its middle, and you will be attacked by head and tail both.

30. 敢問：“兵可使如率然乎？”曰：“可。”夫吳人與越人相
惡也, 當其同舟而濟, 遇風, 其相救也, 如左右手。

31. 是故方馬埋輪, 未足恃也。

30. Asked if an army can be made to imitate the *shuairan*,[50] I should answer, Yes. For the men of Wu and the men of Yue are enemies;[51] yet if they are crossing a river in the same boat and are caught by a storm, they will come to each other's assistance just as the left hand helps the right.[52]

31. Hence it is not enough to put one's trust in the tethering of horses,[53] and the burying of chariot wheel in the ground.[54]

32. 齊勇若一, 政之道也。

33. 剛柔皆得, 地之理也。
34. 故善用兵者, 攜手若使一人, 不得已也。

32. The principle on which to manage an army is to set up one standard of courage which all must reach.[55]

33. How to make the best of both strong and weak—that is a question involving the proper use of ground.[56]

34. Thus the skilful general conducts his army just as though he were leading a single man, willy-nilly, by the hand.[57]

35. 將軍之事：靜以幽, 正以治。
36. 能愚士卒之耳目, 使之無知。

35. It is the business of a general to be quiet and thus ensure secrecy; upright and just, and thus maintain order.[58]

36. He must be able to mystify his officers and men by false reports and appearances,[59] and thus keep them in total ignorance.[60]

37. 易其事, 革其謀, 使人無識。易其居, 迂其途, 使人不得慮。

37. By altering his arrangements and changing his plans,[61] he keeps the enemy without definite knowledge.[62] By shifting his camp and taking circuitous routes, he prevents the enemy from anticipating his purpose.[63]

38. 帥與之期, 如登高而去其梯。帥與之深入諸侯之地, 而發其機。
39. 焚舟破釜, 若驅群羊而往, 驅而來, 莫知所之。

38. At the critical moment, the leader of an army acts like one who has climbed up a height and then kicks away the ladder behind him.[64] He carries his men deep into hostile territory before he shows his hand.[65]

39. He burns his boats and breaks his cooking-pots;[66] like

a shepherd driving a flock of sheep, he drives his men this way and that, and none knows whither he is going.[67]

40. 聚三軍之眾, 投之於險, 此謂將軍之事也。
41. 九地之變, 屈伸之力, 人情之理, 不可不察也。
42. 凡為客之道：深則專, 淺則散。
43. 去國越境而師者, 絕地也；四達者, 衢地也。

40. To muster his host and bring it into danger: this may be termed the business of the general.[68]

41. The different measures suited to the nine varieties of ground;[69] the expediency of aggressive or defensive tactics; and the fundamental laws of human nature: these are things that must most certainly be studied.

42. When invading hostile territory, the general principle is, that penetrating deeply brings cohesion; penetrating but a short way means dispersion.[70]

43. When you leave your own country behind, and take your army across neighboring territory,[71] you find yourself on critical ground.[72] When there are means of communication[73] on all four sides, the ground is one of intersecting highways.[74]

44. 入深者, 重地也；入淺者, 輕地也。
45. 背固前隘者, 圍地也；無所往者, 死地也。
46. 是故散地, 吾將一其志；輕地, 吾將使之屬。

44. When you penetrate deeply into a country, it is serious ground. When you penetrate but a little way, it is facile ground.

45. When you have the enemy's strongholds on your rear,[75] and narrow passes in front, it is hemmed-in ground. When there is no place of refuge at all, it is desperate ground.

46. Therefore, on dispersive ground, I would inspire my men with unity of purpose.[76] On facile ground, I would see that there is close connection between all parts of my army.[77]

47. 爭地, 吾將趨其後。

47. On contentious ground, I would hurry up my rear.[78]

48. 交地, 吾將謹其守；衢地, 吾將固其結。
49. 重地, 吾將繼其食；圮地, 吾將進其塗。
50. 圍地, 吾將塞其闕；死地, 吾將示之以不活。

48. On open ground, I would keep a vigilant eye on my defenses.[79] On ground of intersecting highways, I would consolidate my alliances.[80]

49. On serious ground, I would try to ensure a continuous stream of supplies.[81] On difficult ground, I would keep pushing on along the road.[82]

50. On hemmed-in ground, I would block any way of retreat.[83] On desperate ground, I would proclaim to my soldiers the hopelessness of saving their lives.[84]

51. 故兵之情：圍則禦, 不得已則鬥, 過則從。

51. For it is the soldier's disposition to offer an obstinate resistance when surrounded, to fight hard when he cannot help himself, and to obey promptly when he has fallen into danger.[85]

52. 是故不知諸侯之謀者, 不能預交。不知山林、險阻、沮澤之形者, 不能行軍。不用鄉導, 不能得地利。
53. 四五者, 不知一, 非霸王之兵也。

52. We cannot enter into alliance with neighboring princes until we are acquainted with their designs. We are not fit to lead an army on the march unless we are familiar with the face of the country—its mountains and forests, its pitfalls and precipices, its marches and swamps. We shall be unable to turn natural advantages to account unless we make use of local guides.[86]

53. To be ignorant of any one of the following four or five

principles[87] does not befit a warlike prince.[88]

54. 夫霸王之兵, 伐大國, 則其眾不得聚; 威加於敵, 則其
交不得合。

55. 是故不爭天下之交, 不養天下之權, 信己之私, 威加
於敵, 故其城可拔, 其國可隳。

54. When a warlike prince attacks a powerful state, his generalship shows itself in preventing the concentration of the enemy's forces. He overawes his opponents,[89] and their allies are prevented from joining against him.[90]

55. Hence he does not strive[91] to ally himself with all and sundry,[92] nor does he foster the power of other states. He carries out his own secret designs,[93] keeping his antagonists in awe.[94] Thus he is able to capture their cities and overthrow their kingdoms.[95]

56. 施無法之賞, 懸無政之令, 犯三軍之眾, 若使一人。

56. Bestow rewards without regard to rule,[96] issue orders[97] without regard to previous arrangement;[98] and you will be able to handle a whole army[99] as though you had to do with but a single man.[100]

57. 犯之以事, 勿告以言。犯之以利, 勿告以害。

58. 投之亡地然後存, 陷之死地然後生。

57. Confront your soldiers with the deed itself; never let them know your design.[101] When the outlook is bright, bring it before their eyes; but tell them nothing when the situation is gloomy.

58. Place your army in deadly peril, and it will survive; plunge it into desperate straits, and it will come off in safety.[102]

59. 夫眾陷于害, 然後能為勝敗。

60. 故為兵之事, 在於順詳敵之意。

61. 并敵一向, 千里殺將。

62. 此謂巧能成事者也。

59. For it is precisely when a force has fallen into harm's way that is capable of striking a blow for victory.[103]

60. Success in warfare is gained by carefully accommodating ourselves to the enemy's purpose.[104]

61. By persistently hanging on the enemy's flank,[105] we shall succeed in the long run[106] in killing the commander-in-chief.[107]

62. This is called ability to accomplish a thing by sheer cunning.[108]

63. 是故政舉之日, 夷關折符, 無通其使。
64. 勵於廊廟之上, 以誅其事。

63. On the day that you take up your command,[109] block the frontier passes,[110] destroy the official tallies,[111] and stop the passage of all emissaries.[112]

64. Be stern in the council-chamber,[113] so that you may control the situation.[114]

65. 敵人開闔, 必亟入之。
66. 先其所愛, 微與之期。

65. If the enemy leaves a door open, you must rush in.[115]

66. Forestall your opponent by seizing what he holds dear,[116] and subtly contrive to time his arrival on the ground.[117]

67. 踐墨隨敵, 以決戰事。
68. 是故始如處女, 敵人開戶, 後如脫兔, 敵不及拒。

67. Walk in the path defined by rule,[118] and accommodate yourself to the enemy until you can fight a decisive battle.[119]

68. At first, then, exhibit the coyness of a maiden, until the enemy gives you an opening; afterwards emulate the rapidity of a running hare, and it will be too late for the enemy to oppose you.[120]

# CHAPTER 12

# The Attack By Fire[1]
## 火攻篇第十二

1. 孫子曰：凡火攻有五：一曰火人，二曰火積，三曰火輜，四曰火庫，五曰火隊。

1. Sun Tzŭ said: There are five ways of attacking with fire. The first is to burn soldiers in their camp;[2] the second is to burn stores;[3] the third is to burn baggage-trains;[4] the fourth is to burn arsenals and magazines;[5] the fifth is to hurl dropping fire amongst the enemy.[6]

2. 行火必有因，煙火必素具。
3. 發火有時，起火有日。

2. In order carry out an attack with fire, we must have means available;[7] the material for raising fire should always be kept in readiness.[8]

3. There is a proper season for making attacks with fire, and special days for starting a conflagration.[9]

4. 時者，天之燥也。日者，月在箕、壁、翼、軫也。凡此四宿者，風起之日也。
5. 凡火攻，必因五火之變而應之。
6. 火發於內，則早應之於外。

4. The proper season is when the weather is very dry; the special days are those when moon is in the constellations of the Sieve, the Wall, the Wing or the Crossbar;[10] for these four are all days of rising wind.[11]

5. In attacking with fire, one should be prepared to meet five possible developments:[12]

6. (1) When fire breaks out inside the enemy's camp, respond at once[13] with an attack from without.

7. 火發而其兵靜者, 待而勿攻。
8. 極其火力, 可從而從之, 不可從而止。
9. 火可發於外, 無待於內, 以時發之。

7. (2) If there is an outbreak of fire, but the enemy's soldiers remain quiet, bide your time and do not attack.[14]

8. (3) When force of the flames has reached its height, follow it up with an attack, if that is practicable; if not, stay where you are.[15]

9. (4) If it is possible to make an assault with fire from without, do not wait for it to break out within, but deliver your attack at a favorable moment.[16]

10. 火發上風, 無攻下風。
11. 畫風久, 夜風止。
12. 凡軍必知有五火之變, 以數守之。

10. (5) When you start a fire, be to windward of it. Do not attack from the leeward.[17]

11. A wind that rises in the daytime lasts long, but a night breeze soon falls.[18]

12. In every army, the five developments connected with fire must be known, the movements of the stars calculated, and a watch kept for the proper days.[19]

13. 故以火佐攻者明, 以水佐攻者強。
14. 水可以絕不可以奪。

13. Hence those who use fire as an aid to the attack show intelligence;[20] those who use water as an aid to the attack gain an accession of strength.[21]

14. By means of water, an enemy may be intercepted, but not robbed of all his belongings.[22]

15. 夫戰勝攻取, 而不修其功者凶命, 曰"費留"。
16. 故曰:明主慮之, 良將修之。

15. Unhappy is the fate of one who tries to win his battles and succeed in his attacks without cultivating the spirit of enterprise; for the result is waste of time and general stagnation.[23]
16. Hence the saying: The enlightened ruler lays his plans well ahead; the good general cultivates his resources.[24]

17. 非利不動, 非得不用, 非危不戰。
18. 主不可以怒而興師, 將不可以慍而致戰。
19. 合於利而動, 不合於利而止。

17. Move not unless you see an advantage;[25] use not your troops unless there is something to be gained; fight not unless the position is critical.
18. No ruler should put troops into the field merely to gratify his own spleen; no general should fight a battle simply out of pique.[26]
19. If it is to your advantage, make a forward move if not, stay where you are.[27]

20. 怒可以復喜, 慍可以復悅。
21. 亡國不可以復存, 死者不可以復生。
22. 故明君慎之, 良將警之。此安國全軍之道也。

20. Anger may in time change to gladness; vexation may be succeeded by content.[28]
21. But a kingdom that has once been destroyed can never come again into being;[29] nor can the dead ever be brought back to life.
22. Hence the enlightened ruler is heedful, and the good general full of caution.[30] This is the way to keep a country at peace and an army intact.[31]

# CHAPTER 13

# The Use Of Spies[1]
# 用間篇第十三

1. 孫子曰:凡興師十萬, 出征千里, 百姓之費, 公家之奉, 日
費千金。內外騷動, 怠於道路, 不得操事者, 七十萬家。

1.   Sun Tzŭ said: Raising a host of a hundred thousand men and marching them great distances entails heavy loss on the people and a drain on the resources of the State. The daily expenditure will amount to a thousand ounces of silver.[2]

There will be commotion at home and abroad, and men will drop down exhausted on the highways. As many as seven hundred thousand families will be impeded in their labor.[3]

2. 相守數年, 以爭一日之勝, 而愛爵祿百金, 不知敵之情
者, 不仁之至也。

2.   Hostile armies may face each other for years, striving for the victory which is decided in a single day. This being so, to remain in ignorance of the enemy's condition simply because one grudges the outlay of a hundred ounces of silver in hours and emoluments,[4] is the height of inhumanity.[5]

3. 非人之將也, 非主之佐也, 非勝之主也。

3.   One who acts thus is no leader of men, no present help to his sovereign,[6] no master of victory.

4. 故明君賢將, 所以動而勝人, 成功出于眾者, 先知也。
5. 先知者, 不可取於鬼神, 不可象於事, 不可驗於度。

6.　必取於人, 知敵之情者也。

4.　Thus, what enables the wise sovereign and the good general to strike and conquer, and achieve things beyond the reach of ordinary men, is *foreknowledge*.[7]

5.　Now this foreknowledge cannot be elicited from spirit;[8] it cannot be obtained inductively from experience,[9] nor by any deductive calculation.[10]

6.　Knowledge of the enemy's dispositions can only be obtained from other men.[11]

7.　故用間有五：有鄉間, 有內間, 有反間, 有死間, 有生間。

8.　五間俱起, 莫知其道, 是謂神紀, 人君之寶也。

9.　鄉間者, 因其鄉人而用之。

7.　Hence the use of spies, of whom there are five classes: (1) Local spies; (2) inward spies; (3) converted spies; (4) doomed spies; (5) surviving spies.

8.　When these five kinds of spy are all at work, none can discover the secret system.[12] This is called[13] "divine manipulation of the threads."[14] It is the sovereign's most precious faculty.[15]

9.　Having *local spies*[16] means employing the services of the inhabitants of a district.[17]

10.　內間者, 因其官人而用之。

10.　Having *inward spies*, making use of officials of the enemy.[18]

11.　反間者, 因其敵間而用之。

11.　Having *concerted spies*, getting hold of the enemy's spies and using them for our own purposes.[19]

12.　死間者, 為誑事於外, 令吾間知之, 而傳於敵間也。

13. 生間者, 反報也。

12. Having *doomed spies*, doing certain things openly for purposes of deception, and allowing our own spies to know of them and report them to the enemy.[20]

13. *Surviving spies*, finally, are those who bring back news from the enemy's camp.[21]

14. 故三軍之事, 莫親於間, 賞莫厚於間, 事莫密於間。

14. Hence it is that with none in the whole army are more intimate relations to be maintained than with spies.[22] None should be more liberally rewarded.[23] In no other business should greater secrecy be preserved.[24]

15. 非聖智不能用間。

15. Spies cannot be usefully employed[25] without a certain intuitive sagacity.

16. 非仁義不能使間。
17. 非微妙不能得間之實。
18. 微哉！微哉！無所不用間也。
19. 間事未發, 而先聞者, 間與所告者皆死。

16. They cannot be properly managed without benevolence and straightforwardness.[26]

17. Without subtle ingenuity of mind, one cannot make certain of the truth of their reports.[27]

18. Be subtle! Be subtle![28] and use your spies for every kind of business.

19. If a secret piece of news is divulged by a spy before the time is ripe, he must be put to death together with the man to whom the secret was told.[29]

20. 凡軍之所欲擊, 城之所欲殺, 人之所欲殺, 必先知其守
　　 將、左右、謁者、門者、舍人之姓名, 令吾間必索知之。

20. Whether the object be to crush an army, to storm a city,
or to assassinate an individual, it is always necessary to begin by
finding out the names of the attendants,[30] the aides-de-camp,[31]
the doorkeeper and sentries[32] of the general in command.[33] Our
spies must be commissioned to ascertain these.[34]

21. 必索敵人之間來間我者, 因而利之, 導而舍之, 故反
　　 間可得而用也。
22. 因是而知之, 故鄉間、內間可得而使也。
23. 因是而知之, 故死間為誑事可使告敵。
24. 因是而知之, 故生間可使如期。

21. The enemy's spies who have come to spy on us must be
sought out,[35] tempted with bribes, led away, and comfortably
housed.[36] Thus they will become converted spies and available
for our service.

22. It is through the information brought by the converted spy
that we are able to acquire and employ local and inward spies.[37]

23. It is owing to his information, again, that we can cause
the doomed spy to carry false tidings to the enemy.[38]

24. Lastly, it is by his information that the surviving spy can
be used on appointed occasions.[39]

25. 五間之事, 主必知之, 知之必在於反間, 故反間不可
　　 不厚也。
26. 昔殷之興也, 伊摯在夏;周之興也, 呂牙在殷。

25. The end and aim of spying in all its five varieties is knowledge of the enemy;[40] and this knowledge can only be derived, in
the first instance, from the converted spy.[41] Hence it is essential
that the converted spy be treated with the utmost liberality.

26. Of old, the rise of the Yin dynasty[42] was due to I Chih[43]

who had served under the Hsia. Likewise, the rise of the Chou dynasty was due to Lü Ya who had served under the Yin.[44]

27. 故惟明君賢將能以上智為間者, 必成大功。此兵之要, 三軍之所恃而動也。

27. Hence it is only the enlightened ruler and the wise general who will use the highest intelligence of the army for purposes of spying,[45] and thereby they achieve great results. Spies are a most important element in war, because on them depends an army's ability to move.[46]

PART TWO

# Critical Notes
# and
# Commentaries

# CHAPTER 1

# Laying Plans
# 計篇第一

1. This is the only possible meaning of 計, which M. Amiot and Capt. Calthrop wrongly translate "Fondements de l'art militaire" and "First principles" respectively. Cao Gong says it refers to the deliberations in the temple selected by the general for his temporary use, or as we should say, in his tent. See § 26.

2. The old text of the *Tong Dian* has 故經之以五校之計 etc. Later editors have inserted 事 after 五, and 以 before 計. The former correction is perhaps superfluous, but the latter seems necessary in order to make sense, and is supported by the accepted reading in § 12, where the same words recur. I am inclined to think, however, that the whole sentence from 校 to 情 is an interpolation and has no business here at all. If it be retained, Wang Xi must be right in saying that 計 denotes the "seven considerations" in (§ 13. 情 are the circumstances or conditions likely to bring about victory or defeat. The antecedent of the first 之 is 兵者; of the second, 五. 校 contains the idea of "comparison with the enemy," which cannot well be brought out here, but will appear in § 12. Altogether, difficult though it is, the passage is not so hopelessly corrupt as to justify Capt. Calthrop in burking it entirely.

3. It appears from what follows that Sun Tzǔ means by 道 a principle of harmony, not unlike the Tao of Laozi in its moral aspect. One might be tempted to render it by "morale," were it not considered as an attribute of the *ruler* in § 13.

4 . The original text omits 令民, inserts an 以 after each 可, and omits 民 after 而. Capt. Calthrop translates: "If the ruling authority be upright, the people are united"—a very pretty sentiment, but wholly out of place in what purports to be a translation of Sun Tzǔ.

5. The commentators, I think, make an unnecessary mystery of 陰

陽. Thus Meng Shi defines the words as "the hard and the soft, waxing and waning," 剛柔盈縮 which does not help us much. Wang Xi, however, may be right in saying that what is meant is "the general economy of Heaven," 總天道 including the five elements, the four seasons, wind and clouds, and other phenomena.

6. 死生 (omitted by Capt. Calthrop) may have been included here because the safety of an army depends largely on its quickness to turn these geographical features to account.

7. The five cardinal virtues of the Chinese are (1) 仁 humanity or benevolence; (2) 義 uprightness of mind; (3) 禮 self-respect, self-control, or "proper feeling;" (4) 智 wisdom; (5) 信 sincerity or good faith. Here 智 and 信 are put before 仁, and the two military virtues of "courage" and "strictness" substituted for 義 and 禮.

8. The Chinese of this sentence is so concise as to be practically unintelligible without commentary. I have followed the interpretation of Cao Gong, who joins 曲制 and again 主用. Others take each of the six predicates separately. 曲 has the somewhat uncommon sense of "cohort" or division of an army. Capt. Calthrop translates: "Partition and ordering of troops," which only covers 曲制.

9. The *Yu Lan* has an interpolated 五 before 計. It is obvious, however, that the 五者 just enumerated cannot be described as 計. Capt. Calthrop, forced to give some rendering of the words which he had omitted in § 3, shows himself decidedly hazy: "Further, with regard to these and the following seven matters, the condition of the enemy must be compared with our own." He does not appear to see that the seven queries or considerations that follow arise directly out of the Five heads, instead of being supplementary to them.

10. I.e., "is in harmony with his subjects." Cf. § 5.

11. See §§ 7, 8.

12. Du Mu alludes to the remarkable story of Cao Cao (A.D. 155-220), who was such a strict disciplinarian that once, in accordance with his own severe regulations against injury to standing crops, he condemned himself to death for having allowed his horse to shy into a field of corn! However, in lieu of losing his head, he was persuaded to satisfy his sense of justice by cutting off his hair. Cao Cao's own comment on the present passage is characteristically curt: 設而不犯

犯必誅 "When you lay down a law, see that it is not disobeyed; if it is disobeyed, the offender must be put to death."

13. Morally as well as physically. As Mei Yaochen puts it, 內和外附, which might be freely rendered "*esprit de crops* and 'big battalions.'"

14. Du You quotes 王子 as saying: "Without constant practice, the officers will be nervous and undecided when mustering for battle; without constant practice, the general will be wavering and irresolute when the crisis is at hand."

15. 明, literally "clear;" that is, on which side is there the most absolute certainly that merit will be properly rewarded and misdeeds summarily punished?

16. The form of this paragraph reminds us that Sun Tzŭ's treatise was composed expressly for the benefit of his patron 闔閭 He Lü, king of the Wu State. It is not necessary, however, to understand 我 before 留之 (as some commentators do), or to take 將 as "generals under my command."

17. Capt. Calthrop blunders amazingly over this sentence: "Wherefore, with regard to the foregoing, considering that with us lies the advantage, and the generals agreeing, we create a situation which promises victory." Mere logic should have kept him from penning such frothy balderdash.

18. Sun Tzŭ, as a practical soldier, will have none of the "bookish theoric." He cautions us here not to pin our faith to abstract principles; "for," as Zhang Yu puts it, "while the main laws of strategy can be stated clearly enough for the benefit of all and sundry, you must be guided by the actions of the enemy in attempting to secure a favorable position in actual warfare." On the eve of the battle of Waterloo, Lord Uxbridge, commanding the cavalry, went to the Duke of Wellington in order to learn what plans and calculations were for the morrow, because, as he explained, he might suddenly find himself Commander-in-chief and would be unable to frame new plans in a critical moment. The Duke listened quietly and then said: "Who will attack the first tomorrow—I or Bonaparte?" "Bonaparte," replied Lord Uxbridge. "Well," continued the Duke, "Bonaparte has not given me any idea of his projects; and as my plans will depend upon his, how can you expect me to tell you what mine are?"[1]

---

[1] "Words on Wellington," by Sir W. Fraser.

19. The truth of this pithy and profound saying will be admitted by every soldier. Col. Henderson tells us that Wellington, great in so many military qualities, was especially distinguished by "the extraordinary skill with which he concealed his movements and deceived both friend and foe."

20. 取, as often in Sun Tzŭ, is used in the sense of 擊. It is rather remarkable that all the commentators, with the exception of Zhang Yu, refer 亂 to the enemy: "when he is in disorder, crush him." It is more natural to suppose that Sun Tzŭ is still illustrating the uses of deception in war.

21. The meaning of 實 is made clear from chap. VI, where it is opposed to 虛 "weak or vulnerable spots." 強, according to Du You and other commentators, has reference to the keenness of the men as well as to numerical superiority. Capt. Calthrop evolves an extraordinarily far-fetched translation: "If there are defects, give an appearance of perfection, and awe the enemy. Pretend to be strong, and so cause the enemy to avoid you"!

22. I follow Zhang Yu in my interpretation of 怒. 卑 is expanded by Mei Yaochen into 示以卑弱. Wangzi, quoted by Du You, says that a good tactician plays with his adversary as a cat plays with a mouse, first feigning weakness and immobility, and then suddenly pouncing upon him.

23. This is probably the meaning, though Mei Yaochen has the note: "while we are taking our ease, wait for the enemy to tire himself out." 以我之佚待彼之勞. The *Yu Lan* has "Lure him on and tire him out." 引而勞之. This would seem also to have been Cao Gong's text, judging by his comment 以利勞之.

24. Less plausible is the interpretation favored by most of the commentators: "If sovereign and subject are in accord, put division between them."

25. This seems to be the way in which Cao Gong understood the passage, and is perhaps the best sense to be got out of the text as it stands. Most of the commentators give the following explanation: "It is impossible to lay down rules for warfare before you come into touch with the enemy." This would be very plausible if it did not ignore 此, which unmistakably refers to the maxims that Sun Tzŭ *has* been laying down.

It is possible, of course, that 此 may be a later interpolation, in which case the sentence would practically mean: "Success in warfare cannot be taught." As an alternative, however, I would venture to suggest that a second 不 may have fallen out after 可, so that we get: "These maxims for succeeding in war are the first that ought to be imparted."

26. Zhang Yu tells us that in ancient times it was customary for a temple to be set apart for the use of a general who was about to take the field, in order that he might there elaborate his plan of campaign. Capt. Calthrop misunderstands it as "the shrine of the ancestors," and gives a loose and inaccurate rendering of the whole passage.

# CHAPTER 2

# Waging War
## 作戰篇第二

1. Cao Gong has the notes: 欲戰必先算其費務 "He who wishes to fight must first count the cost," which prepares us for the discovery that the subject of the chapter is not what we might expect from the title, but is primarily a consideration of ways and means.

2. The 馳車 were lightly built and, according to Zhang Yu, used for the attack; the 革車 were heavier, and designed for purposes of defense. Li Quan, it is true, says that the latter were light, but this seems hardly probable. Capt. Calthrop translates "chariots" and "supply wagons" respectively, but is not supported by any commentator. It is interesting to note the analogies between early Chinese warfare and that of the Homeric Greeks. In each case, the war-chariot was the important factor, forming as it did the nucleus round which was grouped a certain number of foot soldiers. With regard to the numbers given here, we are informed that each swift chariot was accompanied by 75 footmen, and each heavy chariot by 25 footmen, so that the whole army would be divided up into a thousand battalions, each consisting of two chariots and a hundred men.

3. 2.78 modern *li* go to a mile. The length may have varied slightly since Sun Tzŭ's time.

4. 則, which follows 糧 in the *textus receptus*, is important as indicating the apodosis. In the text adopted by Capt. Calthrop it is omitted, so that he is led to give this meaningless translation of the opening sentence: "Now the requirements of War are such that we need 1,000 chariot," etc. The second 費, which is redundant, is omitted in the *Yu-lan*. 千金, like 千里 above, is meant to suggest a large but indefinite number. As the Chinese have never possessed gold coins, it is incorrect to translate it "1000 pieces of gold."

5. Capt. Calthrop adds: "You have the instruments of victory," which he seems to get from the first five characters of the next sentence.

6. The *Yulan* omits 勝; but though 勝久 is certainly a bold phrase, it is more likely to be right than not. Both in this place and in § 4, the *Tong Dian* and *Yulan* read 頓 (in the sense of "to injure") instead of 鈍.

7. As synonyms to 屈 are given 盡, 殫, 窮 and 困.

8. 久暴師 means literally, "If there is long exposure of the army." Of 暴 in this sense Kang Xi cites an instance from the biography of 竇融 Dou Rong in the *Hou Han Shu*, where the commentary defines it by 露. Cf. also the following from the 戰國策: 將軍九暴露於外 "General, you have long been exposed to all weather."

9. Following Du You, I understand 善 in the sense of "to make good," i.e. to mend. But Du Mu and He Shi explain it as "to make good plans" for the future.

10. This concise and difficult sentence is not well explained by any of the commentators. Cao Gong, Li Quan, Meng Shi, Du You, Du Mu and Mei Yaochen have notes to the effect that a general, though naturally stupid, may nevertheless conquer through sheer force of rapidity. He Shi says: "Haste may be stupid, but at any rate it saves expenditure of energy and treasure; protracted operations may be very clever, but they bring calamity in their train." Wang Xi evades the difficulty by remarking: "Lengthy operations mean an army growing old, wealth being expended, an empty exchequer, and distress among the people; true cleverness insure against the occurrence of such calamities." Zhang Yu says: "So long as victory can be attained, stupid haste is preferable to clever dilatoriness." Now Sun Tzǔ says nothing whatever, except possibly by implication, about ill-considered haste being better than ingenious but lengthy operations. What he does say is something much more guarded, namely that, while speed may sometimes be injudicious, tardiness can never be anything but foolish—if only because it means impoverishment to the nation. Capt. Calthrop indulges his imagination with the following: "Therefore it is acknowledged that war cannot be too short in duration. But though conducted with the utmost art, if long continuing, misfortunes do always appear." It is hardly worthwhile to note the total disappearance of 拙速 in this precious concoction. In considering the point raised here by Sun Tzǔ,

the general deliberately measured the endurance of Rome against that of Hannibal's isolated army, because it seemed to him that the latter was more likely to suffer from a long campaign in a strange country. But it is quite a moot question whether his tactics would have proved successful in the long run. Their reversal, it is true, led to Cannae; but this only establishes a negative presumption in their favor.

11. The *Yulan* has 圖 instead of 國—evidently the mistake of a scribe.

12. That is, with rapidity. Only one who knows the disastrous effects of a long war can realize the supreme importance of rapidity in bringing it to a close. Only two commentators seem to favor this interpretation, but it fits well into the logic of the context, where as the rendering "He who does not know the evils of war cannot appreciate its benefits," is distinctly pointless.

13. Once war is declared, he will not waste precious time in waiting for reinforcements, nor will he turn his army back for fresh supplies, but crosses the enemy's frontier without delay. This may seem an audacious policy to recommend, but with all great strategists, from Julius Caesar to Napoleon Bonaparte, the value of time—that is, being a little ahead of your opponent—has counted for more than either numerical superiority or the nicest calculations with regard to commissariat. 籍 is used in the sense of 賦. The *Tong Dian* and *Yulan* have the inferior reading 籍. The commentators explain 不三載 by saying that the wagons are loaded once before passing the frontier, and that the army is met by a further consignment of supplies on the homeward march. The *Yulan*, however, reads 再 here as well.

14. 用, "things to be used," in the widest sense. It includes all the impedimenta of an army, apart from provisions.

15. The beginning of this sentence does not balance properly with the next, though obviously intended to do so. The arrangement, moreover, is so awkward that I cannot help suspecting some corruption in the text. It never seems to occur to Chinese commentators that an emendation may be necessary for the sense, and we get no help from them here. Sun Tzŭ says that the cause of the people's impoverishment is 遠輸; it is clear, therefore, that the words have reference to some system by which the husbandmen sent their contributions of corn to the army direct. But why should it fall on them to maintain an army

this way, except because the State or Government is too poor to do so? Assuming that 貧 ought to stand first in the sentence in order to balance 近 (the fact that the two words rhyme is significant), and thus getting rid of 國之, we are still left with 於師, which later words seem to me an obvious mistake for 國 "Poverty in the army" is an unlikely expression, especially as the general has just been warned not to encumber his army with a large quantity of supplies. If we suppose that 師 somehow got written here instead of 國 (a very simple supposition, as we have 近於師 in the next sentence), and that later on somebody, scenting a mistake, prefixed the gloss 國之 to 貧, without however erasing 於師, the whole muddle may be explained. My emended text then would be 貧於國者, etc.

16. 近, that is, as Wang Xi says, before the army has left its own territory. Cao Gong understands it of an army that has already crossed the frontier. Capt. Calthrop drops the 於, reading 近師者, but even so it is impossible to justify his translation "Repeated wars cause high prices."

17. Cf. Mencius VII. 2. xiv. 2, where 丘民 has the same meaning as 丘役. 丘 was an ancient measure of land. The full table, given in the 司馬法, may not be out of place here: 6 尺 1 步; 100 步 1 畝; 100 畝 1 夫; 3 夫 1 屋; 3 屋 1 井; 4 井 1 邑; 4 邑 1 丘; 4 丘 1 甸. According to the *Zhou Li*, there where nine husbandmen to a 井, which would assign to each men the goodly allowance of 100 畝 (of which 6.6 now go to an acre). What the values of these measures were in Sun Tzǔ's time is not known with any certainty. The lineal 尺, however, is supposed to have been about 20 cm. 急, may include levies of men, as well as other exactions.

18. The *Yulan* omits 財殫. I would propose the emended reading 力屈則中, etc. in view of the fact that we have 財竭 in the two preceding paragraphs, it seems probable that 財 is a scribe's mistake for 則, 殫 having been added afterwards to make sense. 中原內虛於家, literally: "Within the middle plains there is emptiness in the homes." For 中原 cf. *Shi Jing* II. 3. VI. 3 and II. 5. II. 3. with regard to 十去 其七, Du Mu says: 家業十耗其七也, and Wang Xi: 民費大半矣; that is, the people are mulcted not of $3/10$ but of $7/10$, of their income. But this is hardly to be extracted from our text. He Shi has a characteristic tag: 國以民為本民以食為天居人上者宜乎重惜 "The

*people* being regarded as the essential part of the State, and *food* as the people's heaven, is it not right that those in authority should value and be careful of both?"

19. The *Yulan* has several various readings here, the more important of which are 疲 for the less common 罷, 干 for 蔽, and 兵牛 for 丘牛, which latter, if right, must mean "oxen from the country districts" (cf. *supra*, § 12). For the meaning of 櫓, see note on II, § 4. Capt. Calthrop omits to translate 丘牛大車.

20. Because twenty cartloads will be consumed in the process of transporting one cartload to the front. According to Cao Gong, a 鐘=6 斛 4, or 64, but according to Meng Shi, 10 斛 make a 鐘. The 石 picul consisted of 70 斤 catties (Du Mu and others say 120). 箕杆, literally, "beanstalks and straw."

21. These are two difficult sentences, which I have translated in accordance with Mei Yaochen's paraphrase. We may incontinently reject Capt. Calthrop's extraordinary translation of the first: "Wantonly to kill and destroy the enemy must be forbidden." Cao Gong quotes a jingle current in his day: 軍無財士不來軍無賞士不往. Du Mu says: "Rewards are necessary in order to make the soldiers see the advantage of beating the enemy; thus, when you capture spoils from the enemy, they must be used as rewards, so that all your men may have a keen desire to fight, each on his own account. Zhang Yu takes 利 as the direct object of 取, which is not so good.

22. Capt. Calthrop's rendering is "They who are the first to lay their hands on more than ten of the enemy's chariots, should be encouraged." We should have expected the gallant captain to see that such Samson-like prowess deserved something more substantial than mere encouragement. *Tu Shu* omits 故, and has 以上 in place of the more archaic 已上.

23. As He Shi remarks: "Soldiers are not to be used as playthings. War is not a thing to be trifled with." 兵不可玩武不可黷 Sun Tzŭ reiterates the main lesson, which this chapter is intended to enforce.

24. In the original text, there is a 生 before the 民.

# CHAPTER 3

# Attack By Strategem
## 謀攻篇第三

1. A 軍 "army corps," according to the *Sima Fa*, consisted nominally of 12,500 men; according to Cao Gong, a 旅 contained 500 men, a 卒 any number between 100 to 500, and a 伍 any number between 5 and 100. For the last two, however, Zhang Yu gives the exact figures of 100 and 5 respectively.

2. Here again, no modern strategist but will approve the words of the old Chinese general. Moltke's greatest triumph, the capitulation of the huge French army at Sedan, was won practically without bloodshed.

3. I.e., as Li Quan says (伐其始謀也), in their very inception. Perhaps the word "baulk" falls short of expressing the full force of 伐, which implies not an attitude of defense, whereby one might be content to foil the enemy's stratagems one after another, but an active policy of counter-attack. He Shi puts this very clearly in his note: "When an enemy has made a plan of attack against us, we must anticipate him by delivering our own attack first."

4. Isolating him from his allies. We must not forget that Sun Tzǔ, in speaking of hostilities, always has in mind the numerous states or principalities into which the China of his day was split up. When he is already in full strength.

5. The use of the word 政 is somewhat unusual, which may account for the reading of the modern text: 其下攻城.

6. Another sound piece of military theory. Had the Boers acted upon it in 1899, and refrained from dissipating their strength before Kimberly, Mafeking, or even Ladysmith, it is more than probable that they would have been masters of the situation before the British were ready to seriously oppose them.

7. It is not quite clear what 櫓 were. Cao Gong simply defines them

as "large shields" 大楯, but we get a better idea from Li Quan, who says they were to protect the heads of those who were assaulting the city walls at close quarters. This seems to suggest a sort of Roman testudo, ready made. Du Mu says they were "what are now termed 彭排" (wheeled vehicles used in repelling attacks, according to Kang Xi), but this is denied by Chen Hao. See supra II.14. The name is also applied to turrets on city walls. Of (*fen yun*) 轒輼 we get a fairly clear description from several commentators. They were wooden missile-proof structures on fourwheels, propelled from within, covered over with raw hides, and used in sieges to convey parties of men to and from the walls, for the purpose of filling up the encircling moat with earth. Du Mu adds that they are now called 木驢 "wooden donkeys." Capt. Calthrop wrongly translates the term, "battering-rams." I follow Cao Gong in taking 具 as a verb, co-ordinate and synonymous with 修. Those commentators who regard 修 as an adjective equivalent to "long," 長 make 具 presumably into a noun.

8. The 距闉 (or 堙, in the modern text) were great mounds or ramparts of earth heaped up to the level of the enemy's walls in order to discover the weak points in the defense, and also to destroy the 樓櫓 fortified turrets mentioned in the preceding note. Du You quotes the Zuo Zhuan: 楚司馬子反乘堙而窺宋城也.

9. Capt. Calthrop unaccountably omits this vivid simile, which, as Cao Gong says, is taken from the spectacle of an army of ants climbing a wall. The meaning is that the general, losing patience at the long delay, may make a premature attempt to storm the place before his engines of war are ready.

10. We are reminded of the terrible losses of the Japanese before Port Arthur, in the most recent siege which history has to record. The *Tong Dian* reads 不勝心之忿 … 則殺士卒 … 攻城之災. For 其忿 the *Yulan* has 心怒. Capt. Calthrop does not translate 而城不拔者, and mistranslates 此攻之災.

11. Jia Lin notes that he only overthrows the 國, that is, the Government, but does not harm the individuals. The classical instance is Wu Wang, who after having put an end to the Yin dynasty was acclaimed "Father and mother of the people."

12. Owing to the double meanings of 兵, 頓 [=鈍] and 利, the

latter part of the sentence is susceptible of quite a different meaning: "And thus, the weapon not being blunted by use, its keenness remains perfect." Zhang Yu says that 利 is "the advantage of a prosperous kingdom and a strong army."

13. Straightaway, without waiting for any further advantage.

14. Note that 之 does not refer to the enemy, as in the two preceding clauses. This sudden change of object is quite common in Chinese. Du Mu takes exception to the saying; and at first sight, indeed, it appears to violate a fundamental principle of war. Cao Gong, however, gives a clue to Sun Tzǔ's meaning: "Being two to the enemy's one, we may use one part of our army in the regular way, and the other for some special diversion" 以二敵一則一術為正一術為奇. [For explanation of 正 and 奇, see V.3, note.] Zhang Yu thus further elucidates the point: "If our force is twice as numerous as that of the enemy, it should be split up into two divisions, one to meet the enemy in front, and one to fall upon his rear; if he replies to the frontal attack, he may be crushed from behind; if to the rearward attack, he may be crushed in front. This is what is meant by saying that "one part may be used in the regular way, and the other for some special diversion." Du Mu does not understand dividing one's army is simply an irregular, just as concentrating it is the regular, strategical method, and he is too hasty in calling this a mistake."

15. Li Quan, followed by He Shi, gives the following paraphrases: "If attackers and attacked are equally matched in strength, only the able general will fight" 主客力敵惟善者戰. He thus takes 能 as though it were 能者, which is awkward.

16. The *Tu Shu* has 守 instead of 逃, which is hardly distinguishable in sense from 避 in the next clause. The meaning, "we can *watch* the enemy," is certainly a great improvement on the above; but unfortunately there appears to be no very good authority for the variant. Zhang Yu reminds us that the saying only applies if the other factors are equal; a small difference in numbers is often more than counterbalanced by superior energy and discipline.

17. In other words: "C'est magnifique; mais ce n'est pas la guerre."

18. 隙 cannot be restricted to anything so particular as in Capt. Calthrop's translation, "divided in his allegiance." It is simply keeping

up the metaphor suggested by 周. As Li Quan tersely puts it: 隙缺也 將才不備兵必弱 "*Xi*, gap, indicates deficiency; if the general's ability is not perfect (i.e. if he is not thoroughly versed in his profession), his army will lack strength."

19. Cao Gong weakly defines 縻 as 御 "control," " direct." Cf. § 17 *ad fin*. But in reality it is one of those graphic metaphors which from time to time illuminate Sun Tzǔ's work, and is rightly explained by Li Quan as = 絆. He adds the comment: "It is like tying together the legs of a thoroughbred, so that it is unable to gallop" 如絆驥足無馳驟 也. One would naturally think of the "ruler" in this passage as being at home, and trying to direct the movements of his army from a distance. But the commentators understand just the reverse, and quote the saying of Tai Gong: "A kingdom should not be governed from without, an army should not be directed from within" 國不可以從外治軍不可 以從中御. Of course it is true that, during an engagement, or when in close touch with the enemy, the general should not be in the thick of his own troops, but a little distance apart. Otherwise, he will liable to misjudge the position as a whole, and give wrong orders.

20. Cao Gong's note is: 軍容不入國國容不入軍禮不可以治 兵也, which may be freely translated: "The military sphere and the civil sphere are wholly distinct; you can't handle an army in kid gloves." And Zhang Yu says: "Humanity and justice (仁義) are the principles to govern a state, but not an army; opportunism and flexibility (權變), on the other hand, are military rather than civic virtues." 同三軍之 政, "to assimilate the governing of an army"—to that of a State, understood. The *Tong Dian* has 欲 inserted before 同, here in § 15.

21. That is, he is not careful to use the right man in the right place.

22. I follow Mei Yaochen here. The other commentators make 不 知 etc. refer, not to the ruler, as in §§ 13, 14, but to officers he employs. Thus Du You says: "If a general is ignorant of the principle of adaptability, he must not be entrusted with a position of authority" 將若 不知權變不可付以勢位. Du Mu quotes 黃石公: "The skillful employer of men will employ the wise man, the brave man, the covetous man, and the stupid man. For the wise man delights in establishing his merit, the brave man likes to show his courage in action, the covetous man is quick at seizing advantages, and the stupid man has no fear of

death." The *Tong Dian* reads 軍覆疑, which Du You explains as 覆敗 "is utterly defeated." Capt. Calthrop gives a very inaccurate rendering: "Ignorant of the situation of the army, to interfere in its disposition."

23. Most of the commentators take 引 in the sense of 奪, which it seems to bear also in the *Li Ji*, 玉藻, I. 18. [卻 is there given as its equivalent, but Legge tries notwithstanding to retain the more usual sense, translating "draw…back," which is hardly defensible.] Du Mu and Wang Xi, however, think 引勝 means "leading to the *enemy's* victory."

24. Zhang Yu says: "If he can fight, he advances and takes the offensive; if he cannot fight, he retreats and remains on the defensive. He will invariably conquer who knows whether it is right to take the offensive or the defensive."

25. This is not merely the general's ability to estimate numbers correctly, as Li Quan and others make out. Zhang Yu expounds the saying more satisfactory: "By applying the art of war, it is possible with a lesser force to defeat a greater, and *vice versa*. The secret lies in an eye for locality, and in not letting the right moment slip. Thus Wuzi says: 'With a superior force, make for easy ground; with an inferior one, make for a difficult ground.'"

26. Cao Gong refers 上下 less well to sovereign and subjects.

27. Du You quotes 王子 as saying: "it is the sovereign's function to give broad instructions, but to decide from battle is the function of the general" 指授在君決戰在將也. It is needless to dilate on the military disasters that have been caused by undue interference with operations in the field on the part of the home government. Napoleon undoubtedly owed much of his extraordinary success to the fact that he was not hampered by any central authority,—that he was, in fact, 將 and 君 in one.

28. Literally, "These five things are knowledge of the principle of victory."

29. Li Quan cites the case of Fu Jian 苻堅, prince of Qin 秦, who in 383 A.D. marched with a vast army against the Jin 晉 Emperor. When warned not to despise an enemy who could command the services of such men as Xie An 謝安 and Huan Chong 桓沖, he boastfully replied: "I have the population of eight provinces at my back, infantry and horsemen to the number of one million; why, they could dam

up the Yangtsze River itself by merely throwing their whips into the stream. What danger have I to fear?" Nevertheless, his forces where soon after disastrously routed at the Fei 淝 River, and he was obliged to beat the hasty retreat.

30. The modern text, represented the 北堂書鈔 and *Tu Shu*, has 必敗, which I should be inclined to adopt in preference to 殆 here, though the *Tong Dian* and *Yulan* both have the latter. Zhang Yu offers the best commentary on 知彼知己. He says that these words "have reference to attack the defense: knowing the enemy enables you to take the offensive, knowing yourself enables you to stand the defensive." He adds: "Attack is the secret of defense; defense is the planning of an attack" 攻是守之機守是攻之策. It would be hard to find a better epitome of the root-principle of war.

# CHAPTER 4

# Tactical Dispositions
## 形篇第四

1. 形 is a very comprehensive and somewhat vague term. Literally, "from," "body," it comes to mean "appearance," "attitude" or "disposition;" and here it is best taken as something between, or perhaps combining, "tactics" and "disposition troops." Cao Gong explains it as 軍之形也，我動彼應兩敵相察情也 "marching and counter-marching on the part of the two armies with a view to discovering each other's condition." Du Mu says: "It is through the 形 disposition of an army that its condition may discovered. Conceal your dispositions (無形), and your condition will remain secret, which leads to victory; show your dispositions, and your condition will become patent, which leads to defeat." Wang Xi remarks that the good general can "secure success by modifying his tactics to meet those of the enemy" 變化其形因敵以制勝. In the modern text, the title of the chapter appears as 軍形, which Capt. Calthrop incorrectly translates "the order of battle."

2. That is, of course, by a mistake on his part. Capt. Calthrop has: "The cause of defeat come from within; victory is born in the enemy's camp," which, though certainly an improvement on his previous attempt, is still incorrect.

3. "By concealing the disposition of his troops, covering up his tracks, and taking unremitting precautions" (Zhang Yu).

4. The original text reads 使敵之可勝, which the modern text has further modified into 使敵之必可勝. Capt. Calthrop makes out the impossible meaning, "and further render the enemy incapable of victory."

5. Capt. Calthrop translates: "The conditions necessary for victory may be present, but they cannot always be obtained," which is more or less unintelligible.

6. For 不可勝 I retain the sense that it undoubtedly bears in §§ 1-3, in spite of the fact that the commentators are all against me. The meaning they give, "he who cannot conquer takes the defensive," is plausible enough, but it is highly improbable that 勝 should suddenly become active in this way. An incorrect variant in the *Yu Lan* is 不可勝則守可勝則攻.

7. Literally, "hides under the ninth earth," which is a metaphor indicating the outmost secrecy and concealment, so that the enemy may not know his whereabouts. The 九地 of this passage have of course no connection with the "Nine situations" 九地 of chap. XI.

8. Another metaphor, implying that he falls on his adversary like a thunderbolt, against which there is no time to prepare. This is the opinion of most of the commentators, though Cao Gong, followed by Du You, explains 地 as the hills, rivers, and other natural features which will afford shelter or protection to the attacked, and 天 as the phase of weather which may be turned to account by the attacking party. Capt. Calthrop's "The skillful in attack push to the top most heaven" conveys no meaning at all.

9. Capt. Calthrop draws on a fertile imagination for the following: "If these precepts be observed, victory is certain."

10. As Cao Gong remarks, "the thing is to see the plant before it has germinated" 當見未萌, to foresee the event before the action has begun. Li Quan alludes to the victory of Han Xin who, when about to attack the vastly superior army of Zhao 趙, which was strongly entrenched in the city of Cheng'an 成安, said to his officers: "Gentlemen, we are going to annihilate the enemy, and shall meet again at dinner." The officers hardly took his word seriously, and gave a very dubious assent. But Han Xin had had already worked out in his mind the details of a clever stratagem, whereby, as he foresaw, he was able to capture the city and inflict a crushing defeat on his adversary. For the full story, see 前漢書, chap. 34, 韓信傳. Capt. Calthrop again blunders badly with: "A victory, even if popularly proclaimed as such by the common folk, may not be a true success."

11. True excellence being, as Du Mu says: "To plan secretly, to move surreptitiously, to foil the enemy's intentions and baulk his schemes, so that at last the day may be won without shedding a drop of blood" 陰

謀潛運攻心伐謀勝敵之日曾不血刃. Sun Tzŭ reserves his probation for things that

> "the world's coarse thumb
> And finger fail to plumb."

12. 秋毫 is explained as the fur of a hare, which is finest in autumn, when it begins to grow afresh. The phrase is a very common one in Chinese writers. Cf. Mencius, I. 1. vii. 10, and Zhuangzi, 知北遊 , *et al.*

13. He Shi gives as real instances of strength, sharp sight and quick hearing: Wu Huo 烏獲, who could lift a tripod weighing 250 stone; Li Zhu 離朱, who at a distance of a hundred paces could see objects no bigger than a mustard seed; and 師曠 Shi Kuang, a blind musician who could hear the footstep of a mosquito.

14. The original text, followed by the *Tu Shu*, has 勝於易勝者也. But this is an alteration evidently intended to smooth the awkwardness of 勝于易勝者也, which means literally: "one who conquering excels in easy conquering." Mei Yaochen says: "He who only sees the obvious, wins his battle with difficultly; he who looks below the surface of things, wins with ease."

15. Du Mu explains this very well: "In as much as his victories are gained over circumstances that have not come to light, the world at large knows nothing of them, and he wins no reputation for wisdom; inasmuch as the hostile state submits before there has been any bloodshed, receives no credit for courage."

16. Chen Hao says: "He plans no superfluous marches, he devises no futile attacks." The connection of ideas is thus explained by Zhang Yu: "One who seeks to conquer by the sheer strength, clever though he may be at winning pitched battles, is also liable on occasion to be vanquished; whereas he who can look into the future and discern conditions that are not yet manifest, will never make a blunder and therefore invariably win." Li Quan thinks that the character 忒 should be 貳 "to have doubts." But it is better not to tamper with the text, especially when no improvement in sense is the result.

17. The *Tu Shu* omits 必. 措 is here = 置. Jia Lin says it is put for 錯 in the sense of 雜; but this is far-fetched. Capt. Calthrop altogether ignores the important word 忒.

18. A "counsel of perfection" 不可為之計, as Du Mu truly ob-

serves. 地 need not be confined strictly to the actual ground occupied by the troops. It includes all the arrangement and preparations which a wise general will make to increase the safety of his army.

19. He Shi thus expounds paradox: "In warfare, first lay plans that will ensure victory, and then lead your army to the battle; if you will not begin with stratagem but rely on brute strength alone, victory will no longer be assured."

20. For 道 and 法, see *supra*, I. 4 sqq. I think that Zhang Yu is wrong in altering their signification here, and taking them as 為戰之道 and 制敵之法 respectively.

21. It is not easy to distinguish the four terms 度量數稱 very clearly. The first seems to be surveying and measurement of the ground, which enable us to 量 form an estimate of the enemy's strength, and to 數 make calculations based on the data thus obtained; we are thus led to 稱 a general weighing-up, or comparison of the enemy's chances with our own; if the latter turn the scale, then 勝 victory ensues. The chief difficulty lies in 數, which some commentators take as a calculation of *numbers*, thereby making it nearly synonymous with 量. Perhaps 量 is rather a consideration of the enemy's general position or condition (情 or 形勢), while 數 is the estimate of his numerical strength. On the other hand, Du Mu defines 數 as 機數, and adds: "the question of relative strength having been settled, we can bring the varied resources of cunning into play" 強弱已定然後能用機變數也. He Shi seconds this interpretation, which is weakened, however, by the fact that 稱 is given as logically consequent on 數; this certainly points to the latter being a calculation of numbers. Of Capt. Calthrop's version the less said the better.

22. Literally, "a victorious army is like an 鎰 *i* (20 oz.) weighed against a 銖 *shu* (2¼ oz.); a routed army as a *shu* weighed against an *i*." The point is simply the enormous advantage that a disciplined force, flushed with victory, has over one demoralized by defeat. Legge, in his note on Mencius, I. 2. ix. 2, makes the 鎰 to be 24 Chinese ounces, and corrects Zhu Xi's statement that it equaled 20 oz. only. But Li Quan of the Tang dynasty here gives the same figure as Zhu Xi.

23. The construction here is slightly awkward and elliptical, but the general sense is plain. The *Tu Shu* omits 民也. A 仞 = 8 尺 or Chinese feet.

# CHAPTER 5

# Energy
# 埶篇第五

1. 埶 here is said to be an older form of 勢; Sun Tzŭ, however, would seem to have used the former in the sense of "power," and the latter only in the sense of "circumstances." The fuller title 兵勢 is found in the *Tu Shu* and the modern text. Wang Xi expands it into "the application, in various ways, of accumulated power;" 積勢之變 and Zhang Yu says: "When the soldiers' energy has reached its height, it be used to secure victory" 兵勢以成然後任勢以取勝. Cf. X, 2, where 勢 is translated "strength," though it might also be "conditions". The three words 埶, 執 and 勢 have been much confused. It appears from the *Shuowen* that the last character is post-classical, so that Sun Tzŭ must have used either 埶 or 執 in all senses.

2. That is, cutting up the army into regiments, companies, etc., with subordinate officers in command of each. Du Mu reminds us of Han Xin's famous reply to the first Han Emperor, who once said him: "How large an army do you think I can lead?" "Not more than 100,000 men, your Majesty." "And you?" asked the Emperor. "Oh!" he answered, "the more the better" (多多益辦耳). Zhang Yu gives the following curious table of the subdivisions of an army: 5 men make a 列; 2 列 make a 火; 5 火 make a 隊; 2 隊 make a 官; 2 官 make a 曲; 2 曲 make a 部; 2 部 make a 校; 2 校 make a 裨; 2 裨 make a 軍. A 軍 or army corps thus works out at 3200 men. But cf. III. § 1, note. Note for 曲, see I. § 10. It is possible that 官 in that paragraph may also be used in the above technical senses.

3. One must be careful to avoid translating "*fighting against* a large number" 鬥眾, no reference to the enemy being intended. 形 is explained by Cao Gong as denoting flags and banners, by means of which every soldier may recognize his own particular regiment or

company, and thus confusion may be prevented. 名 he explains as drums and gongs, which from the earliest times were used to sound the advance and the retreat respectively. Du Mu defines as 陳形 "marshalling the troops in order," and takes as the flags and banners. Wang Xi also dissents from Cao Gong, referring 形 to the ordering of the troops by means of banners, drums, and gongs, and 名 to the various names by which the regiment might be distinguished. There is much to be said for this view.

4. For 必, there is another reading 畢, "all together," adopted by Wang Xi and Zhang Yu. We now come to one of the most interesting parts of Sun Tzǔ's treatise, the discussion of the 正 and the 奇. As it is by no means easy to grasp the full signification of these two terms, or to render them at all consistently by good English equivalents, it may be as well to tabulate some of the commentators' remarks on the subject before proceeding further. Li Quan: "Facing the enemy is *zheng*, making literal diversion is *qi*" 當敵為正傍出為奇. Jia Lin: "In his presence of the enemy, your troops should be arrayed in normal fashion, but in order to secure victory abnormal maneuvers must be employed" 當敵以正陳取勝以奇兵. Mei Yaochen: "*Qi* is active, zheng is passive; passivity means waiting for an opportunity, activity brings the victory itself" 動為奇靜為正靜以待之動以勝之. He Shi: "We must cause the enemy to regard our straightforward attack as one that is secretly designed, and *vice versa*; thus *zheng* may also be *qi*, and *qi* may also be *zheng*" 我之正使敵視之為奇我之奇使敵視之為正正亦為奇奇亦為正. He instances the famous exploit of Han Xin, who when marching ostensibly against Linjin 臨晉 (now Zhaoyi 朝邑 in Shaanxi), suddenly threw a large force across the Yellow River in wooden tubs, utterly disconcerting his opponent. [*Qian Han Shu, chap. 34.*] Here, we are told, the march on Linjin was 正, and the surprise maneuver was 奇. Zhang Yu gives the following summary of opinions on the words: "Military writers do not all agree with regard to the meaning of *qi* and *zheng*. Weiliaozi 尉繚子 [4th cent. B.C.] says: 'Direct warfare favors frontal attacks, indirect warfare attacks from the rear' 正兵貴先奇兵貴後. Cao Gong says: 'Going straight out to join battle is a direct operation; appearing on the enemy's rear is an indirect maneuver.' Li Weigong 李衛公 [6th and 7th cent. A.D.] says:

'In war, to march straight ahead is *zheng*; turning movements, on the other hand, are *qi*.' These writers simply regard *zheng* as *zheng*, and *qi* as *qi*; they do not note that the two are mutually interchangeable and run into each other like the sides of a circle [see *infra*, § II]. A comment of the Tang Emperor Taizong goes to the root of the matter: 'A *qi* maneuver may be *zheng*, if we make the enemy look upon it as *zheng*; then our real attack will be *qi*, and *vice versa*. The whole secret lies in confusing the enemy, so that he cannot fathom our real intent.'" To put it perhaps a little more clearly: any attack or other operation is 正, on which the enemy has had his attention fixed; whereas that is 奇, which takes him by surprise or comes from an unexpected quarter. If the enemy perceives a moment that is meant to be 奇, it immediately becomes 正.

5. 虛實, literally "the hollow and the solid," is the title of chap. VI. *Duan* 碬 is the *Tu Shu* reading, *xia* 碬 that of the standard text. It appears from Kangxi that there has been much confusion between the two characters, and indeed, it is probable that one of them has really crept into the language as a mistake for the other.

6. Zhang Yu says: "Steadily develop indirect tactics, either by pounding the enemy's flanks or falling on his rear" 徐發奇兵或擣其旁或擊其後. A brilliant example of "indirect tactics" which decided the fortunes of a campaign was Lord Roberts' night march round the Peiwar Kotal in the second Afghan war.[1]

7. 奇 is the universally accepted emendation for 兵, the reading of the 北堂書鈔.

8. Du You and Zhang Yu understand this of the permutations of 奇 and 正. But at present Sun Tzǔ is not speaking of 正 at all, unless, indeed, we suppose with Zheng Youxian 鄭友賢 that a clause relating to it has fallen out of the text. Of course, as has already been pointed out, the two are so inextricably interwoven in all military operations, that they cannot really be considered apart. Here we simply have an expression, in figurative language, of the almost infinite resource of a great leader.

---

[1] "Forty-one Years in India," chap. 46

9. 宮商角微羽

10. 青黃赤白黑 blue, yellow, red, white and black.

11. 酸辛鹹甘苦 sour, acid, salt, sweet, bitter.

12. The *Tu Shu* adds 哉. The final 之 may refer either to the circle or more probably, to the 奇正之變 understood. Capt. Calthrop is wrong with: "They are a mystery that none can penetrate."

13. For 疾 the *Yulan* reads 擊, which is also supported by a quotation in the 呂氏春秋 [3rd cent B.C.]. 節 in this context is a word that really defies the best efforts of the translators. Du Mu says that it is equivalent to 節量遠近 "the measurement or estimation of distance." But this meaning does not quite fit the illustrative simile in § 15. As applied to the falcon, it seems to me to denote that instinct of *self-restraint*, which keeps the bird from swooping on its quarry until the right moment, together with the power of judging when the right moment has arrived. The analogous quality in soldiers is the highly important one of being able to reserve their fire until the very instant at which it will be most effective. When the "Victory" went into action at Trafalgar at hardly more than drifting pace, she was for several minutes exposed to a storm of shot and shell before replying with a single gun. Nelson coolly waited until he was within close range, when the broadside he brought to bear worked fearful havoc on the enemy's nearest ships. That was a case of 節.

14. Du You defines 節 here by the word 斷, which is very like "decision" in English. 短 is certainly used in a very unusual sense, even if, as the commentators say, it = 近. This would have reference to the measurement of distance mentioned above, letting the enemy get near before striking. But I cannot help thinking that Sun Tzŭ meant to use the word in a figurative sense comparable to our own idiom "short and sharp." Cf. Wang Xi's note, which after describing the falcon's mode of attack, proceeds: "This is just how the 'psychological moment' should be seized in war" 兵之乘機當如是耳. I do not care for Capt. Calthrop's rendering: "The spirit of the good fighter is terrifying, his occasions sudden."

15. "Energy" seems to be the best equivalent here for 執, because the comparison implies that the force is potential, being stored up in the bent crossbow until released by the finger on the trigger. None of

the commentators seem to grasp the real point of the simile.

16. 形圓, literally "formation circular", is explained by Li Quan as 無向背也 "without back or front." Mei Yaochen says: "The subdivisions of the army having been previously fixed, and the various signals agreed upon, the separating and joining, the dispersing and collecting which will take place in the course of battle, may give the appearance of disorder when no real disorder is possible. Your formation may be without head or tail, your dispositions all topsy-turvy, and yet a rout of your forces quite out of the question." It is a little difficult to decide whether 鬥亂 and 形圓 should not be taken as imperatives: Fight in disorder (for the purpose of deceiving the enemy), and you will be secure against real disorder." Cf. I. § 20: 亂而取之.

17. In order to make the translation intelligible, it is necessary to tone down the sharply paradoxical form of the original. Cao Gong throws out a hint of the meaning in his brief note: "These things all serve to destroy formation and conceal one's condition" 皆毀形匿情也. But Du Mu is the first to put it quite plainly: "If you wish to feign confusion in order to lure the enemy on, you must first have perfect discipline; if you wish to display timidity in order to entrap the enemy, you must have extreme courage; if you wish to parade your weakness in order to make the enemy overconfident, you must have exceeding strength."

18. See *supra*, § I.

19. It is passing strange that the commentators should understand 執 here as "circumstances"—a totally different sense from that which it has previously borne in this chapter. Thus Du Mu says: "seeing that we are favorably circumstanced and yet make no move, the enemy will believe that we are really afraid" 見有利之勢而不動敵人以我為實怯也. Zhang Yu relates the following anecdote of Gaozu, the first Han Emperor: Wishing to crush the Xiongnu, he sent out spies to report on their condition. But the Xiongnu, forewarned, carefully concealed all their able-bodied men and well-fed horses, and only allowed infirm soldiers and emaciated cattle to be seen. The result was that the spies one and all recommended the Emperor to deliver his attack. Lou Jing 婁敬 alone opposed them, saying: "When two countries go to war, they are naturally inclined to make an ostentatious display of their

strength. Yet our spies have seen nothing but old age and infirmity. This is surely some *ruse* on the part of the enemy, and it would be unwise for us to attack." The Emperor, however, disregarding his advice, fell into the trap and found himself surrounded at Bodeng 白登."

20. Cao Gong's note is "Make a display of weakness and want" 見 羸形也, but Du Mu rightly points out that 形 does not refer only to weakness: "If our force happens to be superior to the enemy's, weakness may be simulated in order to lure him on; but if inferior, he must be led to believe that we are strong, in order that he may keep off. In fact, all the enemy's movements should be determined by the signs that we choose to give him." The following anecdote of Sun Bin 孫 臏, a descendant of Sun Wu, is related at length in the 史記, chap. 65: In 341 B.C., the Qi 齊 state being at war with Wei 魏, sent Tian Ji 田 忌 and Sun Bin against the general Pang Juan 龐涓, who happened to be a deadly personal enemy of the latter. Sun Bin said: "The Qi state has a reputation for cowardice, and therefore our adversary despises us. Let us turn this circumstance to account." Accordingly, when the army had crossed the border into Wei territory, he gave orders to show 100,000 fires on the first night, 50,000 on the next, and the night after only 20,000. Pang Juan pursued them hotly, saying to himself: "I knew these men of Qi were cowards: their numbers have already fallen away by more than half." In his retreat, Sun Bin came to a narrow defile, which he calculated that his pursuers would reach after dark. Here he had a tree stripped of its bark, and inscribed upon it the words: "Under this tree shall Pang Juan die." Then, as night began to fall, he placed a strong body of archers in ambush near by, with orders to shoot directly they saw a light. Later on, Pang Juan arrived at the spot, and noticing the tree, struck a light in order to read what was written on it. His body was immediately riddled by a volley of arrows, and his whole army thrown into confusion. [The above is Du Mu's version of the story; the *Shiji*, less dramatically but probably with more historical truth, makes Pang Juan cut his own throat with an exclamation of despair, after the rout of his army.]

21. 予 here = 與.

22. This would appear to be the meaning if we retain 卒, which Mei Yaochen explains as "men of spirit" 精卒. The *Tu Shu* reads 本, an

emendation suggested by Li Jing 李靖. The meaning then would be, "He lies in wait with the main body of his troops."

23. Du Mu says: "He first of all considers the power of his army in the bulk; afterwards he takes individual talent in the account, and uses each man according to his capabilities. He does not demand perfection from the untalented."

24. Another reading has 之 instead of 埶. It would be interesting if Capt. Calthrop could tell us where the following occurs in the Chinese: "yet, when an opening or advantage shows, he pushes it to its limits."

25. Cao Gong calls this "the use of natural inherent power" 任自 然勢. Capt. Calthrop ignores the last part of the sentence entirely. In its stead he has: "So await the opportunity, and so act when the opportunity arrives"—another absolutely gratuitous interpolation. The *Tongdian* omits 任.

26. The *Tongdian* omits 善. The chief lesson of this chapter, in Du Mu's opinion, is the paramount importance in war of rapid evolutions and sudden rushes. "Great results," he adds, "can thus be achieved with small forces."

# CHAPTER 6

# Weak Points And Strong
## 虛實篇第六

1. Zhang Yu attempts to explain the sequence of the chapters as follows: "Chapter IV, on Tactical Dispositions, treated of the offensive and the defensive; chapter V, on Energy, dealt with direct and indirect methods. The good general acquaints himself first with the theory of attack and defense, and then turns his attention to direct and indirect methods. He studies the art of varying and combining these two methods before proceeding to the subject of weak and strong points. For the use of direct or indirect methods arises out of attack and defense, and the perception of weak and strong points depends again on the above methods. Hence the present chapter comes immediately after the chapter on Energy."

2. Instead of 處, the *Yulan* has in both clauses the stronger word 據. For the antithesis between 佚 and 勞, cf. I. § 23, where however 勞 is used as a verb.

3. The next paragraph makes it clear that 致 does not merely mean, as Du Mu says, "to make the enemy approach me" 令敵來就我, but rather to make him go in any direction I please. Cf. Du Mu's own note on V. § 19. One mark of a great soldier is that he fights on his own terms or fights not at all.

4. In the first case, he will entice him with a bait; in the second, he will strike at some important point which the enemy will have to defend.

5. This passage may be cited as evidence against Mei Yaochen's interpretation of I. § 23.

6. 飢 is probably an older form than 饑, the reading of the original text. Both are given in the 說文. The subject to 能 is still 善戰者; but these clauses would read better as direct admonitions, and in the next sentence we find Sun Tzŭ dropping insensibly into the imperative.

7. The original text, adopted by the *Tu Shu*, has 出其所不趨; it has been altered to suit the context and the commentaries of Cao Gong and He Shi, who evidently read 必趨. The other reading would mean: "Appear at points to which the enemy cannot hasten'" but in this case there is something awkward in the use of 趨. Capt. Calthrop is wrong of course with "appearing where the enemy is not."

8. We must beware of understanding 無人之地 as "uninhabited country." Sun Tzǔ habitually uses 人 in the sense of 敵, e. g. *supra*, § 2. Cao Gong sums up very well: "Emerge from the void [*q. d.* like "a bolt from the blue"] 出空擊虛避其所所守擊其不意, strike at vulnerable points, shun places that are defended, attack in unexpected quarters. The difference of meaning between 空 and 虛 is worth nothing.

9. 所不守 is of course hyperbolical; Wang Xi rightly explains it as "weak points; that is to say, where the general is lacking in capacity, or the soldiers in spirit; where the walls are not strong enough, or the precautions not strict enough; where relief comes too late, or provisions are too scanty, or the defenders are at variance amongst themselves."

10. *I.e.*, where there are none of the weak points mentioned above. There is rather a nice point involved in the interpretation of this latter clause. Du Mu, Chen Hao, and Mei Yaochen assume the meaning to be: "In order to make your defense quite safe, you must defend *even* those places that are not likely to be attacked;" and Du Mu adds: "How much more, then, those that will be attacked." Taken thus, however, the clauses balances less well with the preceding—always a consideration in the highly antithetical style which is natural to the Chinese. Zhang Yu, therefore, seems to come nearer the mark in saying: "He who is skilled in attack flashes forth from the topmost heights of heaven [see IV. § 7], making it impossible for the enemy to guard against him. This being so, the places that I shall attack are precisely those that the enemy cannot defend…. He who is skilled in defense hides in the most secret recesses of the earth, making it impossible for the enemy to estimate his whereabouts. This being so, the places that I shall hold are precisely those that the enemy cannot attack."

11. An aphorism which puts the art of war into a nutshell.

12. Literally, "without form or sound," but it is said of course with reference to the enemy. Zhang Yu, whom I follow, draws no sharp dis-

tinction between 微 and 神, but Du Mu and others think that 微 indicates the secrecy to be observed on the defensive, and 神 the rapidity to be displayed in attack. The *Yulan* differs considerably from ours, reading: 微乎微乎故能隱於常形神乎神乎故能為敵司命.

13. The *Tongdian* has 故能為變化司命. Capt. Calthrop's version of this paragraph is so remarkable that I cannot refrain from quoting it in full: "Now the secrets of the art of offence are not to be easily apprehended, as a certain shape or noise can be understood, of the senses; but when these secrets are once learnt, the enemy is mastered."

14. The second member of the sentence is weak, because 不可及 is nearly tautologous with 不可追. The *Yulan* reads 遠 for 速.

15. Du Mu says: "If the enemy is the invading party, we can cut his line of communications and occupy the roads by which he will have to return; if we are the invaders, we may direct our attack against the sovereign himself." It is clear that Sun Tzŭ, unlike certain generals in the late Boer war, was no believer in frontal attacks.

16. In order to preserve the parallelism with § II, I should prefer to follow the *Tu Shu* text, which inserts 雖 before 畫地. This extremely concise expression is intelligibly paraphrased by Jia Lin: "even though we have constructed neither wall nor ditch" 雖未修壘塹. The real crux of passage lies in 乖其所之也. 之 of course = 至. Cao Gong defines 乖 by the word 戾, which is perhaps a case of *obscurum per obscurius*. Li Quan, however, says: "We puzzle him by strange and unusual dispositions" 設奇異而疑之; and Du Mu finally clinches the meaning by three illustrative anecdotes—one of Zhuge Liang 諸葛亮, who when occupying Yangping 陽平 and about to be attacked by Sima Yi 司馬懿, suddenly struck his colors, stopped the beating of the drums, and flung open the city gates, showing only a few men engaged in sweeping and sprinkling the ground. This unexpected proceeding had the intended effect; for Sima Yi, suspecting an ambush, actually drew off his army and retreated. What Sun Tzŭ is advocating here, therefore, is nothing more nor less than the timely use of "bluff." Capt. Calthrop translates: "and prevent the enemy from attacking by keeping him in suspense," which shows that he has not fully grasped the meaning of 乖.

17. The conclusion is perhaps not very obvious, but Zhang Yu (after

Mei Yaochen) rightly explains it thus: "If the enemy's dispositions are visible, we can make for him in one body; whereas, our own dispositions being kept secret, the enemy will be obliged to divide his forces in order to guard against attack from every quarter." 形 is here used as an active verb: "to make to appear." See IV, note on heading. Capt. Calthrop's "making feints" is quite wrong.

18. The original text has 以敵攻其一也, which in accordance with the *Tongdian* and *Yulan* has been altered as above. I adopt the more plausible reading of the *Tu Shu*: 是以十攻其一也, in spite of having to refer 十 to ourselves and not to the enemy. Thus Du You and Mei Yaochen both regard 十 as the undivided force, consisting of so many parts, and 一 as each of the isolated fractions of the enemy. The alteration of 攻 into 共 can hardly be right, though the true text might conceivably have been 是以十共攻其一也.

19. For 擊, the *Tongdian* and *Yulan* have 敵. Du You, followed by the other commentators, arbitrarily defines 約 as 少而易勝 "few and easy to conquer," but only succeeds thereby in making the sentence absolutely pointless. As for Capt. Calthrop's translation: "In superiority of numbers there is economy of strength," its meaning is probably known to himself alone. In justification of my own rendering of 約, I would refer to *Lunyu* IV. 2 and VII. 25 (3).

20. Sheridan once explained the reason of General Grant's victories by saying that "while his opponents were kept fully employed wondering what he was going to do, *he* was thinking most of what he was going to do himself."

21. In Frederick the Great's *Instructions to his Generals* we read: "A defensive war is apt to betray us into too frequent detachment. Those generals who have had but little experience attempt to protect every point, while those who are better acquainted with their profession, having only the capital object in view, guard against a decisive blow, and acquiesce in smaller misfortunes to avoid greater."

22. The highest generalship, in Col. Henderson's words, is "to compel the enemy to disperse his army, and then to concentrate superior force against each fraction in turn."

23. There is nothing about "defeating" anybody in this sentence, as Capt. Calthrop translates. What Sun Tzŭ evidently has in mind is that

nice calculation of distances and that masterly employment of strategy that enable a general to divide his army for the purpose of a long and rapid march, and afterwards to effect a junction at precisely the right spot and the right hour in order to confront the enemy in overwhelming strength. Among many such successful junctions that military history records, one of the most dramatic and decisive was the appearance of Blücher just at the critical moment on the field of Waterloo.

24. The Chinese of this last sentence is a little lacking in precision, but the mental picture we are required to draw is probably that of an army advancing towards a given rendezvous in separate columns, each of which has orders to be there on a fixed date. If the general allows the various detachments to proceed at haphazard, without precise instructions as to the time and place of meeting, the enemy will be able to annihilate the army in detail. Zhang Yu's note may be worth quoting here: "If we do not know the place where our opponents mean to concentrate or the day on which they will join battle, our unity will be forfeited through our preparations for defense, and the positions we hold will be insecure. Suddenly happening upon a powerful foe, we shall be brought to battle in a flurried condition, and no mutual support will be possible between wings, vanguard, or rear, especially if there is any great distance between the foremost and hindmost divisions of the army."

25. Capt. Calthrop omits 以吾度之, and his translation of the remainder is flabby and inaccurate. As Sun Tzŭ was in the service of the Wu 吳 State, it has been proposed to read 吳 instead of 吾 — a wholly unnecessary tampering with the text. Yue coincided roughly with the present province of Zhejiang. Li Quan very strangely takes 越 not as the proper name, but in the sense of "to surpass" 過. No other commentator follows him. 勝敗 belongs to the class of expressions like 遠近 "distance" 大小 "magnitude," etc., to which the Chinese have to resort in order to express abstract ideas of degree. The *Tu Shu*, however, omits 敗.

26. Alas for these brave words! The long feud between the two states ended in 473 B.C. with the total defeat of Wu by Gou Jian 勾踐 and its incorporation in Yue. This was doubtless long after Sun Tzŭ's death. With his present assertion compare IV. § 4: 勝可知

而不可為 (which is the obviously mistaken reading of the *Yulan* here.) Zhang Yu is the only one to point out the seeming discrepancy, which he thus goes on to explain: "In the chapter on Tactical Dispositions it is said, 'One may *know* how to conquer without being able to *do* it.' Whereas here we have the statement that 'victory can be achieved.' The explanation is, that in the former chapter, where the offensive and defensive are under discussion, it is said that if the enemy is fully prepared, one cannot make certain beating him. But the present passage refers particularly to the soldiers of Yue who, according to Sun Tzŭ's calculations, will be kept in ignorance of the time and place of the impending struggle. That is why he says here that victory can be achieved."

27. Capt. Calthrop quite unwarrantably translates: "*If the enemy be many in number, prevent him*," etc. This is the first of four similarly constructed sentences, all of which present decided difficulties. Zhang Yu explains 知得失之計 as 知其計之得失. This is perhaps the best way of taking the words, though Jia Lin, referring 計 to ourselves and not the enemy, offers the alternative of 我得彼失之計皆先知也 "Know beforehand all plans conductive to our success and to the enemy's failure."

28. Instead of 作, the *Tongdian, Yulan*, and also Li Quan's text have 候, which the latter explains as "the observation of omens," and Jia Lin simply as "watching and waiting." 作 is defined by Du Mu as 激作, and Zhang Yu tells us that by noting the joy or anger shown by the enemy on being thus disturbed, we shall be able to conclude whether his policy is to lie low or the reverse. He instances the action of Zhuge Liang, who sent the scornful present of a woman's head-dress to Sima Yi, in order to goad him out of his Fabian tactics.

29. Two commentators, Li Quan and Zhang Yu, take 形之 in the sense of 示之 "put on specious appearances." The former says: "You may either deceive the enemy by a show of weakness—striking your colors and silencing your drums; or by a show of strength—making a hollow display of camp-fires and regimental banners." And the latter quotes V. 19, where 形之 certainly seems to bear this sense. On the other hand, I would point to § 13 of this chapter, where 形 must with equal certainty be active. It is hard to choose between the two inter-

pretations, but the context here agrees better, I think, with the one that I have adopted. Another difficulty arises over 死生之地, which most of the commentators, thinking no doubt of the 死地 in XI. §1, refer to the actual *ground* on which the enemy is encamped. The notes of Jia Lin and Mei Yaochen, however, seem to favor my view. The same phrase has a somewhat different meaning in I. § 2.

30. Du You is right, I think, in attributing this force to 角; Cao Gong defines it simply as 量. Capt. Calthrop surpasses himself with the staggering translation "Flap the wings"! Can the Latin *cornu* (in its figurative sense) have been at the back of his mind?

31. Cf. IV. § 6.

32. The piquancy of the paradox evaporates in translation. 無形 is perhaps not so much actual invisibility (see *supra*, § 9) as "showing no sign" of what you mean to do, of the plans that are formed in your brain.

33. 深閒 is expanded by Du Mu into 雖有閒者深來窺我 (For 閒 see, XIII note on heading.) He explains 知者 in like fashion: "though the enemy may have clever and capable officers, they will not be able to lay any plans against us" 雖有智能之士亦不能謀我也.

34. All the commentators except Li Quan make 形 refer to the enemy. So Cao Gong: 因敵形而立勝. 錯 is defined as 置. The *Tu Shu* has 措, with the same meaning. See IV. § 13. The *Yulan* reads 作, evidently a gloss.

35. *I.e.*, everybody can see superficially how a battle is won; what they cannot see is the long series of plans and combinations that has preceded the battle. It seems justifiable, then, to render the first 形 by "tactics" and the second by "strategy."

36. As Wang Xi sagely remarks: "There is but one root-principle (理) underlying victory, but the tactics (形) which lead up to it are infinite in number." With this compare Col. Henderson; "The rules of strategy are few and simple. They may be learned in a week. They may be taught by familiar illustrations or a dozen diagrams. But such knowledge will no more teach a man to lead an army like Napoleon than a knowledge of grammar will teach him to write like Gibbon."

37. 行 is 劉晝子 Liu Zhouzi's reading for 形 in the original text.

38. Like water, taking the line at least resistance.

39. The *Tongdian* and *Yulan* read 制形,—the latter also 制行. The present text is derived from Zheng Youxian.

40. Water, fire, wood, metal, earth.

41. That is, as Wang Xi says: "they predominate alternately" 迭相克也.

42. Literally, "have no invariable seat."

43. Cf. V. § 6. The purport of the passage is simply to illustrate the want of fixity in war by the changes constantly taking place in nature. The comparison is not very happy, however, because the regularity of the phenomena which Sun Tzŭ mentions is by no means paralleled in war.

# CHAPTER 7

# Maneuvering
# 軍爭篇第七

1. The commentators, as well as the subsequent text, make it clear that this is the real meaning of 軍爭. Thus, Li Quan says that 爭 means "marching rapidly to seize an advantage" 趨利; Wang Xi says: "'Striving' means striving for an advantage; this being obtained, victory will follow" 爭者爭利得利則勝; and Zhang Yu: "The two armies face to face, and each striving to obtain a tactical advantage over the other" 兩軍相對而爭利也. According to the latter commentator, then, the situation is analogous to that of two wrestlers maneuvering for a "hold," before coming to actual grips. In any case, we must beware of translating 爭 by the word "fighting" or "battle," as if it were equivalent to 戰. Capt. Calthrop falls into this mistake.

2. For 君 there is another reading 天, which Li Quan explains as "being the reverent instrument of Heaven's chastisement" 恭行天罰.

3. Cao Gong takes 和 as referring to the 和門 or main gate of the military camp. This, Du You tells us, was formed with a couple of flags hung across. [Cf. *Zhou Li*, chap. xxvii. Fol. 31 of the Imperial edition: 直旌門.] 交和 would then mean "setting up his 和門 opposite that of the enemy." But Jia Lin's explanation, which has been adopted above, is on the whole simpler and better. Zhang Yu, while following Cao Gong, adds that the words may also be taken to mean "the establishment of harmony and confidence between the higher and lower ranks before venturing into the field;" and he quotes a saying of Wuzi (chap. 1 *ad init*): "Without harmony in the army, no battle array can be formed." In the historical romance 東周列國, chap. 75, Sun Tzǔ himself is represented as saying to Wu Yuan 伍員: "As a general rule, those who are waging war should get rid of all domestic troubles before proceeding to attack the external foe" 大凡行兵之法先除內

患然後方可外征. 舍 is defined as 止. It here conveys the notion of encamping after having taken the field.

4. I have departed slightly from the traditional interpretation of Cao Gong, who says: "From the time of receiving the sovereign's instructions until our encampment over against the enemy, the tactics to be pursued are most difficult" 從始受命至於交和軍爭難也. It seems to me that the 軍爭 tactics or maneuvers can hardly be said to begin until the army has sallied forth and encamped, and Chen Hao's note gives color to this view: "For levying, concentrating, harmonizing and entrenching an army, there are plenty of old rules that will serve. The real difficulty comes when we engage in tactical operations." Du You also observes that "the great difficulty is to be beforehand with the enemy in seizing favorable positions."

5. 以迂為直 is one of those highly condensed and somewhat enigmatical expressions of which Sun Tzŭ is so fond. This is how it is explained by Cao Gong: "Make it appear that you are a long way off, then cover the distance rapidly and arrive on the scene before your opponent" 示以遠速其道里先敵至也. Du You says: "Hoodwink the enemy, so that he may be remiss and leisurely while you are dashing along with the utmost speed." Heshi gives a slightly different turn to the sentence: "Although you may have difficult ground to transverse and natural obstacles to encounter, this is a drawback which can be turned into actual advantage by celerity of movement." Signal examples of this saying are afforded by the two famous passages across the Alps—that of Hannibal, which laid Italy at his mercy, and that of Napoleon two thousand years later, which resulted in the great victory of Marengo.

6. Jia Lin understands 途 as the *enemy's* line of march, thus: "If our adversary's course is really a short one, and we can manage to divert him from it (迂之) either by stimulating weakness or by holding out some small advantage, we shall be able to beat him in the race for good positions." This is quite a defensible view, though not adopted by any other commentator. 人 of course = 敵, and 後 and 先 are to be taken as verbs. Du You cites the famous march of Zhao She 趙奢 in 270 B.C. to relieve the town of Eyu 閼與, which was closely invested by a Qin 秦 army. [It should be noted that the above is the correct pronunciation of 閼與, as given in the commentary on the *Qian Han Shu*,

chap. 43. Giles' dictionary gives "Yuyu," and Chavannes, I know not on what authority, prefers to write "Yanyu." The name is omitted altogether from Playfair's "Cities and Towns."] The King of Zhao first consulted Lian Po 廉頗 on the advisability of attempting a relief, but the latter thought the distance too great, and the intervening country too rugged and difficult. His Majesty then turned to Zhao She, who fully admitted the hazardous nature of the march, but finally said: "We shall be like two rats fighting in a hole—and the pluckier one will win!" So he left the capital with his army, but had only gone a distance of 30 *li* when he stopped and began throwing up entrenchments. For 28 days he continued strengthening his fortifications, and took care that spies should carry the intelligence to the enemy. The Qin general was overjoyed, and attributed his adversary's tardiness to the fact that the beleaguered city was in the Han State, and thus not actually part of Zhao territory. But the spies had no sooner departed than Zhao She began a forced march lasting for two days and one night, and arrived on the scene of action with such astonishing rapidity that he was able to occupy a commanding position on the "North hill" 北山 before the enemy had got wind of his movements. A crushing defeat followed for the Qin forces, who were obliged to raise the siege of Eyu in all haste and retreat across the border. (See 史記, chap. 81.)

7. I here adopt the reading of the *Tongdian*, Zheng Youxian and the *Tu Shu*, where 眾 appears to supply the exact nuance required in order to make sense. The standard text, on the other hand, in which 軍 is repeated, seems somewhat pointless. The commentators take it to mean that maneuvers may be profitable, or they may be dangerous: it all depends on the ability of the general. Capt. Calthrop translates 眾爭 "the wrangles of a multitude"!

8. The original text has 故 instead of 舉; but a verb is needed to balance 委.

9. 委軍 is evidently unintelligible to the Chinese commentators, who paraphrase the sentence as though it began with 棄輜. Absolute tautology in the apodosis can then only be avoided by drawing an impossible fine distinction between 棄 and 捐. I submit my own rendering without much enthusiasm, being convinced that there is some deep-seated corruption in the text. On the whole, it is clear that Sun

Tzǔ does not approve of a lengthy march being undertaken without supplies. Cf. *infra*, §11.

10. 卷甲 does not mean "to discard one's armor," as Capt. Calthrop translates, but implies on the contrary that it is to be carried with you. Zhang Yu says: "This means, in full panoply" 猶悉甲也.

11. The ordinary day's march, according to Du You, was 30 *li*, but on one occasion, when pursuing Liu Bei 劉備, Cao Cao is said to have covered the incredible distance of 300 *li* within twenty-four hours.

12. For 罷, see II. § 14. The moral is, as Cao Gong and others point out: Don't march a hundred *li* to gain a tactical advantage, either with or without impedimenta. Maneuvers of this description should be confined to short distances. Stonewall Jackson said: "The hardships of forced marches are often more painful than the dangers of battle." He did not often call upon his troops for extraordinary exertions. It was only when he intended a surprise, or when a rapid retreat was imperative, that he sacrificed everything to speed."[1]

13. 蹶 is explained as similar in meaning to 挫: literally, "the leader of the first division will be *torn away*." Cf. Zuozhuan, 襄 19th year: "This is a case of [the falling tree] tearing up its roots" 是謂蹶其本.

14. In the *Tongdian* is added: "From this we may know the difficulty of maneuvering" 以是知軍爭之難.

15. 委積 is explained by Du You as "fodder and the like" 芻草之 屬; by Du You and Zhang Yu as "goods in general" 財貨; and by Wang Xi as "fuel, salt, foodstuff, etc" 薪鹽蔬材之屬. But I think what Sun Tzǔ meant was "stores accumulated in depots," as distinguished from 輜重 and 糧食, the various impedimenta accompanying an army on its march. Cf. *Zhou Li*, chap. Xvi. Fol. 10: 委人... 斂薪芻凡疏材木 材凡畜聚之物.

16. 豫 = 先. Li Quan understands it as "guard against" 備, which is hardly so good. An original interpretation of 交 is given by Du You, who says it stands for 交兵 or 合戰 "join in battle."

17. 險, defined as (Cao Gong) 坑塹 or (Zhang Yu) 坑坎.

18. 阻, defined as 一高一下.

19. 沮, defined as 水草漸洳者.

---

20. 澤, defined as 眾水所歸而不流者.

21. §§12–14 are repeated in chap. XI. § 52

22. According to Du You, 立 stands for 立勝. Cf. I. § 18. In the tactics of Turenne, deception of the enemy, especially as to the numerical strength of his troops, took a very prominent position.

23. This is the interpretation of all the commentators except Wang Xi, who has the brief note "Entice out the enemy" 誘之也 (by offering him some apparent advantage).

24. The simile is doubly appropriate, because the wind is not only swift but, as Mei Yaochen points out, "invisible and leaves no tracks" 無形跡.

25. It is hardly possible to take 徐 here in its ordinary sense of "sedate" as Du You tries to do. Mengshi comes nearer the mark in his note: "When slowly marching, order and ranks must be preserved" 緩行須有行列—so as to guard against surprise attacks. But natural forests do not grow in rows, whereas they do generally possess the quality of density or compactness. I think then that Mei Yaochen uses the right adjective in saying 如林之森然.

26. Cf. *Shijing*, IV. 3 iv. 6: 如火烈烈則莫我敢曷 "Fierce as a blazing fire which no man can check."

27. That is, when holding a position from which the enemy is trying to dislodge you, or perhaps, as Du You says, when he is trying to entice you into a trap.

28. The original text has 震 instead of 霆. Cf. IV. § 7. Du You quotes a saying of Tai Gong that has passed into a proverb: "You cannot shut your ears to the thunder or your eyes to the lightning—so rapid are they" 疾雷不及掩耳疾電不及瞑目. Likewise, an attack should be made so quickly that it cannot be parried.

29. The reading of Du You, Jia Lin, and apparently Cao Gong, is 指向分眾, which is explained as referring to the subdivision of the army, mentioned in V. §§ 1, 2, by means of banners and flags, serving to point out (指) to each man the way he should go (向). But this is very forced, and the ellipsis is too great, even for Sun Tzǔ. Luckily, the *Tongdian* and *Yulan* have the variant 嚮, which not only suggests the true reading 鄉, but affords some clue to the way in which the corruption arose. Some early commentator having inserted 向 as the

sound of 鄉, the two may afterwards have been read as one character; and this being interchangeable with 向, 鄉 must finally have disappeared altogether. Meanwhile, 掠 would have been altered to 指 in order to make sense. As regards 分眾, I believe that Heshi alone has grasped the real meaning, the other commentators understanding it as "dividing the men into parties" to search for plunder. Sun Tzŭ wishes to lessen the abuses of indiscriminate plundering by insisting that all booty shall be thrown into a common stock, which may afterward be fairly divided amongst all.

30. That this is the meaning may be gathered from Du You's note: 開土拓境則分割與有功者. The 三略 gives the same advice: 獲地裂之. 廓 means "to enlarge" or "extend"—at the expense of the enemy, understood. Cf. *Shijing*, III. 1. vi. 1: "hating all the great States" 憎其式廓. Chen Hao also says "quarter your soldiers on the land, and let them sow and plant it" 屯兵種蒔. It is by acting on this principle, and harvesting the lands they invaded, that the Chinese have succeeded in carrying out some of their most memorable and triumphant expeditions, such as that of Ban Chao 班超 who penetrated to the Caspian, and in more recent years those of Fukang'an 福康安 and Zuo Zongtang 左宗棠. (M. Chavannes writes in the *T'ong Pao*, 1906, p. 210: "Le général Pan Tch'ao n'a jamais porté les armes chinoises jusque sur les bords de la mer Caspienne." I hasten to correct my statement on this authority.)

31. Note that both these words, like the Chinese 懸權, are really metaphors derived from the use of scales.

32. Zhang Yu quotes 尉繚子 as saying that we must not break camp until we have gauged the resisting power of the enemy and the cleverness of the opposing general. Cf. the "seven comparisons" in I. § 13. Capt. Calthrop omits this sentence.

33. See *supra*, §§ 3, 4.

34. With these words, the chapter would naturally come to an end. But there now follows a long appendix in the shape of an extract from an earlier book on War, now lost, but apparently extant at the time when Sun Tzŭ wrote. The style of this fragment is not noticeably different from that of Sun Tzŭ himself, but no commentator raises a doubt as to its genuineness.

35. It is perhaps significant that none of the earlier commentators give us any information about this work. Mei Yaochen calls it "an ancient military classic" 軍之舊典, and Wang Xi, "an old book on war" 古軍書. Considering the enormous amount of fighting that had gone on for centuries before Sun Tzŭ's time between the various kingdoms and principalities of China, it is not in itself improbable that a collection of military maxims should have been made and written down at some earlier period.

36. Implied, though not actually in the Chinese.

37. I have retained the words 金鼓 of the original text, which recur in the next paragraph, in preference to the other reading "drums and bells" 鼓鐸, which is found in the *Tongdian, Beitang Shuchao* and *Yulan.* 鐸 is a bell with a clapper. See *Lunyu* III. 24, *Zhou Li* XXIX. 15, 29. 金 of course would include both gongs and bells of every kind. The *Tu Shu* inserts a 之 after each 為.

38. The original text, followed by the *Tu Shu*, has 人 for 民 here and in the next two paragraphs. But, as we have seen, 人 is generally used in Sun Tzŭ for the enemy.

39. Note the use of 一 as a verb. Zhang Yu says: "If sight and hearing converge simultaneously on the same object, the evolutions of as many as a million soldiers will be like those of a single man" 視聽均齊則雖百萬之眾進退如一矣!

40. Zhang Yu quotes a saying: "Equally guilty are those who advance against orders and those who retreat against orders" 令不進而進與令不退而退厥罪惟均. Du You tells a story in this connection of Wu Qi 吳起, when he was fighting against the Qin state. Before the battle had begun, one of his soldiers, a man of matchless daring, sallied forth by himself, captured two heads from the enemy, and returned to camp. Wu Qi had the man instantly executed, whereupon an officer ventured to remonstrate, saying: "This man was a good soldier, and ought not to have been beheaded," Wu Qi replied: "I fully believe he was a good soldier, but I had him beheaded because he acted without orders."

41. The *Tongdian* has the bad variant 便 for 變. With regard to the latter word, I believe I have hit off the right meaning, the whole phrase being slightly elliptical for "influencing the movements of the

army through their senses of sight and hearing." Li Quan, Du You and Jia Lin certainly seem to understand it thus. The other commentators, however, take 民 (or 人) as the enemy, and 變 as equivalent to "to perplex" or "confound" 變惑 or 變亂. This does not agree so well with what has gone before, though on the other hand it renders the transition to § 27 less abrupt. The whole question, I think, hinges on the alternative readings 民 and 人. The latter would almost certainly denote the enemy. Chen Hao alludes to Li Guangbi's 李光弼 night ride to Heyang 河陽 at the head of 500 mounted men; they made such an imposing display with torches, that though the rebel leader Shi Siming 史思明 had a large army, he did not dare to dispute their passage. (Chen Hao gives the date as A.D. 756 天寶末; but according to the New Tang History 新唐書, 列傳 61, it must have been later than this, probably 760.)

42. "In war," says Zhang Yu, "if a spirit of anger can be made to pervade all ranks of an army at one and the same time, its onset will be irresistible. Now the spirit of the enemy's soldiers will be keenest when they have newly arrived on the scene, and it is therefore our cue not to fight at once, but to wait until their ardor and enthusiasm have worn off, and then strike. It is in this way that they may be robbed of their keen spirit." Li Quan and others tell an anecdote (to be found in the *Zuozhuan*, 莊公 year 10, § 1) of Cao Gui 曹劌, *a protégé* of Duke Zhuang of Lu. The latter State was attacked by Qi and the Duke was about to join battle at Changzhuo 長勺, after the first roll of the enemy's drums, when Cao said: "Not just yet." Only after their drums had beaten for the third time, did he give the word for attack. Then they fought, and the men of Qi were utterly defeated. Questioned afterwards by the Duke as to the meaning of his delay, Cao Gui replied: "In battle, a courageous spirit is everything. Now the first roll of the drums tend to create this spirit, but with the second it is already on the wane, and after the third it is gone altogether. I attacked when their spirit was gone and ours was at its height. Hence our victory." 吳子 (chap. 4) puts "spirit" first among the "four important influences" in war, and continues: "The value of a whole army—a mighty host of a million men—is dependent on one man alone: such is the influence of spirit" 三軍之眾百萬之師張設輕重在於一人是謂氣機.

43. Capt. Calthrop goes woefully astray with "defeat his general's ambition." Zhang Yu says: "Presence of mind is the general's most important asset. It is the quality which enables him to discipline disorder and to inspire courage into the panic-stricken>" 心者將之所主也夫 治亂勇怯皆主於心. The great general Li Jing 李靖 (A.D. 571-649) has a saying: "Attacking does not merely consist in assaulting walled cities or striking at an army in battle array; it must include the art of assailing the enemy's mental equilibrium" 夫攻者不止攻其城擊其 陳而已必有攻其心之術焉. [問對, pt. 3.]

44. Always provided, I suppose, that he has had breakfast. At the battle of the Trebia, the Romans were foolishly allowed to fight fasting, whereas Hannibal's men had breakfasted at their leisure. See Livy, XXI. Liv. 8, lv. 1 and 8.

45. The 故, which certainly seems to be wanted here, is omitted in the *Tu Shu*.

46. The *Tongdian*, for reasons of 避諱 "avoidance of personal names of the reigning dynasty," reads 理 for 治 in this and the two next paragraphs.

47. The *Tongdian* has 逸 for 佚. The two characters are practically synonymous, but according to the commentary, the latter is the form always used in Sun Tzŭ.

48. 邀 is the reading of the original text. But the 兵書要訣 quotes the passage with 要 yao (also meaning "to intercept"), and this is supported by the *Beitang shuchao*, the *Yulan*, and Wang Xi's text.

49. For this translation of 堂堂, I can appeal to the authority of Du Mu, who defines the phrase as 無懼. The other commentators mostly follow Cao Gong, who says 大, probably meaning "grand and imposing". Li Quan, however, has "in subdivisions" 部分, which is somewhat strange.

50. I have not attempted a uniform rendering of the four phrases 治氣, 治心, 治力, and 治變, though 治 really bears the same meaning in each case. It is to be taken, I think, not in the sense of "to govern" or "control," but rather, as Kangxi defines it, = 簡習 "To examine and practice," hence "look after," "keep a watchful eye upon." We may find an example of this use in the *Zhou Li*, XVIII. Col. 46: 治其大 禮. Sun Tzŭ has not told us to control or restrain the quality that he

calls 氣, but only to observe the time at which it is strongest. As for 心, it is important to remember that in the present context it can only mean "presence of mind." To speak of "controlling presence of mind" is absurd, and Capt. Calthrop's "to have the heart under control" is hardly less so. The whole process recommended here is that of VI. § 2: 致人而不致於人.

51. Li Quan and Du Mu, with extraordinary inability to see a metaphor, take these words quite literally of food and drink that have been poisoned by the enemy. Chen Hao and Zhang Yu carefully point out that the saying has a wider application. The *Tongdian* reads 貪 "to covet" instead of 食. The similarity of the two characters sufficiently accounts for the mistake.

52. The commentators explain this rather singular piece of advice by saying that a man whose heart is set on returning home will fight to the death against any attempt to bar his way, and is therefore too dangerous an opponent to be attacked. Zhang Yu quotes the words of Han Xin: "Invincible is the soldier who hath his desire and returneth homewards" 從思東歸之士何所不克. A marvelous tale is told of Cao Cao's courage and resource in chap. I of the *Sanguozhi*, 武帝紀: In 198 A.D., he was besieging Zhang Xiu 張繡 in Rang 穰, when Liu Biao 劉表 sent reinforcement with a view to cutting off Cao's retreat. The latter was obliged to draw off his troops, only to find himself hemmed in between two enemies, who were guarding each outlet of a narrow pass in which he had engaged himself. In this desperate plight Cao waited until nightfall, when he bored a tunnel into the mountainside and laid an ambush in it. The he marched on with his baggage-train, and when it grew light, Zhang Xiu, finding that the bird had flown, pressed after him in hot pursuit. As soon as the whole army had passed by, the hidden troops fell on his rear, while Cao himself turned and met his pursuers in front, so that they were thrown into confusion and annihilated. Cao Cao said afterwards: "The brigands tried to check my army in its retreat and brought me to battle in a desperate position: hence I knew how to overcome them" 虜遏吾歸師而與吾死地戰吾是以知勝矣.

53. This does not mean that the enemy is to be allowed to escape. The object, as Du Mu puts it, is "to make him believe that there is a

road to safety, and thus prevent his fighting with the courage of despair" 示以生路令無必死之心. Du Mu adds pleasantly: "After that,
you may crush him" 因而擊之.

54. For 迫, the *Tu Shu* reads "pursue" 追. Chen Hao quotes the
saying: "Birds and beasts when brought to bay will use their claws and
teeth" 鳥窮則搏獸窮則噬. Zhang Yu says: "If your adversary has
burned his boats and destroyed his cook-pots, and is ready to stake
all on the issue of the battle, he must not be pushed to extremities"
敵若焚舟破釜決一戰則不可逼迫來. The phrase 窮寇 doubtless
originated with Sun Tzŭ. The *Peiwen yunfu* gives four examples of its
use, the earliest being from the *Qian Han Shu*, and I have found another in chap. 34 of the same work. Heshi illustrates the meaning by
a story taken from the life of Fu Yanqing 符彥卿 in chap. 251 of the
宋史. The general, together with his colleague Du Zhongwei 杜重
威, was surrounded by a vastly superior army of Khitans in the year
945 A.D. The country was bare and desert-like, and the little Chinese
force was soon in dire straits for want of water. The wells they bored
ran dry, and then men were reduced to squeezing lumps of mud and
sucking out the moisture. Their ranks thinned rapidly, until at last Fu
Yanqing exclaimed: "We are desperate men. Far better to die for our
country rather than to go with fettered hands into captivity." A strong
gale happened to be blowing from the northeast and darkening the air
with dense clouds of sandy dust. Du Zhongwei was for waiting until
this had abated before deciding on a final attack; but luckily another
officer, Li Shouzhen 李守貞 by name, was quicker to see an opportunity, and said: "They are many and we are few, but in the midst of this
sandstorm our numbers will not be discernible; victory will go to the
strenuous fighter, and the wind will be our best ally." Accordingly, Fu
Yanqing made a sudden and wholly unexpected onslaught with his
cavalry, routed the barbarians, and succeeded in breaking through to
safety. (Certain details in the above account have been added from the
歷代紀事年表, juan 78.)

55. Zheng Youxian in his 遺說 inserts 妙 after 法. I take it that
these words conclude the extract from the 軍政, which began at § 23.

# CHAPTER 8

# Variation Of Tactics
# 九變篇第八

1. The heading means literally "The Nine Variations," but as Sun Tzŭ does not appear to enumerate these, and as, indeed, he has already told us (V. §§ 6-11) that such deflections from the ordinary course are practically innumerable, we have a little option but to follow Wang Xi, who says "Nine" stands for an indefinitely large number. "All it means is that in warfare 當極其變 we ought to vary our tactics to the utmost degree…I do not know what Cao Gong makes these Nine Variations out to be [the latter's note is 變其正得其所用九也], but it has been suggested that they are connected with the Nine Situations"—of chap. XI. This is the view adopted by Zhang Yu: see note on 死地, § 2. The only other alternative is to suppose something has been lost—a supposition to which the unusual shortness of the chapter lends some weight.

2. Repeated from VII. § I. where it is certainly more in place. It may have been interpolated here merely in order to supply a beginning to the chapter.

3. For explanation of 圯地, see XI. § 8.

4. See XI, §§ 6, 12 Capt. Calthrop omits 衢地.

5. 絕地 is not one of the Nine Situations as given in the beginning of chap. XI, but occurs later on (*ibid* § 43, *q.v.*). We may compare it with 重地 (XI § 7). Zhang Yu calls it a 危絕之地, situated across the frontier, in hostile territory. Li Quan says it is "country in which there are no springs or wells, flocks or herds, vegetables or firewood;" Jia Lin, "one of gorges, chasms and precipices, without a road by which to advance."

6. See XI. § § 9, 14. Capt. Calthrop has "mountainous and wooded country," which is a quite inadequate translation of 圍.

7. See XI. § § 10, 14. Zhang Yu has an important note here, which must be given in full. "From 圯地無舍," he says, "down to this point,

the Nine Variations are presented to us. The reason why only five are given is that the subject is treated *en précis* (舉其大略也). So in chap. XI, where he discusses the variations of tactics corresponding to the Nine Grounds, Sun Tzǔ mentions only six variations; there again we have an abridgement. (I cannot understand what Zhang Yu means by this statement. He can only be referring to §§ 11-14 or §§ 46-50 of chap. IX; but in both places all the nine grounds are discussed. Perhaps he is confusing these with the Six 地形 of chap. X.) All kinds of ground have corresponding military positions, and also a variation of tactics suitable to each (凡地有勢有變). In chap. XI, what we find enumerated first [§§ 2-10] are the situations; afterwards [§§ 11-14] the corresponding tactics. Now, how can we tell that 'Nine Variations' 九變 are simply the 'variations of tactics corresponding to the Nine Grounds' 九地之變? It is said further on [§ 5] that 'the general who does not understand the nine variations of tactics may be well acquainted with the features of the country, yet he will not be able to turn his knowledge to practical account.' Again, in chap. XI [§ 41] we read: 'The different measures adapted to the nine varieties of ground (九地之變) and the expediency of aggressive or defensive tactics must be carefully examined.' From a consideration of these passages the meaning is made clear. When later on the nine grounds are enumerated, Sun Tzǔ refers to these nine variations. He wishes here to speak of the Five Advantages [see *infra*, § 6], so he begins by setting forth the Nine Variations. These are inseparably connected in practice, and therefore they are dealt with together." The weak point of this argument is the suggestion that "five things" 五事 can stand as a 大畧, that is, an abstract or abridgment, of nine, when those that are omitted are not less important than those that appear, and when one of the latter is not included amongst the nine at all.

8. "Especially those leading through narrow defiles," says Li Quan, "where an ambush is to be feared."

9. More correctly, perhaps, "there are times when an army must not be attacked." Chen Hao says: "When you see your way to obtain a trivial advantage, but are powerless to inflict a real defeat, refrain from attacking, for fear of overtaxing your men's strength."

10. Capt. Calthrop says "castles"—an unfortunate attempt to introduce local color.

11. Cf. III. § 4. Cao Gong gives an interesting illustration from his own experience. When invading the territory of Xuzhou 徐州, he ignored the city of Huabi 華費, which lay directly in his path, and pressed on into the heart of the country. This excellent strategy was rewarded by the subsequent capture of no fewer than fourteen important district cities. Zhang Yu says: "No town should be attacked which, if taken, cannot be held, or if let alone, will not cause any trouble." Xun Ying 荀罃, when urged to attack Biyang 偪陽, replied: "The city is small and well-fortified; even if I succeed in taking it, it will be no great feat of arms; whereas if I fail, I shall make myself a laughingstock." In the seventeenth century, sieges still formed a large proportion of war. It was Turenne who directed attention to the importance of marches, countermarches, and maneuvers. He said: "It is a great mistake to waste men in taking a town when the same expenditure of soldiers will gain a province."[1]

12. This is a hard saying for the Chinese, with their reverence for authority, and Weiliaozi (quoted by Du Mu) is moved to exclaim: "Weapons are baleful instruments, strife is antagonistic to virtue, a military commander is the negation of civil order!" 兵者凶器也爭者逆德也將者死官也. The unpalatable fact remains, however, that even Imperial wishes must be subordinated to military necessity. Cf. III. § 17. (5), X. § 23. The *Tongdian* has 將在軍 before 君命, etc. This is a gloss on the words by Zhuge Liang, which being repeated by Du You became incorporated with the text. Zhang Yu thinks that these five precepts are the 五利 referred to in § 6. Another theory is that the mysterious 九變 are here enumerated, starting with 圮地無舍 and ending at 地有所不爭, while the final clause 君命有所不受 embraces and as it were sums up all the nine. Thus Heshi says: "Even if it be your sovereign's command to encamp in difficult country, linger in isolated positions, etc., you must not do so." The theory is perhaps a little too ingenious to be accepted with confidence.

13. Before 利 in the original text there is a 地, which is obviously not required.

14. Literally, "get the advantage of the ground," which means not only securing good position, but availing oneself of natural advantages in eve-

---

[1] *See* Col. Henderson, *op. cit.* vol. 1. p. 426.

ry possible way. Zhang Yu says: "Every kind of ground is characterized by certain natural features, and also gives scope for a certain variability of plan. How is it possible to turn these natural features to account unless topographical knowledge is supplemented by versatility of mind?"

15. Cao Gong says that the 五利 are "the five things that follow" 下五事也; but this cannot be right. We must rather look back to the five "variations" contained in § 3. Jia Lin (who reads 五變 here to balance the 五利) tells us that these imply five obvious and generally advantageous lines of action, namely: "if a certain road is short, it must be followed; if any army is isolated, it must be attacked; if a town is in a parlous condition, it must be besieged; if a position can be stormed, it must be attempted; and if consistent with military operations, the ruler's commands must be obeyed." But there are circumstances that sometimes forbid a general to use these advantages. For instance, "a certain road may be the shortest way for him, but if he knows that it abounds in natural obstacles, or that the enemy has laid an ambush on it, he will not follow that road. A hostile force may be open to attack, but if he knows that it is hard-pressed and likely to fight with desperation, he will refrain from striking," and so on. Here the 變 comes in to modify the 利, and hence we see the uselessness of knowing the one without the other—of having an eye for weakness in the enemy's armor without being clever enough to recast one's plans on the spur of the moment. Capt. Calthrop offers this slovenly translation: "In the management of armies, if the art of the Nine Changes be understood [*sic*], a knowledge of the Five Advantages is of no avail."

16. "Whether in an advantageous position or a disadvantageous one," says Cao Gong, "the opposite state should be always present to your mind."

17. 信, according to Du Mu, is equivalent to 申, and 務可信也 is paraphrased by Zhang Yu as 可以伸己之事. Du Mu goes on to say: "If we wish to wrest an advantage from the enemy, we must not fix our minds on that alone, but allow for the possibility of the enemy also doing some harm to us, and let this enter as a factor into our calculations."

18. A translation cannot emulate the conciseness of "to blend [thoughts of advantage] with disadvantage" 雜於害, but the meaning is as given. Du Mu says: "If I wish extricate myself from a dangerous

position, I must consider not only the enemy's ability to injure me, but also my own ability to gain an advantage over the enemy. If in my counsels these two considerations are properly blended, I shall succeed in liberating myself…For instance, if I am surrounded by the enemy and only think of effecting an escape, the nervelessness of my policy will incite my adversary to pursue and crush me; it would be far better to encourage my men to deliver a bold counter-attack, and use the advantage thus gained to free myself from the enemy's toils." See the story of Cao Cao, VII. § 35, note. In this first edition, Capt. Calthrop translated §§ 7-9 as follows: "The wise man perceives clearly wherein lies advantage and disadvantage. While recognizing an opportunity, he does not overlook the risk, and saves future anxiety." This has now been altered into: "the wise man considers well both advantage and disadvantage. He sees now out of adversity, *and on the day of victory to danger is not blind.*" Owing to a needless inversion of the Chinese, the words that I have italicized are evidently intended to represent § 8!

19. Jia Lin enumerates several ways of inflicting this injury: "Entice away the enemy's best and wisest men, so that he may be left without counselors. Introduce traitors into his country that the government policy may be rendered futile. Foment intrigue and deceit, and thus sow dissension between the ruler and his ministers. By means of every artful contrivance, cause deterioration amongst his men and waste of his treasure. Corrupt his morals by insidious gifts leading him into excess. Disturb and unsettle his mind by presenting him with lovely women." Zhang Yu (after Wang Xi) considers the 害 to be military chastisement: "Get the enemy," he says, "into a position where he must suffer injury, and he will submit of his own accord." Capt. Calthrop twists Sun Tzŭ's words into an absurdly barbarous precept: "In reducing an enemy to submission, inflict all possible damage upon him."

20. 業 is defined by Cao Gong as 事, and his definition is generally adopted by the commentators. Du Mu, however, seems to take it in the sense of "assets," which he considers to be "a large army, a rich exchequer, harmony amongst the soldiers, punctual fulfillment of commands" 兵眾國富人和令行. These give us a whip hand over the enemy.

21. 役, literally, "make servants of them." Du You says "prevent them from having any rest" 令不得安佚.

22. Mengshi's note contains an excellent example of the idiomatic use of 變: "cause them to forgot bian (the reasons for acting otherwise than on their first impulse), and hasten in our direction" 令忘變而速至.

23. The *Tongdian* and *Yulan* read 有能以待之也, but the conciser form is more likely to be right.

24. The *Tongdian* and *Yulan* insert 吾也 after the first 攻, and omit 有所.

25. "Bravely without forethought," 勇而無慮, as Cao Gong analyses it, which causes a man to fight blindly and desperately like a mad bull. Such an opponent, says Zhang Yu, "must not be encountered with brute force, but may be lured into an ambush and slain." Cf. Wuzi, chap. IV *ad init.*: "In estimating the character of a general, men are wont to pay exclusive attention to his courage, forgetting that courage is only one out of many qualities which a general should possess. The merely brave man is prone to fight recklessly; and who fights recklessly, without any perception of what is expedient, must be condemned." 凡人論將常觀於勇勇之於將乃數分之一耳夫勇者必輕合輕合而不知利未可也. The *Sima Fa*, too, makes the incisive remark "Simply going to one's death does not bring about victory." 上死不勝.

26. 必生 is explained by Cao Gong of the man "whom timidity prevents from advancing to seize an advantage," and Wang Xi adds, "Who is quick to flee at the sight of danger." Mengshi gives the closer paraphrase "he who is bent on returning alive" 志必生反, that is, the man who will never take a risk. But, as Sun Tzǔ knew, nothing is to be achieved in war unless you are willing to take a risks. Tai Gong said: "He who lets advantage slip will subsequently bring upon himself real disaster" 失利後時反受其殃. In 404 A.D., Liu Yu 劉裕 pursued the rebel Huan Xuan 桓玄 up the Yangtse and fought a naval battle with him at the island of Zhengrong 峥嶸洲. The loyal troops numbered only a few thousand, while their opponents were in great force. But Huan Xuan, fearing the fate which was in store for him should he be overcome, had a light boat made fast to the side of his war-junk, so that he might escape, if necessary, at a moment's notice. The natural result was that the fighting spirit of his soldiers was utterly quenched, and when the loyalists made an attack from windward with fire ships, all striving with the outmost ardor to be first in the fray, Huan Xuan's forces were routed,

had to burn all their baggage and fled for two days and nights without stopping. [*See* 晉書, chap. 99, fol. 13.] Zhang Yu tells a somewhat similar story of Zhao Yingqi 趙嬰齊, a general of the Jin state who during a battle with the army of Chu in 597 B.C. had a boat kept in readiness for him on the river, wishing in case of defeat to be the first to get across.

27. I fail to see the meaning of Capt. Calthrop's "which *brings* insult." Du Mu tells us that Yao Xiang 姚襄, when opposed in 357 A.D. by Huang Mei 黃眉, Deng Qiang 鄧羌 and others, shut himself up behind his walls and refused to fight. Deng Qiang said: "Our adversary is of a choleric temper and easily provoked; let us make constant sallies and break down his walls, then he will grow angry and come out. Once we can bring his force to battle, it is doomed to be our prey." This plan was acted upon, Yao Xiang came out to fight, was lured on as far as Sanyuan 三原 by the enemy's pretended flight, and finally attacked and slain.

28. This need not be taken to mean that a sense of honor is really a defect in a general. What Sun Tzǔ condemns is rather an exaggerated sensitiveness to slanderous report, the thin-skinned man who is stung by opprobrium, however undeserved. Mei Yaochen truly observes, though somewhat paradoxically; "The seeker after glory should be careless of public opinion." 徇名不顧.

29. Here again, Sun Tzǔ does not mean that the general is to be careless of the welfare of his troops. All he wishes to emphasize is the danger of sacrificing any important military advantage to the immediate comfort of his men. This is a shortsighted policy, because in the long run the troops will suffer more from the consequence. A mistaken feeling of pity will often induce a general to relieve a beleaguered city, or to reinforce a hard-pressed detachment, contrary to his military instincts. It is now generally admitted that our repeated efforts to relieve Ladysmith in the South African War were so many strategical blunders which defeated their own purpose. And in the end, relief came through the very man who started out with the distinct resolve no longer to subordinate the interests of the whole to sentiment in favor of a part. An old soldier of one of our generals who failed most conspicuously in this war, tried once, I remember, to defend him to me on the ground that he was always "so good to his men." By this plea, had he known it, he was only condemning him out of Sun Tzǔ's mouth.

# CHAPTER 9

# The Army On The March
## 行軍篇第九

1. The contents of this interesting chapter are better indicated in § I than by this heading.

2. The discussion of 處軍, as Zhang Yu points out, extends from here down to 伏姦之所藏處也 (§§ 1-17), and 相敵 from that point down to 必謹察之 (§§ 18-39). The rest of the chapter consists of a few desultory remarks, chiefly on the subject of discipline.

3. For this use of 絕, cf. *infra*, § 3. See also 荀子, chap. 1. fol. 2 (standard edition of 1876): 絕江河; *Shiji*, chap. 27 ad *init*.: 後六星 絕漢. Du Mu says that 依 here = 近. The idea is, not to linger among barren uplands, but to keep close to supplies of water and grass. Capt. Calthrop translates "camp in valleys," heedless of the very next sentence. Cf. Wuzi, chap. 3: "Abide not in natural ovens" 無當天竈, *i.e.* "the opening of large valleys" 大谷之口. Zhang Yu tells the following anecdote: "Wudu Qiang 武都羌 was a robber captain in the time of the Later Han, and Ma Yuan 馬援 was sent to exterminate his gang. Qiang having found a refuge in the hills, Ma Yuan made no attempt to force a battle, but seized all the favorable positions commanding supplies of water and forage. Qiang was soon in such a desperate plight for want of provision that he was forced to make a total surrender. He did not know the advantage of keeping in the neighborhood of valleys."

4. Not on high hills, but on knolls or hillocks elevated above the surrounding country.

5. 視生 = 面陽. Du Mu takes this to mean "facing south," and Chen Hao "facing east." Cf. *infra*, §§ 11, 13.

6. 隆 is here simply equivalent to 高. The *Tongdian* and *Yulan* read 降.

7. After 山, the *Tongdian* and *Yulan* insert 谷.

8. "In order to tempt the enemy to cross after you," according to

Cao Gong, and also, says Zhang Yu, "in order not to be impeded in your evolution." The *Tongdian* reads 敵若絕水, "If *the enemy* crosses a river," etc. But in view of the next sentence, this is almost certainly an interpolation.

9. The *Tongdian* and *Yulan* read 度 for 濟, without change of meaning. Wuzi plagiarizes this passage twice over: chap. 11 *ad fin.* 涉水半渡可擊; chap. V, 敵若絕水半渡而擊. Li Quan alludes to the great victory won by Han Xin over Long Ju 龍且 at the Wei 濰 River. Turning to the *Qian Han Shu*, chap. 34, fol. 6 *verso*, we find the battle described as follows: "The two armies were drawn up on opposite sides of the river. In the night, Han Xin ordered his men to take some ten thousand sacks filled with sand and construct a dam a little higher up. Then, leading half his army across, he attacked Long Ju; but after a time, pretending to have failed in his attempt, he hastily withdrew to the other bank. Long Ju was much elated by this unlooked-for success, and exclaiming: "I felt sure that Han Xin was really a coward!" he pursued him and began crossing the river in his turn. Han Xin now sent a party to cut open the sandbags, thus releasing a great volume of water, which swept down and prevented the greater portion of Long Ju's army from getting across. He then turned upon the force that had been cut off, and annihilated it, Long Ju himself being amongst the slain. The rest of the army, on the further bank, also scattered and fled in all directions."

10. For fear of preventing his crossing. Capt. Calthrop makes the injunction ridiculous by omitting 欲戰者.

11. See *supra*, § 2. The repetition of these words in connection with water is very awkward. Zhang Yu has the note: "Said either of troops marshaled on the riverbank, or of boats anchored in the stream itself; in either case it is essential to be higher than the enemy and facing the sun." 或岸邊為陳或水上泊舟皆須面陽而居高. The other commentators are not at all explicit. One is much tempted to reject their explanation of 視生 altogether, and understand it simply as "seeking safety." (Cf. 必生 in VIII. § 12, and *infra*, § 9.) It is true that this involves taking 視 in an unusual, though not, I think, an impossible sense. Of course the earlier passage would then have to be translated in like manner.

12. Du Mu says: "As water flows downwards, we must not pitch our camp on the lower reaches of a river, for the fear the enemy should open the sluices and sweep us away in a flood. This is implied above in the words 視生處高. Zhuge Wuhou has remarked that 'in river warfare we must not advance against the stream,' which is as much as to say that our fleet must not be anchored below that of the enemy, for then they would be able to take advantage of the current and make short work of us." There is also the danger, noted by other commentators, that the enemy may throw poison on the water to be carried down to us. Capt. Calthrop's first version was: "Do not cross rivers in the face of the stream"—a sapient piece of advice, which made one curious to know what the correct way of crossing rivers might be. He has now improved this into: "Do not fight when the enemy is between the army and the source of the river."

13. Because of the lack of fresh water, the poor quality of the herbage, and last but not least, because they are low, flat, and exposed to attack.

14. Li Quan remarks that the ground is less likely to be treacherous where there are trees, while Du You says that they will serve to protect the rear. Capt. Calthrop, with a perfect genius for going wrong, says "in the neighborhood of a marsh." For 若 the Tongdian and Yulan wrongly read 為, and the latter also has 倍 instead of 背.

15. This is doubtless the force of 易, its opposite being 險. Thus, Du Mu explains it as "ground that is smooth and firm" 坦易平穩之處, and therefore adapted for cavalry; Zhang Yu as "level ground, free from depressions and hollows" 坦易無坎陷之處. He adds later on that although Sun Tzŭ is discussing flat country, there will nevertheless be slight elevations and hillocks.

16. The Yulan again reads 倍 for 背. Du Mu quotes Tai Gong as saying: "An army should have a stream or a marsh on its left, and a hill or tumulus on its right."

17. Wang Xi thinks that 後生 contradicts the saying 視生 in § 2, and therefore suspects a mistake in the text.

18. Those, namely, concerned with (1) mountains, (2) rivers, (3) marshes, and (4) plains. Compare Napoleon's "Military Maxims," no. 1.

19. Mei Yaochen asks, with some plausibility, whether 帝 is not a mistake for "armies" 軍, as nothing is known of Huang Di having con-

quered four other Emperors. The *Shiji* (chap. I *ad init.*) speaks only of his victories over Yan Di 炎帝 and Chi You 蚩尤. In the 六稻 it is mentioned that he "fought seventy battles and pacified the Empire." Cao Gong's explanation is, that the Yellow Emperor was the first to institute the feudal system of vassal princes, each of whom (to the number of four) originally bore the title of Emperor. Li Quan tells us that the art of war originated under Huang Di, who received it from his Minister Feng Hou 風后.

20. "High ground," says Mei Yaochen, "is not more agreeable and salubrious, but more convenient from a military point of view; low ground is not only damp and unhealthy, but also disadvantageous for fighting." The original text and the *Tu Shu* have 好 instead of 喜.

21. Cao Gong says: "Make for fresh water and pasture, where you can turn out your animals to graze" 向水草可放牧養畜. And the other commentators follow him, apparently taking 生 as = 牲. Cf. Mencius, V. 1. ix. 1, where 養牲者 means a cattle-keeper. But here 養生 surely has reference to the health of the troops. It is the title of Zhuangzi's third chapter, where it denotes moral rather than physical well being.

22. 實 must mean dry and solid, as opposed to damp and marshy, ground. This is to be found as a rule in high places, so the commentators explain 實 as practically equivalent to 高.

23. Zhang Yu says: "The dryness of the climate will prevent the outbreak of illness."

24. The *Tongdian* and *Yulan* have a superfluous 下 before 水.

25. 絕澗, explained by Mei Yaochen as 前後險峻水橫其中.

26. 天井, explained as "places enclosed on every side by steep banks, with pools of water at the bottom" 四面峻坂澗壑所歸.

27. 天牢, "natural pens or prisons," explained as "places surrounded by precipices on three sides—easy to get into, but hard to get out of" 三面環絕易入難出.

28. 天羅, explained as "places covered with such dense undergrowth that spears cannot be used" 草木蒙密鋒鏑莫施.

29. 天陷 explained as "low-lying places, so heavy with mud as to be impassible for chariots and horsemen" 卑下汙濊車騎不通.

30. 天隙, is explained by Mei Yaochen as "a narrow difficult way

between beetling cliffs" 兩山相向洞道狹惡, but Cao Gong says 山澗迫狹地形深數尺長數丈者, which seems to denote something on a much smaller scale. Du Mu's note is "ground covered with trees and rocks, and intersected by numerous ravines and pitfalls" 地多溝坑坎陷木石. This is very vague, but Jia Lin explains it clearly enough as a defile or narrow pass: 兩邊險絕形狹長而數里, and Zhang Yu takes much the same view. On the whole, the weight of the commentators certainly inclines to the rendering "defile". But the ordinary meaning of 隙 (a crack or fissure) and the fact that 絕澗 above must be something in the nature of a defile, make me think that Sun Tzŭ is here speaking of crevasses. The *Tongdian* and *Yulan* read 郄 for 隙, with the same meaning; the latter also has 大害 after 天郄—a palpable gloss.

31. The original text has 軍行, but 旁 has been generally adopted as yielding much better sense.

32. 險阻 is 邱阜之地, according to Zhang Yu.

33. The original text omits 蔣 and 生, so that 潢 and 井 join to make a pair: "ponds and basins." This is plausible enough at first sight, but there are several objections to the reading: (1) 蔣 is unlikely to have got into the text as a gloss on 潢; (2) it is easy to suppose, on the other hand, that 蔣 and afterwards 生 (to restore the balance of the sentence) were omitted by a copyist who jumped to the conclusion that 潢 and 井 must go together; (3) the sense, when one comes to consider it, actually requires 蔣, for it is absurd to talk of pools and ponds as in themselves suitable places for an ambush; (4) Li Jing (571-649 A.D.) in his "Art of War" 兵法 has the words: 蔣潢蘙薈則必索其伏. This is evidently a reminiscence of Sun Tzŭ, so there can be little doubt that 蔣 stood in the text at this early date. It may be added that the *Tongdian* and *Yulan* both have 蔣, and the latter also reads 并 for 井.

34. I read 小林 with the *Yulan* in preference to 山林, given in the original text, which is accepted by the commentators without question. The text of the *Tu Shu* up to this point runs as follows: 潢井兼葭林木蘙薈者. The original text omits 藏, which has been restored from the *Tongdian* and *Yulan*. The *Tu Shu* omits 處 as well, making 所 a substantive. On 姦 Zhang Yu has the note: "We must also be on our guard against traitors who may lie in close covert, secretly spying

out our weaknesses and overhearing our instructions. Fu and *jian* are to be taken separately." 又慮姦細潛隱覘我虛實聽我號令伏姦當為兩事.

35. Here begin Sun Tzŭ's remarks on the reading of signs, much of which is so good that it could almost be included in a modern manual like Gen. Baden-Powell's "Aids to Scouting."

36. Probably because we are in a strong position from which he wishes to dislodge us. "If he came close up to us," says Du Mu, "and tried to force a battle, he would seem to despise us, and there would be less probability of our responding to the challenge."

37. 易 is here the opposite of 險 in § 18. The reading of the *Tongdian* and *Yulan*, 其所處者居易利也, is pretty obviously corrupt. The original text, which transposes 易 and 者, may very possibly be right. Du Mu tells us that there is yet another reading: 士爭其所居者易利也.

38. Cao Gong explains this as "felling trees to clear a passage," and Zhang Yu says: "Every army sends out scouts to climb high places and observe the enemy. If a scout sees that the trees of a forest are moving and shaking, he may know that they are being cut down to clear a passage for the enemy's march."

39. Whenever the meaning of a passage happens to be somewhat elusive, Capt. Calthrop seems to consider himself justified in giving free rein to the imagination. Thus, though his text is here identical with ours, he renders the above: "Broken branches and trodden grass, as of the passing of a large host, must be regarded with suspicion." Du You's explanation, borrowed from Cao Gong, is as follows: "The presence of a number of screens or sheds in the midst of thick vegetation is a sure sign that the enemy has fled and, fearing pursuit, has constructed these hiding-places in order to make us suspect an ambush." It appears that these "screens" were hastily knotted together out of any long grass that the retreating enemy happened to come across.

40. Zhang Yu's explanation is doubtless right: "When birds that are flying along in a straight line suddenly shoot upwards, it means that soldiers are in ambush at the spot beneath."

41. An example of 覆 *fu* in the meaning of "ambuscade" may be found in the *Zuozhuan*, 隱 9th year: 君為三覆以待之. In the present passage however, it is to be distinguished from 伏 just above, in that

it implies onward motion on the part of the attacking force. Thus, Li Quan defines it as 不意而至, and Du Mu as 來襲我也.

42. "High and sharp" 高而銳, or rising to a peak, is of course somewhat exaggerated as applied to dust. The commentators explain the phenomenon by saying that horses and chariots, being heavier than men, raise more dust, and also follow one another in the same wheel-track, whereas foot-soldiers would be marching in ranks, many abreast. According to Zhang Yu, "every army on the march must have scouts (探候之人) some way in advance, who on sighting dust raised by the enemy, will gallop back and report it to the commander-in-chief." Cf. Gen. Baden-Powell ("Aids to Scouting," p. 26): "As you move along, say, in a hostile country, your eyes should be looking afar for the enemy or any signs of him: figures, dust rising, birds getting up, glitter of arms, etc."[1]

43. There is some doubt about the reading 樵採. The *Tongdian* and *Yulan* have 薪採, and Li Quan proposes 薪來.

44. Zhang Yu says: "In apportioning the defenses for a cantonment, light horse will be sent out to survey the position and ascertain the weak and strong points all along its circumference. Hence the small quantity of dust and its motion."

45. "As though they stood in great fear of us," says Du Mu. "Their object is to make us contemptuous and careless, after which they will attack us." Zhang Yu alludes to the story of 田單 Tian Dan of the Qi State, who in 279 B.C. was hard-pressed in his defense of Jimo 即墨 against the Yan forces, led by Qi Jie 騎劫. In chap. 82 of the *Shiji* we read: "Tian Dan openly said: 'My only fear is that the Yen army may cut off the noses of their Qi prisoners and place them in the front rank to fight against us; that would be the undoing of our city.' The other side being informed of this speech, at once acted on the suggestion; but those within the city were enraged at seeing their fellow-countrymen thus mutilated, and fearing only lest they should fall into the enemy's hands, were nerved to defend themselves more obstinately than ever. Once again Tian Dan sent back converted spies who reported these words to the enemy: 'What I dread most is that the men of Yan may

---

[1] "Aids to Scouting," p. 26.

dig up the ancestral tombs outside the town, and by inflicting this in-
dignity on our forefathers cause us to become faint-hearted.' Forthwith
the besiegers dug up all the graves and burned the corpses lying in
them. And the inhabitants of Jimo, witnessing the outrage from the
city-walls, wept passionately and were all impatient to go out and fight,
their fury being increased tenfold. Tian Dan knew then that his soldiers
were ready for any enterprise. But instead of a sword, he himself took
a mattock in his hands, and ordered others to be distributed amongst
his best warriors, while the ranks were filled up with their wives and
concubines. He then served out all the remaining rations and bade his
men eat their fill. The regular soldiers were told to keep out of sight,
and the walls were manned with the old and weaker men and with
women. This done, envoys were dispatched to the enemy's camp to ar-
range terms of surrender, whereupon the Yan army began shouting for
joy. Tian Dan also collected 20,000 ounces of silver from the people,
and got the wealthy citizens of Jimo to send it to the Yan general with
the prayer that, when the town capitulated, he would not allow their
homes to be plundered or their women to be maltreated. Qi Jie, in high
good humor, granted their prayer; but his army now became increas-
ingly slack and careless. Meanwhile, Tian Dan got together a thousand
oxen, decked them with pieces of red silk, painted their bodies, drag-
on-like, with colored stripes, and fastened sharp blades on their horns
and well-greased rushes on their tails. When night came on, he lighted
the ends of the rushes, and drove the oxen through a number of holes
which he had pierced in the walls, backing them up with a force of 5000
picked warriors. The animals, maddened with pain, dashed furiously
into the enemy's camp where they caused the utmost confusion and
dismay; for their tails acted as torches, showing up the hideous pattern
on their bodies, and the weapons on their horns killed or wounded any
with whom they came into contact. In the meantime, the band of 5000
had crept up with gags in their mouths, and now threw themselves on
the enemy. At the same moment a frightful din arose in the city itself,
all those that remained behind making as much noise as possible by
banging drums and hammering on bronze vessels, until heaven and
earth were convulsed by the uproar. Terror-stricken, the Yan army fled
in disorder, hotly pursued by the men of Qi, who succeeded in slaying

their general Qi Jie...The result of the battle was the ultimate recovery of some seventy cities which had belonged to the Qi State."

46. I follow the original text here, also adopted by the *Tu Shu*. The standard text reads 辭詭而強進驅者退也 on the strength of Cao Gong's commentary 詭詐也, which shows that his text included the word 詭. Strong as this ground is, I do not think it can counterbalance the obvious superiority of the other reading in point of sense. 詭 not only provides no antithesis to 卑, but makes the whole passage absurd; for if the language of the enemy is calculated to deceive, it cannot be known as deceitful at the time, and can therefore afford no "sign." Moreover, the extra word in 強進驅者 (an awkward locution, by the way) spoils the parallelism with 益備者.

47. The same, according to Du You, as the 馳車 of II. § 1.

48. The *Tongdian* omits 出.

49. Du You defines 約 as 要約, and Li Quan as "a treaty confirmed by oaths and hostages" 質盟之約. Wang Xi and Zhang Yu, on the other hand, simply say "without reason" 無故, "on a frivolous pretext," as though 約 bore the rather unusual sense of "important." Capt. Calthrop has "without consultation," which is too loose.

50. Every man hastening to his proper place under his own regimental banner.

51. I follow the *Tu Shu* in omitting 車 after 兵. Du Mu quotes the *Chou Li*, chap. Xxix. Fol. 31: 車驟徒趨及表乃止.

52. What Jia Lin calls 晷刻之期, as opposed to 尋常之期.

53. Capt. Calthrop is hardly right in translating: "An advance, followed by sudden retirement." It is rather a case of feigned confusion. As Du Mu says: 偽為雜亂不整之狀.

54. 仗 is here probably not a synonym for 倚, but = "a weapon" 兵. The original text has 杖而立者, which has been corrected from the *Tongdian* and *Yulan*.

55. As Du Mu remarks: "One may know the condition of a whole army from the behavior of a single man" 覩一人三軍可知也. The 先 may mean either that they drink before drawing water for the army, or before they return to camp. Zhang Yu takes the latter view. The Tongdian has the faulty reading 汲役先飲者, and the Yulan, worse still, 汲設飲者.

56. Not necessarily "booty," as Capt. Calthrop translates it. The *Tongdian* and *Yulan* read 向人見利, etc.

57. A useful fact to bear in mind when, for instance, as Chen Hao says, the enemy has secretly abandoned his camp.

58. Owing to false alarms; or, as Du Mu explains it: "Fear makes men restless; so they fall to shouting at night in order to keep up their courage." 恐懼不安故夜呼以自壯也. The *Tongdian* inserts 喧 before 呼.

59. The *Tongdian* and *Yulan* omit 旌.

60. And therefore, as Capt. Calthrop says, slow to obey. Du You understands the sentence differently: "If all the officers of an army are angry with their general, it means that they are broken with fatigue" [owing to the exertions which he has demanded from them].

61. 粟馬肉食 is expanded by Mei Yaochen (following Du Mu) into 給糧以秣乎馬殺畜以饗乎士, which is the sense I have given above. In the ordinary course of things, the men would be fed on grain and the horses chiefly on grass.

62. The *Tongdian* reads 缶, which is much the same as 瓵, and the *Yulan* 筆, which is manifestly wrong.

63. For 返, the *Tongdian* and *Yulan* both read 及.

64. For 窮寇, see VII. § 36. I may quote here the illustrative passage from the Hou Han Shu, chap. 71, given in abbreviated form by the *Peiwen yunfu*: 'The rebel Wang Guo 王國 of Liang 梁 was besieging the town of Chencang 陳倉, and Huangfu Song 皇甫嵩, who was in supreme command, and Dong Zhuo 董卓 were sent out against him. The latter pressed for hasty measures, but Song turned a deaf ear to his counsel. At last the rebels were utterly worn out, and began to throw down their weapons of their own accord. Song was now for advancing to the attack, but Zhuo said: 'It is a principle of war not to pursue desperate men and not to press a retreating host.' Song answered: 'That does not apply here. What I am about to attack is a jaded army, not a retreating host; with disciplined troops I am falling on a disorganized multitude, not a band of desperate men.' Thereupon he advanced to the attack unsupported by his colleague, and routed the enemy, Wang Guo being slain." The inferior reading of the *Tu Shu* for § 34 is as follows: 殺馬肉食者軍無糧也懸瓵不返其舍者窮寇也. The first

clause strikes me as rather shallow for Sun Tzǔ and it is hard to make anything of 懸瓿 in the second without the negative. Capt. Calthrop, nothing daunted, set down in his first edition: "When they *cast away* their cooking-pots." He now has: "When the cooking-pots are hung up on the wall."

65. 諄諄 is well explained by Du Mu as "speaking with bated breath" 乏氣聲促. The *Shuowen* rather strangely defines 翕 by the word 起, but the *Erya* says "to join" or "contract" 合, which is undoubtedly its primary meaning. Zhang Yu is right, then, in explaining it here by the word 聚. The other commentators are very much at sea: Cao Gong says 失志貌, Du You 不真, Du Mu 顛倒失次貌, Jia Lin 不安貌, Mei Yaochen 曠職事, Wang Xi 患其上.

66. 入入 is said to be the same as 如如. 失眾 is equivalent to 失其眾心, the subject of course being "the general," understood. In the original text, which seems to be followed by several commentators, the whole passage stands thus: 諄諄翕翕徐與人言者失眾也. Here it would be the general who is talking to his men, not the men amongst themselves. For 翕, which is the chief stumbling block in the way of this reading, the *Tu Shu* gives the very plausible emendation 諰 (also read *xi*, and defined by Kangxi as "to speak fast" 疾言). But this is unnecessary if we keep to the standard text.

67. Because, when an army is hard pressed, as Du Mu says, there is always a fear of mutiny, and lavish rewards are given to keep the men in good temper.

68. Because in such case discipline becomes relaxed, and unwonted severity is necessary to keep the men to their duty.

69. I follow the interpretation of Cao Gong: 先輕敵後聞其眾則心惡之也, also adopted by Li Quan, Du Mu and Zhang Yu. Another possible meaning, set forth by Du You, Jia Lin, Mei Yaochen and Wang Xi, is: "The general who is first tyrannical towards his men, and then in terror lest they should mutiny, etc." This would connect the sentence with what went before about rewards and punishments. The Tongdian and Yulan read "affection" 情 instead of 精.

70. Du Mu says: "If the enemy open friendly relations by sending hostages, it is a sign that they are anxious for an armistice, either because their strength is exhausted or for some other reason." 所以委質

來謝此乃勢已窮或有他故必欲休息也. But it hardly needs a Sun Tzŭ to draw such an obvious inference; and although Du Mu is supported by Mei Yaochen and Zhang Yu, I cannot think that hostages are indicated by the word 委.

71. Capt. Calthrop falls into a trap which often lurks in the word 相. He translates: "When both sides, eager for a fight, face each other for a considerable time, neither advancing nor retiring," etc. Had he reflected a little, he would have seen that this is meaningless as addressed to a commander who has control over the movements of his own troops. 相迎, then, does not mean that the two armies go to meet each other, but simply that the other side comes up to us. Likewise with 相去. If this were not perfectly clear of itself, Mei Yaochen's paraphrase would make it so: 怒而來逆我, etc. As Cao Gong points out, a maneuver of this sort may be only a *ruse* to gain time for an unexpected flank attack or the laying of an ambush.

72. Wang Xi's paraphrase, partly borrowed from Cao Gong, is 權力均足矣. Another reading, adopted by Jia Lin and the *Tu Shu*, is 兵非貴益多, which Capt. Calthrop renders, much too loosely: "Numbers are no certain mark of strength."

73. Literally, "no martial advance." That is to say, "*zheng*" 正 tactics and frontal attacks must be eschewed, and stratagem resorted to instead.

74. This is an obscure sentence, and none of the commentators succeed in squeezing very good sense out of it. The difficulty lies chiefly in the words 取人, which have been taken in every possible way. I follow Li Quan, who appears to offer the simplest explanation: 惟得人者勝也 "Only the side that gets more men will win." Cao Gong's note, concise as usual to the verge of incomprehensibility, is 廝養足也. Fortunately we have Zhang Yu to expound its meaning to us in language which is lucidity itself: "When the numbers are even, and no favorable opening presents itself, although we may not be strong enough to deliver a sustained attack, we can find additional recruits amongst our settlers and camp-followers, and then, concentrating our forces and keeping a close watch on the enemy, contrive to snatch the victory. But we must avoid borrowing foreign soldiers to help us" 兵力即均又未見便雖未足剛進足以取人於廝養之中以并兵合力察敵而取勝不必假他兵以助己. He then quotes from Weiliaozi, chap. 3:

"The nominal strength of mercenary troops may be 100,000, but their real value will be not more than half that figure." 助卒名為十萬其實不過數萬耳. According to this interpretation, 取人 means "to get recruits," not from outside, but from the tag-rag and bobtail which follows in the wake of a large army. This does not sound a very soldierly suggestion, and I feel convinced that it is not what Sun Tzǔ meant. Jia Lin, on the other hand, takes the words in a different sense altogether, namely "to conquer the enemy" (cf. I. § 20). But in that case they could hardly be followed by 而已. Better than this would be the rendering "to make isolated captures," as opposed to "a general attack" 武進.

75. The force of 夫惟 is not easy to appreciate. Chen Hao says 殊無遠慮但輕敵者, thus referring 惟 to the second verb. He continues, quoting from the *Zuozhuan*: "If bees and scorpions carry poison, how much more will a hostile state! [僖公, XXII. 3.] Even a puny opponent, then, should not be treated with contempt." 蜂蠆有毒而況國乎則小敵亦不可輕.

76. This is wrongly translated by Capt. Calthrop: "If troops know the general, but are not affected by his punishments, they are useless."

77. 文 and 武, according to Cao Gong, are here equivalent to 仁 and 法 respectively. Compare our two uses of the word "civil." Yanzi 晏子 [d. B.C. 493] said of Sima Rangju 司馬穰苴: "His civil virtues endeared him to the people; his martial prowess kept his enemies in awe" 文能附眾武能威敵也. Cf. Wuzi, chap. 4 *init.*: "The ideal commander unities culture with a warlike temper; the profession of arms requires a combination of hardness and tenderness." 夫總文武者軍之將也兼剛柔者兵之事也. Again I must find fault with Capt. Calthrop's translation: "By humane treatment we obtain obedience; authority brings uniformity."

78. The Tongdian and Yulan read: 令素行以教其人者也令素行則人服令素不行則人不服.

79. The original text has 令素行者. 令素 is certainly awkward without 行, but on the other hand it is clear that Du Mu accepted the *Tongdian* text, which is identical with ours. He says: "A general ought in time of peace to show kindly confidence in his men and also make his authority respected, so that when they come to face the enemy, orders may be executed and discipline maintained, because they all trust

and look up to him." What Sun Tzǔ has said in § 44, however, would lead one rather to expect something like this: "If a general is always confident that his orders will be carried out," etc. Hence I am tempted to think that they may have written 令素信行者. But this is perhaps too conjectural.

80. Zhang Yu says: "The general has confidence in the men under his command, and the men are docile having confidence in him. Thus the gain is mutual." 上以信使民民以信服上是上下相得也. He quotes a pregnant sentence from Weiliaozi, chap. 4: "The art of giving orders is not to try to rectify minor blunders and not to be swayed by petty doubts" 令之之法小過無更小疑無中. Vacillation and fussiness are the surest means of sapping the confidence of an army. Capt. Calthrop winds up the chapter with a final mistranslation of a more than usually heinous description: "Orders are always obeyed, if general and soldiers are in sympathy." Besides inventing the latter half of the sentence, he has managed to invert protasis and apodosis.

# CHAPTER 10

# Terrain
## 地行篇第十

1. Only about a third of the chapter, comprising §§ 1-13, deal with 地形, the subject being more fully treated in chap. XI. The "six calamities" are discussed in §§ 14-20, and the rest of the chapter is again a mere string of desultory remarks, though not less interesting, perhaps, on that account.

2. Mei Yaochen says: "plentifully provided with roads and means of communication" 道路交達.

3. The same commentator says: "Net-like country, venturing into which you become entangled" 網羅之地往必掛綴.

4. Du You explains 支 as 久. This meaning is still retained in modern phrases such as 支托, "stave off" 支演, "delay." I do not know why Capt. Calthrop calls 支地 "suspended ground," unless he is confusing it with 掛地.

5. The root idea in 隘 is narrowness; in 險, steepness.

6. It is hardly necessary to point out the faultiness of this classification. A strange lack of logical perception is shown in unquestioning acceptance of glaring cross-divisions such as the above.

7. Generally speaking, "level country" 平陸 is meant. Cf. IX. § 9: 處易.

8. The *Tongdian* reads 居通地.

9. See IX. § 2. The *Tongdian* reads 先據其地.

10. A curious use of 利 as a verb, if our text is right. The general meaning is doubtless, as Du You says, "not to allow the enemy to cut your communications" 無使敵絕己糧道. Du Mu, who was not a soldier and can hardly have had any practical experience of fighting, goes more into detail and speaks of protecting the line of communications by a wall (壘), or enclosing it by embankments on each side (作甬

道)! In view of Napoleon's dictum, "the secret of war lies in the communications,"[1] we could wish that Sun Tzŭ had done more than skirt the edge of this important subject here and in I. § 10, VII. § 11. Col. Henderson says: "The line of supply may be said to be as vital to the existence of an army as the heart to the life of a human being. Just as the duellist who finds his adversary's point menacing him with certain death, and his own guard astray, is compelled to confirm to his adversary's movements, and to content himself with warding off his thrusts, so the commander whose communications are suddenly threatened finds himself in a false position, and he will be fortunate if he has not to change all his plans, to split up his force into more or less isolated detachments, and to fight with inferior numbers on ground which he has not had time to prepare, and where defeat will not be an ordinary failure, but will entail the ruin or the surrender of his whole army."[2]

11. Omitted by Capt. Calthrop.

12. Capt. Calthrop is wrong in translating 返 "retreat from it."

13. 不利 (an example of litotes) is paraphrased by Mei Yaochen as "you will receive a check" 必受制.

14. "Each side finds it inconvenient to move, and the situation remains at a deadlock." 俱不便九相持也 (Du You).

15. Du You says "turning their backs on us and pretending to flee" 佯背我去. But this is only one of the lures that might induce us to quit our position. Here again 利 is used as a verb, but this time in a different sense: "to hold out an advantage to." Mei Yaochen paraphrases the passage in a curious jingle, the scheme of rhymes being *abcbdd*: 各居所險、先出必敗、利而誘我、我不可愛、偽去引敵、半出而擊.

16. Capt. Calthrop says: "Defiles, make haste to occupy." But this is a conditional clause, answering to 若敵先居之 in the next paragraph. Because then, as Du You observes, "the initiative will lie with us, and by making sudden and unexpected attacks we shall have the enemy at our mercy." 皆制在我然後出奇以制敵. The commentators make a great pother about the precise meaning of 盈, which to the foreign reader seems to present no difficulty whatever.

---

[1] See "Pensées de Napoléon Ier," no. 47.
[2] "The Science of War," chap. 2.

17. Cao Gong says: "The particular advantage of securing height and defiles is that your actions cannot then be dictated by the enemy." 地形險隘尤不可致於人. (For the enunciation of the grand principle alluded to, see VI § 2). Zhang Yu tells the following anecdote of Pei Xingjian 裴行儉 (A.D. 619-682), who was sent on a punitive expedition against the Turkic tribes. "At nightfall he pitched his camp as usual, and it had already been completely fortified by wall and ditch, when suddenly he gave orders that the army should shift its quarters to a hill near by. This was highly displeasing to his officers, who protested loudly against the extra fatigue that it would entail on the men. Pei Xingjian, however, paid no heed to their remonstrances and had the camp moved as quickly as possible. The same night, a terrific storm came on, which flooded their former place of encampment to the depth of over twelve feet. The recalcitrant officers were amazed at the sight, and owned that they had been in the wrong. 'How did you know what was going to happen?' they asked. Pei Xingjian replied: 'From this time forward be content to obey orders without asking unnecessary questions.' (See *Jiu Tang Shu*, chap. 84, fol. 12 *r*o., and *Xin Tang Shu* chap. 108, fol. 5 *v*o.) From this it may be seen," Zhang Yu continues, "that high and sunny places are advantageous not only for fighting, but also because they are immune from disastrous floods."

18. The turning-point of Li Shimin's 李世民 campaign in 621 A.D. against the two rebels, Dou Jiande 竇建德, King of Xia 夏, and Wang Shichong 王世充, Prince of Zheng 鄭, was his seizure of the heights of Wulao 武牢, in spite of which Dou Jiande persisted in his attempt to relieve his ally in Luoyang, was defeated and taken prisoner. (See *Jiu Tang Shu*, chap. 2, fol 5 *v*o., and also chap. 54.)

19. The *Tongdian* reads 夫通形均勢.

20. Cao Gong says that 挑戰 means "challenging the enemy" 迎敵. But the enemy being far away, that plainly involves, as Du You says, "going to meet him." The point of course is, that we must not think of undertaking a long and wearisome march, at the end of which "we should be exhausted and our adversary fresh and keen" 是我困敵銳.

21. Or perhaps, "the principles relating to ground." See, however, I. § 8.

22. Capt. Calthrop omits 至任. Out of the foregoing six 地形, it will be noticed that nos. 3 and 6 have really no reference to the con-

figuration of the country, and that only 4 and 5 can be said to convey any definite geographical idea.

23. The *Tu Shu* reads 天地之災.

24. I take exception to Capt. Calthrop's rendering of 陷 and 崩 as "distress" and "disorganization," respectively.

25. Cf. III. § 10. The general's fault here is that of "not calculating the enemy's strength" 不料力. It is obvious that 勢 cannot have the same force as in § 12, where it was equivalent to 兵力. I should not be inclined, however, to limit it, with Zhang Yu, to "the wisdom and valor of the general and the sharpness of the weapons" 將之智勇兵之利銳. As Li Quan very justly remarks, "Given a decided advantage in position, or the help of some stratagem such as a flank attack or an ambuscade, it would be quite possible [to fight in the ratio of one to ten]" 若得形便之地用奇伏之計則可矣.

26. 弛 "laxity"—the metaphor being taken from an unstrung bow. Capt. Calthrop's "relaxation" is not good, on account of its ambiguity. Du Mu cites the unhappy case of 田布 Tian Bu (*Xin Tang Shu*, chap. 148), who was sent to Wei 魏 in 821 A.D. with orders to lead an army against Wang Tingzou 王延湊. But the whole time he was in command, his soldiers treated him with the utmost contempt, and openly flouted his authority by riding about the camp on donkeys, several thousands at a time. Tian Bu was powerless to put a stop to this conduct, and when, after some months had passed, he made an attempt to engage the enemy, his troops turned tail and dispersed in every direction. After that, the unfortunate man committed suicide by cutting his throat.

27. Cao Gong says: "The officers are energetic and want to press on, the common soldiers are feeble and suddenly collapse" 吏強欲進卒弱輒陷. Note that 弱 is to be taken literally of physical weakness, whereas in the former clause it is figurative. Li Quan makes 陷 equivalent to 敗, and Du Mu explains it as "stumbling into a death-trap" 陷沒於死地.

28. 大吏, according to Cao Gong, are the "generals of inferior rank" 小將. But Li Quan, Chen Hao, and Wang Xi take the term as simply convertible with 將 or 大將.

29. Cao Gong makes 大將, understood, the subject of 怒, which

seems rather far-fetched. Wang Xi's note is: "This means, the general is angry without just cause, and at the same time does not appreciate the ability of his subordinate officers; thus he arouses fierce resentment and brings an avalanche of ruin upon his head." 謂將怒不以理且不知裨佐之才激致其凶懟如山之崩壞也. He takes 能, therefore, in the sense of 才; but I think that Chen Hao is right in his paraphrase "they don't care if it be possible or not." 不顧能否. My interpretation of the whole passage is that of Mei Yaochen and Zhang Yu. Du Mu gives a long extract from the *Zuozhuan*, 宣公, XII. 3, showing how the great battle of Bi 邲 [597 B.C.] was lost for the Jin 晉 State through the contumacy of Xian Hu 先縠 and the resentful spite of Wei Yi 魏錡 and Zhao Zhan 趙旃. Zhang Yu also alludes to the mutinous conduct of Luan Yan 欒黶 [*ibid.* 襄公, XIV. 3].

30. Weiliaozi (chap. 4) says: "If the commander gives his orders with decision, the soldiers will not wait to hear them twice; if his moves are made without vacillation, the soldiers will not be in two minds about doing their duty" 上無疑令、則眾不二聽、動無疑事、則眾不二志. General Baden-Powell says, italicizing the words: "The secret of getting successful work out of your trained men lies in one nutshell— in the clearness of the instructions they receive."[1] Assuming that clear instructions beget confidence, this is very much what Weiliaozi (*loc. cit.*) goes on to say: 未有不信其心而能得其力者也. Cf. also Wuzi chap. 3: "the most fatal defect in a military leader is diffidence; the worst calamities that befall an army arise from hesitation" 用兵之害猶豫最大三軍之災生於狐疑.

31. "Neither officer nor men have any regular routine." 吏卒皆不拘常度 (Du Mu).

32. Zhang Yu paraphrases the latter of the sentence 不選驍勇之士使為先鋒兵必敗北也, and continues: "Whenever there is fighting to be done, the keenest spirits should be appointed to serve in the front ranks, both in order to strengthen the resolution of our own men and to demoralize the enemy." 凡戰必用精銳為前鋒者一則壯吾志一則挫敵威也. Cf. the primi ordines of Caesar ("De Bello Gallico," V. 28, 44 *et al.*). There seems little to distinguish 北 from 走 in §

---

15, except that 北 is a more forcible word.

33. Chen Hao makes them out to be: (1) "neglect to estimate the enemy's strength" 不量寡眾; (2) "want of authority" 本乏刑德; (3) "defective training" 失於訓練; (4) "unjustifiable anger" 非理興怒; (5) "non-observance of discipline" 法令不行; (6) "failure to use picked men" 不擇驍果.

34. See *supra*, § 13.

35. Jia Lin's text has the reading 易 for 助. Chen Hao says: "The advantages of weather and season are not equal to those connected with ground." 天時不如地利.

36. The insertion of a "but" is necessary to show the connection of thought here. A general should always utilize, but never rely wholly on natural advantages of terrain.

37. 制勝 is one of those condensed expressions that mean so much in Chinese, and so little in an English translation. What it seems to imply is complete mastery of the situation from the beginning.

38. The *Tongdian* and *Yulan* read 計極險易利害遠近. I am decidedly puzzled by Capt. Calthrop's translation: "an eye for steepness, *command* and distances." Where did he find the word that I have put in italics?

39. A somewhat free translation of 道. As Zhang Yu remarks, these are "the essentials of soldiering" 兵之本, ground being only a helpful accessory.

40. Cf. VIII § 3 *fin*. Huangshi Gong of the Qin dynasty, who is said to have been the patron of Chang Liang 張良 and to have written the 三略, has these words attributed to him: "The responsibility of setting an army in motion must devolve on the general alone; if advance and retreat are controlled from the Palace, brilliant result will hardly be achieved. Hence the god-like ruler and the enlightened monarch are content to play a humble part in furthering their country's cause (*lit*., kneel down to push the chariot wheel)" 出軍行師將在自專進退內御則功難成故聖主明王跪而推轂. This means that "in matters lying outside the zenana, the decision of the military commander must be absolute" 閫外之事將軍裁之. Zhang Yu also quotes the saying: "Decrees of the Son of Heaven do not penetrate the walls of a camp" 軍中不聞天子之詔.

41. It was Wellington, I think, who said that the hardest thing of all for a soldier is to retreat.

42. 合, which is omitted by the *Tu Shu*, is said by Chen Hao to be equivalent to 歸. If it had to be separately translated, it would be something like our word "accrue."

43. A noble presentment, in few words, of the Chinese "happy warrior." Such a man, says Heshi, "even if he had to suffer punishment, would not regent his conduct." 罪及其身不悔也.

44. Cf. I. § 6. in this connection, Du Mu draws for us an engaging picture of the famous general Wu Qi, from whose treatise on war I have frequently had occasion to quote: "He wore the same clothes and ate the same food as the meanest of his soldiers, refused to have either a horse to ride or a mat to sleep on, carried his own surplus rations wrapped in a parcel, and shared every hardship with his men. One of his soldiers was suffering from an abscess, and Wu Qi himself sucked out the virus. The soldier's mother, hearing this, began wailing and lamenting. Somebody asked her, saying: 'Why do you cry? Your son is only a common soldier, and yet the commander-in-chief himself has sucked the poison from his sore.' The woman replied. 'Many years ago, Lord Wu performed a similar service for my husband, who never left him afterwards, and finally met his death at the hands of the enemy. And now that he has done the same for my son, he too will fall fighting I know not where.'" Li Quan mentions 楚子 the Viscount of Chu, who invaded the small state of Xiao 蕭 during the winter. 申公 The Duke of Shên said to him: "Many of the soldiers are suffering severely from the cold." So he made a round of the whole army, comforting and encouraging the men; and straightway they felt as if they were clothed in garments lined with floss silk. (*Zuozhuan*, 宣公, XII. 5) Zhang Yu alludes to the same passage, saying: 溫言一撫士同挾纊.

45. Capt. Calthrop has got these three clauses quite wrong. The last he translates: "overindulgence may produce disorder."

46. Cf. IX. § 42. We read in the 陰符經, pt. 2: "injury comes out of kindness" 害生于思. Li Jing once said that if you could make your soldiers afraid of you, they would not be afraid of the enemy. Du Mu recalls an instance of stern military discipline that occurred in 219 A.D., when Lü Meng 呂蒙 was occupying the town of Jiangling 江陵.

He had given stringent orders to his army not to molest the inhabitants nor take anything from them by force. Nevertheless, a certain officer serving under his banner, who happened to be a fellow-townsman, ventured to appropriate a bamboo hat (笠) belonging to one of the people, in order to wear it over his regulation helmet as a protection against the rain. Lü Meng considered that the fact of his being also a native of Ru'nan 汝南 should not be allowed to palliate a clear breach of discipline, and accordingly he ordered his summary execution, the tears rolling down his face, however, as he did so. This act of severity filled the army with wholesome awe, and from that time forth even articles dropped in the highway were not picked up. (Sanguozhi, chap. 54, f. 13*r*°. & *v*°.)

47. That is, as Cao Gong says, "the issue in this case is uncertain."

48. Cf. III. § 13 (I).

49. I may take this opportunity of pointing out the rather nice distinction in meaning between 擊 and 攻. The latter is simply "to attack" without any further implication, whereas 擊 is a stronger word which in nine cases out of ten means "to attack with expectation of victory," "to fall upon," as we should say, or even "to crush." On the other hand, 擊 is not quite synonymous with 伐, which is mostly used of operations on a larger scale, as of one State *making war* on another, often with the added idea of invasion. 征, finally, has special reference to the subjugation of rebels. See Mencius, VII. 2. ii. 2.

50. The reason being, according to Du Mu, that he has taken his measures so thoroughly as to ensure victory beforehand. "He does not move recklessly," says Zhang Yu, "so that when he does move, he makes no mistakes." Another reading substitutes 困 for 迷 and 頓 for 窮. The latter variant only is adopted by the *Tongdian* and *Yulan*. Note that 窮 here means "at the end of his *mental* resources."

51. Capt. Calthrop makes the saying end here, which cannot be justified.

52. 天 and 地 are transposed for the sake of the jingle between 天 and 全. The original text, however, has 知天知地, and the correction has been made from the Tongdian. As opposed to 勝之半, above. The original text has 勝乃不窮, the corruption being perhaps due to the occurrence of 不窮 in the preceding sentence. Here, however 不窮

would not be synonymous with 不困, but equivalent to "inexhaustible," "beyond computation" 不可以窮. Cf. V. § 11. The Tongdian has again supplied the true reading. Li Quan sums up as follows: "Given a knowledge of three things—the affairs of man, the seasons of heaven and the natural advantages of earth—victory will invariably crown your battles." 人事天時地利三者同知則百戰百勝.

# CHAPTER 11

# The Nine Situations
九地篇第十一

1. Li Quan is not quite right in calling these 勝敵之地. As we shall see, some of them are highly disadvantageous from the military point of view. Wang Xi more correctly says: "There are nine military situations, good and bad" 用兵之地利害有九地. One would like to distinguish the 九地 from the six 地形 of chap. X by saying that the latter refer to the natural formation or geographical features of the country, while the 九地 have more to do with the condition of the army, being "situations" 地勢 as opposed to "grounds." But it is soon found impossible to carry out the distinction. Both are cross-divisions, for among the 地形 we have "temporizing ground" side by side with "narrow passes," while in the present chapter there is even greater confusion.

2. So called because the soldiers, being near to their homes and anxious to see their wives and children, are likely to seize the opportunity afforded by a battle and scatter in every direction. "In their advance," observes Du Mu, "they will lack valor of desperation, and when they retreat, they will find harbors of refuge." The 者, which appears in the *Tu Shu*, seems to have been accidentally omitted in my edition of the standard text.

3. Li Quan and Heshi say "because of the facility for retreating" 輕於退也, and the other commentators give similar explanations. Du Mu remarks: "When your army has crossed the border, you should burn your boats and bridges, in order to make it clear to everybody that you have no hankering after home." 師出越境必焚舟示民無返顧之心. I do not think that "disturbing ground," Capt. Calthrop's rendering of 輕地, has anything to justify it. If an idiomatic translation is out of the question, one should at least attempt to be literal.

4. I must apologize for using this word in a sense not known to the dictionary, i.e. "to be contended for"—Du Mu's 必爭之地. Cao Gong says: "ground on which the few and the weak can defeat the many and the strong" 可以少勝眾弱勝強, such as "the neck of a pass" 阨喉, instanced by Li Quan. Thus, Thermopylae was a 爭地, because the possession of it, even for a few days only, meant holding the entire invading army in check and thus gaining invaluable time. Cf. Wuzi, chap. V. *ad init.*: "For those who have to fight in the ratio of one to ten, there is nothing better than a narrow pass" 以一擊十莫善於阨. When Lü Guang 呂光 was returning from his triumphant expedition to Turkestan in 385 A.D., and had got as far as Yihe 宜禾, laden with spoils, Liang Xi 梁熙, administrator of Liangzhou 涼州, taking advantage of the death of Fu Jian, King of Qin, plotted against him and was for barring his way into the province. Yang Han 楊翰, governor of Gaochang 高昌, counseled him, saying: "Lü Guang is fresh from his victories in the west, and his soldiers are vigorous and mettlesome. If we oppose him in the shifting sands of the desert, we shall be no match for him, and we must therefore try a different plan. Let us hasten to occupy the defile at the mount of the Gaowu 高梧 pass, thus cutting him off from supplies of water, and when his troops are prostrated with thirst, we can dictate our own terms without moving. Or if you think that the pass I mention is too far off, we could make a stand against him at the Yiwu 伊吾 pass, which is nearer. The cunning and resource of Zifang 子房 himself [i.e. 張良] would be expended in vain against the enormous strength of these two positions." Liang Xi, refusing to act on this advice, was overwhelmed and swept away by the invader. [See 晉書, chap. 122, fol. 3 *r*°, and 歷代紀事年表, chap. 43, fol. 26.]

5. This is only a makeshift translation of 交, which according to Cao Gong stands for "ground covered with a network of roads" 交錯, like a chessboard. Another interpretation, suggested by Heshi, is "ground on which intercommunication is easy" 交通. In either case, it must evidently be "flat country" 平原, and therefore "cannot be blocked" 不可杜絕. Cf. 通形, X. § 2.

6. "Our country adjoining the enemy's and a third country conterminous with both" 我與敵相當而旁有他國也. (Cao Gong.) Mengshi instances the small principally of Zheng 鄭, which was bounded on the

north-east by Qi 齊, on the west by Jin 晉, and on the south by Chu 楚.

7. 天下 of course stands for the loose confederacy of states into which China was divided under the Zhou dynasty. The belligerent who holds this dominating position can constrain most of them to become his allies. See *infra*, § 48. 眾 appears at first sight to be "the masses" or "population" of the Empire, but it is more probably, as Du You says, 諸侯之眾.

8. Capt. Calthrop's "path-ridden ground" might stand well enough for 交地 above, but it does not bring out the force of 衢地, which clearly denotes the central position where important highways meet.

9. After 多, the *Tongdian* intercalates the gloss 難以退. Wang Xi explains the name by saying that "when an army has reached such a point, its situation is serious" 兵至此者事勢重也. Li Quan instances (1) the victorious march of Yue Yi 樂毅 into the capital of Qi in 284 B.C., and (2) the attack on Chu, six years later, by the Qin general Bo Qi 白起.

10. Or simply, "forests." I follow the *Tu Shu* in omitting the 行 before 山林, given in the standard text, which is not only otiose but spoils the rhythm of the sentence.

11. *Pi* 圮 (to be distinguished from 圯 yi) is defined by Kangxi (after the *Shuowen*) as "to destroy" 毀. Hence Jia Lin explains 圮地 as ground "that has been ruined by water passing over it" 經水所毀, and Du You simply as "swampy ground" 沮洳之地. But Chen Hao says that the word is specially applied to deep hollows—what Zhuge Liang, he tells us, used to designate by the expressive term "earth-hells" 地獄. Compare the 天井 of IX § 15.

12. The situation, as pictured by Cao Gong, is very similar to the 圍地, except that here escape is no longer possible: "A lofty mountain in front, a large river behind, advance impossible, retreat blocked." 前有高山後有大水進則不得退則有礙. Chen Hao says: "To be on 'desperate ground' is like sitting in a leaking boat or crouching in a burning house" 人在死地如坐漏船伏燒屋. Du Mu quotes from Li Jing a vivid description of the plight of an army thus entrapped: "Suppose an army invading hostile territory without the aid of local guides: it falls into a fatal snare and is at the enemy's mercy. A ravine on the left, a mountain on the right, a pathway so perilous that the horses

have to be roped together and the chariots carried in slings, no passage open in front, retreat cut off behind, no choice but to proceed in single file (鴈行魚貫之嚴). Then, before there is time to range our soldiers in order of battle, the enemy in overwhelming strength suddenly appears on the scene. Advancing, we can nowhere take a breathing space; retreating, we have no haven of refuge. We seek a pitched battle, but in vain; yet standing on the defensive, none of us has a moment's respite. If we simply maintain our ground, whole days and months will crawl by; the moment we make a move, we have to sustain the enemy's attacks on front and rear. The country is wild, destitute of water and plants; the army is lacking in the necessaries of life, the horses are jaded and the pass so narrow that a single man defending it can check the onset of ten thousand; all means of offence in the hands of the enemy, all point of vantage already forfeited by ourselves: in this terrible plight, even though we had the most valiant soldiers and the keenest of weapons, how could they be employed with the slightest effect?" Students of Greek history may be reminded of the awful close to the Sicilian expedition, and the agony of the Athenians under Nicias and Demosthenes. [*See* Thucydides, VII. 78 sqq.].

13. But rather let all your energies be bent on occupying the advantageous position first. So Cao Gong. Li Quan and others, however, suppose the meaning to be that the enemy has already forestalled us, so that it would be sheer madness to attack. In the 孫子敍錄, when the King of Wu inquires what should be done in this case, Sun Tzǔ replies: "The rule with regard to contentious ground is that those in possession have the advantage over the other side. If a position of this kind is secured first by the enemy, beware of attacking him. Lure him away by pretending to flee—show your banners and sound your drums—make a dash for other places that he cannot afford to lose—trail brushwood and raise a dust—confound his ears and eyes—detach a body of your best troops, and place it secretly in ambuscade. Then your opponent will sally forth to the rescue."

14. Because the attempt would be futile, and would expose the blocking force itself to serious risks. There are two interpretations of 無絕. I follow that of Zhang Yu (不可以兵阻絕其路). The other is indicated in Cao Gong's brief note: "Draw closer together" 相濟屬

也—i.e., see that a portion of your own army is not cut off. Wang Xi points out that 交地 is only another name for the "accessible ground" 通地 of X. § 2, and says that the advice here given is simply a variation of "keep a sharp eye on the line of supplies," 利糧道, be careful that your communications are not cut. The *Tongdian* reads 無相絕.

15. Or perhaps, "form alliances with neighboring states." Thus Cao Gong has: 結諸侯也. Capt. Calthrop's "cultivate intercourse" is much too timid and vague. The original text reads 交合.

16. On this, Li Quan has the following delicious note: "When an army penetrates far into the enemy's country, care must be taken not to alienate the people by unjust treatment. Follow the example of the Han Emperor Gaozu, whose march into Qin territory was marked by no violation of women or looting of valuables. [*Nota bene*: this was in 207 B.C., and may well cause us to blush for the Christian armies that entered Peking in 1900 A.D.] Thus he won the hearts of all. In the present passage, then, I think that the true reading must be, not 'plunder' 掠, but 'do not plunder'" 無掠" 深入敵境不可非義失人心 如漢高祖入秦無犯婦女無取寶貨得人心也此筌以掠字為無 掠字. Alas, I fear that in this instance the worthy commentator's feelings outran his judgment. Du Mu, at least, has no such illusions. He says: "When encamped on 'serious ground,' there being no inducement as yet to advance further, and no possibility of retreat, one ought to take measures for a protracted resistance by bringing in provisions from all sides, and keep a close watch on the enemy." Cf. also II. § 9: 因糧於敵.

17. Or, in the words of VIII. § 2, "do not encamp" 無舍.

18. Cao Gong says: "Try the effect of some unusual artifice" 發奇 謀; and Du You amplifies this by saying: "In such a position, some scheme must be devised which will suit the circumstances, and if we can succeed in deluding the enemy, the peril may be escaped." 居此 則當權謀詐譎可以免難. This is exactly what happened on the famous occasion when Hannibal was hemmed in among the mountains on the road to Casilinum, and to all appearances entrapped by the Dictator Fabius. The stratagem that Hannibal devised to baffle his foes was remarkably like that which Tian Dan had also employed with success exactly 62 years before. (See IX. § 24, note.) When night came

on, bundles of twigs were fastened to the horns of some 2000 oxen and set on fire, the terrified animals being then quickly driven along the mountainside towards the passes that were beset by the enemy. The strange spectacle of these rapidly moving lights so alarmed and discomfited the Romans that they withdrew from their position, and Hannibal's army passed safely through the defile. (See Polybius, III. 93, 94; Livy, XXII. 16, 17.)

19. For, as Jia Lin remarks: "if you fight with all your might, there is a chance of life; whereas death is certain if you cling to your corner" 力戰或生守隅則死.

20. 所謂 is omitted in the *Tu Shu* text.

21. More literally, "cause the front and rear to lose touch with each other."

22. I doubt if 貫賤 can mean "officers and men," as Capt. Calthrop translates. This is wanted for 上下.

23. The reading 扶, derived from the *Yulan*, must be considered very doubtful. The original text has 救, and the *Tu Shu* 收.

24. Capt. Calthrop translates 卒離 "they scattered the enemy," which cannot be right.

25. Mei Yaochen's note makes the sense plain: 或已離而不能合 或雖合而不能齊. All these clauses, of course, down to 不齊, are dependent on 使 in § 15.

26. Mei Yaochen connects this with the foregoing: "Having succeeded in thus dislocating the enemy, they would push forward in order to secure any advantage to be gained; if there was no advantage to be gained, they would remain where they were" 然能使敵若此當須有利則動無利則止.

27. 敢問 is like 或問, introducing a supposed question.

28. Opinions differ as to what Sun Tzŭ had in mind. Cao Gong thinks it is "some strategical advantage on which the enemy is depending" 其所恃之利. Du Mu says: "The three things which an enemy is anxious to do, and on the accomplishment of which his success depends, are: (1) to capture our favorable position; (2) to ravage our cultivated land; (3) to guard his own communications." 據我便地畧我田野利其糧道斯三者敵人之所愛惜倚恃者也. Our object then must be to thwart his plans in these three directions and thus render

him helpless. [Cf. III § 3.] But this exegesis unduly strains the meaning of 奪 and 愛, and I agree with Chen Hao, who says that 所愛 does not refer only to strategical advantages, but is any person or thing that may happen to be of importance to the enemy. By boldly seizing the initiative in this way, you at once throw the other side on the defensive.

29. 兵之情 means "the conditions of war," not, as Capt. Calthrop says, "the spirit of the troops." According to Du Mu, "this is a summary of leading principles in warfare" 此統言兵之情狀, and he adds: "These are the profoundest truths of military science, and the chief business of the general" 此乃兵之深情將之至事也. The following anecdotes, told by Heshi, show the importance attached to speed by two of China's greatest generals. In 227 A.D., Meng Da 孟達, governor of Xincheng 新城 under the Wei Emperor Wendi, was meditating defection to the House of Shu, and had entered into correspondence with Zhuge Liang, Prime Minister of that State. The Wei general Sima Yi was then military governor of Wan 宛, and getting wind of Meng Da's treachery, he at once set off with an army to anticipate his revolt, having previously cajoled him and said: "If Meng Da has leagued himself with Wu and Shu, the matter should be thoroughly investigated before we make a move." Sima Yi replied: "Meng Da is an unprincipled man, and we ought to go and punish him at once, while he is still wavering and before he has thrown off the mask." Then, by a series of forced marched, he brought his army under the walls of Xincheng within the space of eight days. Now Meng Da had previously said in a letter to Zhuge Liang: "Wan is 1200 *li* from here. When the news of my revolt reaches Sima Yi, he will at once inform his Imperial Master, but it will be a whole month before any steps can be taken, and by that time my city will be well fortified. Besides, Sima Yi is sure not to come himself, and the generals that will be sent against us are not worth troubling about." The next letter, however, was filled with consternation: "Though only eight days have passed since I threw off my allegiance, an army is already at the city-gates. What miraculous rapidity is this!" A fortnight later, Xincheng had fallen and Meng Da had lost his head. (See *Jin Shu*. Chap. 1, f. 3.) In 621 A.D., Li Jing was sent from Kuizhou 夔州 in Sichuan to reduce the successful rebel Xiao Xian 蕭銑, who had set up as Emperor at the modern Jingzhou 荊州 Fu in Hubei. It

was autumn, and the Yangtsze being then in flood, Xiao Xian never dreamt that his adversary would venture to come down through the gorges, and consequently made no preparations. But Li Jing embarked his army without loss of time, and was just about to start when the other generals implored him to postpone his departure until the river was in a less dangerous state for navigation. Li Jing replied: "To the soldier, overwhelming speed is of paramount importance, and he must never miss opportunities. Now is the time to strike, before Xiao Xian even knows that we have got an army together. If we seize the present moment when the river is in flood, we shall appear before his capital with startling suddenness, like the thunder which is heard before you have time to stop your ears against it. [*See* VIII,§ 19, note.] This is the great principle in war. Even if he gets to know of our approach, he will have to levy his soldiers in such a hurry that they will not be fit to oppose us. Thus the full fruits of victory will be ours." All came about as he predicted, and Xiao Xian was obliged to surrender, nobly stipulating that his people should be spared and he alone suffer the penalty of death. (See *Xin Tang Shu*, chap. 93, f. 1 *v°*.)

30. Cf. *supra*, § 13. Li Quan does not venture on a note here.

31. 謹養, according to Wang Xi, means: "Pet them, humor them, give them plenty of food and drink, and look after them generally" 撫循飲食周謹之.

32. Du Mu explains these words in a rhyming couplet: 氣全力盛一發取勝; and Chen Hao recalls the line of action adopted in 224 B.C. by the famous general Wang Jian 王翦, whose military genius largely contributed to the First Emperor. He had invaded the Chu State, where a universal levy was made to oppose him. But, being doubtful of the temper of his troops, he declined all invitations to fight and remained strictly on the defensive. In vain did the Chu general try to force a battle: day after day Wang Jian kept inside his walls and would not come out, but devoted his whole time and energy to winning the affection and confidence of his men. He took care that they should be fed, sharing his own meals with them, provided facilities for bathing, and employed every method of judicious indulgence to weld them into a loyal and homogeneous body. After some time had elapsed, he told off certain persons to find out how the men were amusing themselves. The

answer was, that they were contending with one another in putting the weight and long jumping (投石超距). When Wang Jian heard that they were engaged in these athletic pursuits, he knew that their spirits had been strung up to the required pitch and that they were now ready for fighting. By this time the Chu army, after repeating their challenge again and again, had marched away eastwards in disgust. The Qin general immediately broke up his camp and followed them, and in the battle that ensued they were routed with great slaughter. Shortly afterwards, the whole of Chu was conquered by Qin, and the king Fuchu 負芻 led into captivity. (See *Shiji*, chap. 73, f. 5 r°. It should be noted that, 楚 being a taboo character under the Qin dynasty, the name figures as 荊 throughout.)

33. In order that the enemy may never know exactly where you are. It has struck me, however, that the true reading might be, not 運兵, but 連兵 "link your army together" (cf. *supra* § 46, 吾將使之屬), which would be more in keeping with 併氣積力. Capt. Calthrop cuts the Gordian knot by omitting the words altogether.

34. Zhang Yu's paraphrase is: 常為不可測度之計.

35. Cf. Nicias' speech to the Athenians: Τό τε ξύμπαν γνῶτε, ὦ ἄνδρες στρατιῶται, ἀναγκαῖόν τε ὂν ὑμῖν ἀνδράσιν ἀγαθοῖς γίγνεσθαι, ὡς μὴ ὄντος χωρίου ἐγγὺς ὅποι ἂν μαλακισθέντες σωθεῖτε, etc. [Thuc. VII. 77. vii.]

36. 死 by itself constitutes the protasis, and 焉 is the interrogative = 安. Capt. Calthrop makes the protasis end with 得: "If there be no alternative but death." But I do not see how this is to be got out of the Chinese. Zhang Yu gives a clear paraphrase: 士卒死戰安不得志, and quotes his favorite Weiliaozi (chap. 3): "If one man were to run amok with a sword in the marketplace, and everybody else tried to get out of his way, I should not allow that this man alone had courage and that all the rest were contemptible cowards. The truth is, that a desperado and a man who sets some value on his life do not meet on even terms" 一夫仗劍擊於市萬人無不避之者臣謂非一人之獨勇萬人皆不肖也何則必死與必生固不侔也.

37. 士人 appears to stand for the more usual 士卒. Zhang Yu says "If they are in an awkward place together, they will surely exert united strength to get out of it." 同在難地安得不共竭其力.

38. Capt. Calthrop weakly says: "there is unity," as though the text

were 則專, as in § 20. But 拘 introduces quite a new idea—that of tenacity—which Cao Gong tries to explain by the word "to bind fast" 縛.

39. Du Mu says: 不待修整而自戒懼. Capt. Calthrop wrongly translates 不修 "without warning."

40. Literally, "without asking, you will get." Zhang Yu's paraphrase is: 不求索而得情意.

41. Zhang Yu says: 不約束而親上.

42. This last clause is very similar in sense to the one preceding, except that 親 indicates the soldiers' attachment to their leader, and 信 the leader's attitude towards them. I rather doubt if 信 can mean "they will have confidence in their leader," as the commentary seems to indicate. That way, the sense is not nearly so good. On the other hand, it is just possible that here, as in VIII. § 8 and *infra*, § 55, 信 may = 申: "Without orders, they will carry out [their leader's plan]." The whole of this paragraph, of course, has reference to "desperate ground."

43. 祥 is amplified by Cao Gong into 妖祥之言, and 疑 into 疑惑之計. Cf.; the *Sima Fa*, chap. 3: 滅厲祥.

44. The superstitious, "bound in to saucy doubts and fears," degenerate into cowards and "die many times before their deaths." Du Mu quotes Huangshi Gong: 'Spells and incantations should be strictly forbidden, and no officer allowed to inquire by divination into the fortunes of an army, for fear the soldier's minds should be seriously perturbed.' 禁巫祝不得為吏士卜問軍之吉凶恐亂軍士之心. The meaning is, he continues, "that if all doubts and scruples are discarded, your men will never falter in their resolution until they die." The reading of the standard text is "there will be no refuge" 無所之, which does not fit in well here. I therefore prefer to adopt the variant 災, which evidently stood in Li Quan's text.

45. Zhang Yu has the best note on this passage: "Wealth and long life are things for which all men have a natural inclination. Hence, if they burn or fling away valuables, and sacrifice their own lives, it is not that they dislike them, but simply that they have no choice" 貨與壽人之所愛也所以燒擲財寶割棄性命者非憎惡之也不得已也. Sun Tzŭ is slyly insinuating that, as soldiers are but human, it is for the general to see that temptations to shirk fighting and grow rich are not thrown in their way. Capt. Calthrop, mistaking 惡 for the adjective,

has: "not because money is a bad thing...not because long life is evil."

46. The word in the Chinese is "snivel" 涕. This is taken to indicate more genuine grief than tears alone.

47. Not because they are afraid, but because, as Cao Gong says, "all have embraced the firm resolution to do or die" 皆持必死之計. We may remember that the heroes of the Iliad were equality childlike in showing their emotion. Zhang Yu alludes to the mournful parting at the Yi 易 River between Jingke 荊軻 and his friends, when the former was sent to attempt the life of the King of Qin (afterwards First Emperor) in 227 B.C. The tears of all flowed down like rain as he bade them farewell and uttered the following lines: "The shrill blast is blowing, Chilly the burn; Your champion is going—Not to return" 風蕭蕭兮、易水寒、狀士一去兮、不復還.[1]

48. 諸 was the personal name of Zhuan Zhu 專諸, a native of the Wu State and contemporary with Sun Tzŭ himself, who was employed by Gongzi Guang 公子光, better known as He Lü Wang, to assassinate his sovereign Wang Liao 王僚 with a dagger which he secreted in the belly of a fish served up at a banquet. He succeeded in his attempt, but was immediately hacked to pieces by the king's bodyguard. This was in 515 B.C. The other hero referred to, Cao Gui 曹劌 (or Cao Mo 沫), performed the exploit which has made his name famous 166 years earlier, in 681 B.C. Lu had been thrice defeated by Qi, and was just about to conclude a treaty surrendering a large slice of territory, when Cao Gui suddenly seized 桓公 Huan Gong, the Duke of Qi, as he stood on the altar steps and held a dagger against his chest. None of the Duke's retainers dared to move a muscle, and Cao Gui proceeded to demand full restitution, declaring that Lu was being unjustly treated because she was a smaller and weaker state. Huan Gong, in peril of his life, was obliged to consent, whereupon Cao Gui flung away his dagger and quietly resumed his place amid the terrified assemblage without having so much as changed color. As was to be expected, the Duke wanted afterwards to repudiate the bargain, but his wise old counselor Guan Zhong 管仲 pointed out to him the impolicy of breaking his word, and the upshot was that this bold stroke regained for Lu the

---

[1] See Giles' Dictionary, no. 399.

whole of what she had lost in three pitched battles. (For another anecdote of Cao Gui see VII. § 27, note i and for the biographies of these three bravos, Cao, Zhuan and Jing, see *Shiji*, chap. 86.)

49. 率然 means "suddenly" or "rapidly," and the snake in question was doubtless so called owing to the rapidity of its movements. Through this passage, the term has now come to be used in the sense of "military maneuvers." The 常山 have apparently not been identified. Another reading in the *Yulan* for 中 is 腹 "belly."

50. That is, as Mei Yaochen says, "Is it possible to make the front and rear of an army each swiftly responsive to attack on the other, just as though they were parts of a single living body?" 可使兵首尾率然相應如一體乎?

51. Cf. VI. § 21.

52. The meaning is: If two enemies will help each other in a time of common peril, how much more should two parts of the same army, bound together as they are by every tie of interest and fellow-feeling. Yet it is notorious that many a campaign has been ruined through lack of co-operation, especially in the case of allied armies.

53. 方 is said here to be equivalent to 縛.

54. These quaint devices to prevent one's army from running away recall the Athenian hero Sôphanes who carried an anchor with him at the battle of Plataea, by means of which he fastened himself firmly to one spot. (See Herodotus, IX. 74.) It is not enough, says Sun Tzŭ, to render flight impossible by such mechanical means. You will not succeed unless your men have tenacity and unity of purpose, and, above all, a spirit of sympathetic co-operation. This is the lesson that can be learned from the *shuairan*.

55. Literally, "level the courage [of all] as though [it were that of] one." If the ideal army is to form a single organic whole, then it follows that the resolution and spirit of its component parts must be of the same quality, or at any rate must not fall below a certain standard. Wellington's seemingly ungrateful description of his army at Waterloo as "the worst he had ever commanded" meant no more than it was deficient in this important particular—unity of spirit and courage. Had he not foreseen the Belgian defections and carefully kept those troops in the background, he would almost certainly have lost the day.

56. This is rather a hard sentence on the first reading, but the key to it will be found, firstly, in the pause after 得, and next, in the meaning of 得 itself. The best equivalent for this that I can think of is the German "zur Geltung kommen." Mei Yaochen's paraphrase is: "The way to eliminate the differences of strong and weak and to make both serviceable is to utilize accidental features of the ground" 兵無強弱皆得用者是因地之勢也. Less reliable troops, if posted in strong positions, will hold out as long as better troops on more exposed terrain. The advantage of position neutralizes the inferiority in stamina and courage. Col Henderson says: "With all respect to the text books, and to ordinary tactical teaching, I am inclined to think that the study of ground is often overlooked, and that by no means sufficient importance is attached to the selection of positions...and to the immense advantages that are to be derived, whether you are defending or attacking, from the proper utilization of natural features."[1]

57. Du Mu says: "The simile has reference to the ease with which he does it" 喻易也. 不得已 means that he makes it impossible for his troops to do otherwise than obey. Zhang Yu quotes a jingle, to be found in Wuzi, chap. 4: 將之所揮、莫不從移、將之所指、莫不前死.

58. 靜 seems to combine the meanings "noiseless" and "imperturbable," both of which attributes would of course conduce to secrecy. Du Mu explains 幽 as "deep and inscrutable" 幽深難測, and 正 as "fair and unbiased" 平正無偏. Mei Yaochen alone among the commentators takes 治 in the sense of "self-controlled" 自治. 幽 and 治 are causally connected with 靜 and 正 respectively. This is not brought out at all in Capt. Calthrop's rendering: "The general should be calm, inscrutable, just, and prudent." The last adjective, moreover, can in no sense be said to represent 治.

59. Literally, "to deceive their eyes and ears"—愚 being here used as a verb in the sense of 誤.

60. Cao Gong gives us one of his excellent apophthegms: "The troops must not be allowed to share your schemes in the beginning; they may only rejoice with you over their happy outcome" 民可與樂成不可與慮始. "To mystify, mislead, and surprise the enemy,"

---

[1] "The Science of War," p. 333.

is one of the first principles in war, as has been frequently pointed out. But how about the other process—the mystification of one's own men? Those who may think that Sun Tzŭ is over-emphatic on this point would do well to read Col. Herderson's remarks on Stonewall Jackson's Valley campaign: "The infinite pains," he says, "with which Jackson sought to conceal, even from his most trusted staff officers, his movements, his intentions, and his thoughts, a commander less thorough would have pronounced useless"—etc. etc. In the year 88 A.D., as we read in chap. 47 of the *Hou Han Shu*, "Ban Chao took the field with 25,000 men from Khotan and other Central Asian states with the object of crushing Yarkand. The King of Kutcha replied by dispatching his chief commander to succor the place with an army drawn from the kingdoms of Wensu, Gumo and Weitou, totaling 50,000 men. Ban Chao summoned his officers and also the King of Khotan to a council of war, and said: 'Our forces are now outnumbered and unable to make head against the enemy. The best plan, then, is for us to separate and disperse, each in a different direction. The King of Khotan will march away by the easterly route, and I will then return myself towards the west. Let us wait until the evening drum has sounded and then start.' Ban Chao now secretly released the prisoners whom he had taken alive, and the King of Kutcha was thus informed of his plans. Much elated by the news, the latter set off at once at the head of 10,000 horsemen to bar Ban Chao's retreat in the west, while the King of Wensu rode eastwards with 8,000 horses in order to intercept the King of Khotan. As soon as Ban Chao knew that the two chieftains had gone, he called his divisions together, got them well in hand, and at cockcrow hurled them against the army of Yarkand, as it lay encamped. The barbarians, panic-stricken, fled in confusion, and were closely pursued by Ban Chao. Over 5,000 heads were brought back as trophies, besides immense spoils in the shape of horses and cattle and valuables of every description. Yarkand then capitulating, Kutcha and the other kingdoms drew off their respective forces. From that time forward, Ban Chao's prestige completely overawed the countries of the west." In this case, we see that the Chinese general not only kept his own officers in ignorance of his real plans, but actually took the bold step of dividing his army in order to deceive the enemy.

61. Wang Xi thinks that this means, not using the same stratagem twice. He says:治已行之事已施之謀當革易之不可再之.

62. Note that 人 denotes the enemy, as opposed to the 士卒 of § 36. Capt. Calthrop, not perceiving this, joins the two paragraphs into one. Zhang Yu quotes 太白山人 as saying: "The axiom, that war is based on deception, does not apply only to deception of the enemy. You must deceive even your own soldiers. Make them follow you, but without letting them know why" 兵貴詭道者非止詭敵也抑詭我士卒使由而不使知之也.

63. Wang Xi paraphrases 易其居 as "camp on easy ground" 處易者, and Zhang Yu follows him, saying: 其居則去險而就易. But this is an utterly untenable view. For 迂其途, cf. VIII. 4. Jia Lin, retaining his old interpretation of those words, is now obliged to explain 易其居 as "cause the enemy to shift his camp," which is awkward in the extreme.

64. I must candidly confess that I do not understand the syntax of 師與之期, though the meaning is fairly plain. The difficulty has evidently been felt, for Du Mu tells us that one text omits 期如. It is more likely, however, that a couple of characters have dropped out.

65. 發其機, literally, "releases the spring" (see V. § 25). That is, takes some decisive step that makes it impossible for the army to return—like Xiang Yu 項羽, who sunk ships after crossing a river. Chen Hao, followed by Jia Lin, understands the words less well as "puts forth every artifice at his command" 發其心機. But 機 in this derived sense occurs nowhere else in Sun Tzŭ.

66. Omitted in the *Tu Shu*.

67. The *Tu Shu* inserts another 驅 after 羊. Du Mu says: "The army is only cognizant of orders to advance or retreat; it is ignorant of the ulterior ends of attacking and conquering" 三軍但知進退之命不知攻取之端也.

68. Sun Tzŭ means that after mobilization there should be no delay in aiming a blow at the enemy's heart. With 投之於險 cf. *supra*, § 23: 投之無所往. Note how he returns again and again to this point. Among the warring states of ancient China, desertion was no doubt a much more present fear and serious evil than it is in the armies of today.

69. Zhang Yu says: "One must not be hide-bound in interpreting

the rules for the nine varieties of ground" 九地之法不可拘泥. The use of "contraction and expansion" 屈伸 may be illustrated by the saying 屈以求伸, which almost exactly corresponds to the French "il faut reculer pour mieux sauter." Capt. Calthrop, *more suo*, avoids a real translation and has: "the suiting of the means to the occasion."

70. Cf. *supra*, § 20.

71. Zhang Yu's paraphrase is 而用師者.

72. This "ground" is cursorily mentioned in VIII. § 2, but it does not figure among the Nine 地 of the chapter or the Six 地形 in chap. X. One's first impulse would be to translate it "distant ground" (絕域 is commonly used in the sense of "distant lands"), but this, if we can trust the commentators, is precisely what is not meant here. Mei Yaochen says it is "a position not far enough advanced to be called 'facile,' and not near enough to home to be called 'dispersive,' but something between the two." 進不及輕退不及散在二地之間也. That, of course, does not explain the name 絕, which seems to imply that the general has severed his communications and temporarily cut himself off from his base. Thus, Wang Xi says: "It is ground separated from home by an interjacent state, whose territory we have had to cross in order to reach it. Hence it is incumbent in us to settle our business there quickly." He adds that this position is of rare occurrence, which is the reason why it is not included among the 九地. Capt. Calthrop gives but a poor rendering of this sentence: "To leave home and cross the borders is to be free from interference."

73. The *Tu Shu* reads 通 for 達.

74. From 四達 down to the end of § 45, we have some of the definitions of the early part of the chapter repeated in slightly different language. Capt. Calthrop omits these altogether.

75. 固 = 險固.

76. This end, according to Du Mu, is best attained by remaining on the defensive, and avoiding battle. Cf. *supra*, § 11.

77. The *Tongdian* has 其 instead of 之. The present reading is supported by the 遺說 of Zheng Youxian. As Du Mu says, the object is to guard against two possible contingencies: "(1) the desertion of our own troops 一者備其逃逸; (2) a sudden attack on the part of the enemy 二者恐其敵至." Cf. VIII. § 17: 其徐如林. Mei Yaochen says:

"On the march, the regiments should be in close touch; in an encampment, there should be continuity between the fortification" 行則隊校相繼止則螢壘聯屬. He seems to have forgotten, by the way, what Sun Tzŭ says above: 輕地則無止.

78. This is Cao Gong's interpretation. Zhang Yu adopts it, saying: "We must quickly bring up our rear, so that head and tail may both reach the goal" 當疾進其後使首尾俱至. That is, they must not be allowed to straggle up a long way apart. Mei Yaochen offers another equally plausible explanation: "Supposing the enemy has not yet reached the coveted position, and we are behind him, we should advance with all speed in order to dispute its possession" 敵未至其地我若在後則當疾趨以爭之. 其 would thus denote the enemy, 後 being the preposition, and 趨 would retain its usual intransitive sense. Cf. VII. § 4: 後人發先人至. Chen Hao, on the other hand, assuming that the enemy has had time to select his own ground, quotes VI. § 1, where Sun Tzŭ warns us against coming exhausted to the attack. His own idea of the situation is rather vaguely expressed: "If there is a favorable position lying in front of you, detach a picked body of troops to occupy it; then if the enemy, relying on their numbers, come up to make a fight for it, *you may fall quickly on their rear* with your main body, and victory will be assured" 若地利在前先分精銳以據之彼若恃眾來爭我以大眾趨其後無不剋者. It was thus, he adds, that Zhao She beat the army of Qin. (See VII. 4.) Li Quan would read 多 for 趨, it is not easy to see why.

79. As Wang Xi says, "fearing a surprise attack" 懼襲我也. *The Tongdian* reads here 固其結 (see next sentence).

80. The *Tongdian* reads 謹其市, which Du You explains as "watching the market towns," "the hotbeds of revolution" 變事之端. Capt. Calthrop translates 固其結 by the same words as 合交 in § 12: "cultivate intercourse."

81. The commentators take this as referring to forage and plunder, not, as one might expect, to an unbroken communication with a home base. One text indeed, gives the reading 掠其食. Cf. § 13. Capt. Calthrop's "be careful of supplies" fails to render the forces of 繼.

82. Capt. Calthrop's "do not linger" cannot be called a translation, but only a paraphrase of the paraphrase offered by Cao Gong: "Pass

away from it in all haste" 疾過去也.

83. "To make it seem that I mean to defend the position, whereas my real intention is to burst suddenly though the enemy's lines." 意欲突圍示以守固 (Mengshi); "in order to make my soldiers fight with desperation" 使士卒必死戰也 (Mei Yaochen); "fearing lest my men be tempted to run away" 懼人有走心 (Wang Xi). Du Mu points out that this is the converse of VII. § 36, where it is the enemy who is surrounded. In 532 A.D., Gao Huan 高歡, afterwards Emperor and canonized as Shenwu 神武, was surrounded by a great army under Erzhu Zhao 爾朱兆 and others. His own force was comparatively small, consisting only of 2000 horse and something under 30,000 foot. The lines of investment had not been drawn very closely together, gaps being left at certain points. But Gao Huan, instead of trying to escape, actually made a shift to block all the remaining outlets himself by driving into them a number of oxen and donkeys roped together. As soon as his officers and men saw that there was nothing for it but to conquer or die, their spirits rose to an extraordinary pitch of exaltation, and they charged with such desperate ferocity that the opposing ranks broke and crumbled under their onslaught. (See Du Mu's commentary, and 北齊書 chap. 1, fol. 6.)

84. Du You says: "Burn your baggage and impedimenta, throw away your stores and provisions, choke up the wells, destroy your cooking stoves, and make it plain to your men that they cannot survive, but must fight to the death" 焚輜重棄糧食塞井夷竈示之無活必殊死戰也. Mei Yaochen says epigrammatically: "The only chance of life lies in giving up all hope of it" 必死可生. This concludes what Sun Tzŭ has to say about "grounds" and the "variations" corresponding to them. Reviewing the passages, which bear on this important subject, we cannot fail to be struck by the desultory and unmethodical fashion in which it is treated. Sun Tzŭ begins abruptly in VIII. § 2 to enumerate "variations" before touching on "grounds" at all, but only mentions five, namely nos. 7, 5, 8 and 9 of the subsequent list, and one that is not included in it. A few varieties of ground are dealt with in the earlier portion of chap. IX, and then chap. X sets forth six new grounds, with six variations of plan to match. None of these is mentioned again, though the first is hardly to be distinguished from ground no. 4 in the

next chapter. At last, in chap. XI, we come to the Nine Grounds *par excellence*, immediately followed by the variations. This takes us down to § 14. In §§ 43-45, fresh definitions are provided for nos. 5, 6, 2, 8 and 9 (in the order given), as well as for the tenth ground noticed in chap VIII; and finally, the nine variations are enumerated once more from beginning to end, all, with the exception of 5, 6 and 7, being different from those previously given. Though it is impossible to account for the present state of Sun Tzŭ's text, a few suggestive facts may be brought into prominence: (1) Chap. VIII, according to the title, should deal with nine variations, whereas only five appear. (2) It is an abnormally short chapter. (3) Chap. XI is entitled The Nine Grounds. Several of these are defined twice over, besides which there are two distinct lists of the corresponding variations. (4) The length of the chapter is disproportionate, being double that of any other except IX. I do not propose to draw any inferences from these facts, beyond the general conclusion that Sun Tzŭ's work cannot have come down to us in the shape in which it left his hands: chap. VIII is obviously defective and probably out of place, while XI seems to contain matter that has either been added by a later hand or ought to appear elsewhere.

85. 過則從 is rendered by Capt. Calthrop: "to pursue the enemy if he retreat." But 過 cannot mean "to retreat." Its primary sense is to pass over, hence to go too far, to exceed, or to err. Here, however, the word has lost all implication of censure, and appears to mean "to pass the boundary line dividing safety from danger," or as Zhang Yu puts it, "to be deeply involved in a perilous position" 深陷于危難之地. The latter commentator alludes to the conduct of Ban Chao's devoted followers in 73 A.D. The story runs thus in the *Hou Han Shu*, chap. 47, fol. 1 *v*°: "When Ban Chao arrived at Shanshan 鄯善, Guang 廣, the King of the country, received him at first with great politeness and respect; but shortly afterwards his behavior underwent a sudden change, and he became remiss and negligent. Ban Chao spoke about this to the officers of his suite: 'Have you not noticed,' he said, 'that Guang's polite intentions are on the wane? This must signify that envoys have come from the Northern barbarians, and that consequently he is in a state of indecision, not knowing with which side to throw in his lot. That surely is the reason. The truly wise man, we are told, can per-

ceive things before they have come to pass; how much more, then, those that are already manifest!' Thereupon he called one of the natives who had been assigned to his service, and set a trap for him, saying: 'Where are those envoys from the Xiungnu who arrived some days ago?' The man was so taken aback that between surprise and fear he presently blurted out the whole truth. Ban Chao, keeping his informant carefully under lock and key, then summoned a general gathering of his officers, thirty-six in all, and began drinking with them. When the wine had mounted into their heads a little, he tried to rouse their spirit still further by addressing them thus: 'Gentlemen, here we are in the heart of an isolated region, anxious to achieve riches and honor by some great exploit. Now it happens that an ambassador from the Xiungnu arrived in this kingdom only a few days ago, and the result is that the respectful courtesy extended towards us by our royal host has disappeared. Should this envoy prevail upon him to seize our party and hand us over to the Xiungnu, our bones will become food for the wolves of the desert. What are we to do?' With one accord, the officers replied: *'Standing as we do in peril of our lives, we will follow our commander through life and death.'* (今在危亡之地死生從司馬)." For the sequel of this adventure, see chap. XII. § 1, note.

86. These three sentences are repeated from VII. § 12-14, in order to emphasize their importance, the commentators seem to think. I prefer to regard them as interpolated here in order to form an antecedent to the following words. With regard to local guides, Sun Tzŭ might have added that there is always the risk of going wrong, either through their treachery or some misunderstanding such as Livy records (XXII. 13): Hannibal, we are told, ordered a guide to lead him into the neighborhood of Casinum, where was an important pass to be occupied; but his Carthaginian accent, unsuited to the pronunciation of Latin names, caused the guide to understand Casilinum instead of Casinum, and turning from his proper route, he took the army in that direction, the mistake not being discovered until they had almost arrived.

87. Referring, I think, to what is contained in § 54, 55. Cao Gong, thinking perhaps of the 五利 in VIII. § 6, takes them to be "the advantages and disadvantages attendant on the nine varieties of ground." 九地之利害. The *Tu Shu* reads 此五者.

88. "One who rules by force" 罷王, was a term specially used for those princes who established their hegemony over other feudal states. The famous 五罷 of the 7th century B.C. were (1) Duke Huan of Qi 齊桓公 (2) Duke Wen of Jin 晉文公, (3) Duke Xiang of Song 宋襄公, (4) Prince Zhuang of Chu 楚莊王, (5) Duke Mu of Qin 秦穆公. Their reigns covered the period 685-591 B.C.

89. Here and in the next sentence, the *Yulan* inserts 家 after 敵.

90. Mei Yaochen constructs one of the chains of reasoning that are so much affected by the Chinese: "In attacking a powerful state, if you can divide her forces, you will have a superiority in strength; if you have a superiority in strength, you will overawe the enemy; if you overawe the enemy, the neighboring states will be frightened; and if the neighboring states are frightened, the enemy's allies will be prevented from joining her." The following gives a stronger meaning to 威加: "If the great state has once been defeated (before she has had time to summon her allies), then the lesser states will hold aloof and refrain from massing their forces" 若大國一敗則小國離而不聚矣. Chen Hao and Zhang Yu take the sentence in quite another way. The former says: "Powerful though a prince may be, if he attacks a large state, he will be unable to raise enough troops, and must rely to some extent on external aid; if he dispenses with this, and with overweening confidence in his own strength, simply tries to intimidate the enemy, he will surely be defeated." Zhang Yu puts his view thus: "If we recklessly attack a large state, our own people will be discontented and hang back. But if (as will then be the case) our display of military forces is inferior by half to that of the enemy, the other chieftains will take fright and refuse to join us." According to this interpretation, 其 would refer, not to the 大國, but to the 霸王 himself.

91. For 爭 the *Yulan* reads 事.

92. 天下, as in § 6, stands for "the feudal princes" 諸侯, or the states ruled by them.

93. For 信 (read *shen*) in the meaning of 伸, cf. VIII. § 8. The commentators are unanimous on this point, and we must therefore beware of translating 信己之私 by "secretly self-confident" or the like. Capt. Calthrop (omitting 之私) has: "he has confidence in himself."

94. The train of thought appears to be this: Secure against a com-

bination of his enemies, "he can afford to reject entangling alliances and simply pursue his own secret designs, his prestige enabling him to dispense with external friendship" 能絕天下之交惟得伸己之私志威而無外交者. (Li Quan.)

95. This paragraph, though written many years before the Qin State became a serious menace, is not a bad summary of the policy by which the famous Six Chancellors gradually paved the way for her final triumph under Shihuangdi. Zhang Yu, following up his previous note, thinks that Sun Tzŭ is condemning this attitude of cold-blooded selfishness and haughty isolation. He again refers 其 to the warlike prince, thus making it appear that in the end he is bound to succumb.

96. Wuzi (chap. 3) less wisely says: "Let advance be richly rewarded and retreat be heavily punished." 進有重賞退有重刑.

97. 懸, literally, "hang" or "post up."

98. "In order to prevent treachery," 杜姦媮, says Wang Xi. The general meaning is made clear by Cao Gong's quotation from the *Sima Fa*: "Give instructions only on sighting the enemy; give rewards only when you see deserving deeds." 見敵作誓瞻功作賞. 無政, however, present some difficulty. Cao Gong's paraphrase, 軍法令不應預施懸也, I take to mean: "The final instructions you give to your army should not correspond with those that have been previously posted up." Zhang Yu simplifies this into "your arrangements should not be divulged beforehand" 政不預告. And Jia Lin says: "there should be no fixity in your rules and arrangements" 不守常法常政. Not only is there danger in letting your plans be known, but war often necessitates the entire reversal of them at the last moment.

99. 犯, according to Cao Gong, is here equal to 用. The exact meaning is brought out more clearly in the next paragraph.

100. Cf. supra, § 34.

101. Literally, "do not tell them words;" *i.e.* do not give your reasons for any order. Lord Mansfield once told a junior colleague to "give no reasons" for his decision, and the maxim is even more applicable to a general than to a judge. Capt. Calthrop translates this sentence with beautiful simplicity: "Order should direct the soldiers." That is all.

102. Compare the paradoxical saying 亡者存之基死者生之本. These words of Sun Tzŭ were once quoted by Han Xin in explanation

of the tactics he employed in one of his most brilliant battles, already alluded to on p. 83. In 204 B.C., he was sent against the army of Chao, and halted ten miles from the mouth of the Jingxing 井陘 pass, where the enemy had mustered in full force. Here, at midnight, he detached a body of 2000 light cavalry, every man of which was furnished with a red flag. Their instructions were to make their way through narrow defiles and keep a secret watch on the enemy. "When the men of Zhao see me in full flight," Han Xin said, "they will abandon their fortifications and give chase. This must be the sign for you to rush in, pluck down the Zhao standards and set up the red banners of Han 漢 in their stead." Turning then to his other officers, he remarked: "Our adversary holds a strong position, and is not likely to come out and attack us until he sees the standard and drums of the commander-in-chief, for fear I should turn back and escape through the mountains." So saying, he first of all sent out a division consisting of 10,000 men, and ordered them to form in line of battle with their backs to the River Di 漢. Seeing this maneuver, the whole army of Zhao broke into loud laughter. By this time it was broad daylight, and Han Xin, displaying the generalissimo's flag, marched out of the pass with drums beating, and was immediately engaged by the enemy. A great battle followed, lasting for some time; until at length Han Xin and his colleague Zhang Ni 張耳, leaving drums and banner on the field, fled to the division on the river bank, where another fierce battle was raging. The enemy rushed out to pursue them and to secure the trophies, thus denuding their ramparts of men; but the two generals succeeded in joining the army, which was fighting with the utmost desperation. The time had now come for the 2000 horsemen to play their part. As soon as they saw the men of Zhao following up their advantage, they galloped behind the deserted walls, tore up the enemy's flags and replaced them by those of Han. When the Zhao army turned back from the pursuit, the sight of these red flags struck them with terror. Convinced that the Hans had got in and overpowered their king, they broke up in wild disorder, every effort of their leader to stay the panic being in vain. Then the Han army fell on them from both sides and completed the route, killing a great number and capturing the rest, amongst whom was King 歇 Ya himself....After the battle, some of Han Xin's officers came to him and said: "In the Art of War we are told to have a hill or tumulus on the right rear, and a river or marsh on the left front. (This appears to be a blend of Sun Tzŭ and Tai Gong. See IX. § 9, and note.) You, on the contrary, ordered us to draw up our troops with the river at our back. Under these conditions, how did you manage to gain the victory?" The general replied: "I fear you gentlemen have not studied the Art of War with sufficient care. Is it not written there: *'Plunge your army into desperate straits and it will come off in safety; place it in deadly peril and it will survive'?* Had I taken the usual course, I should never have been able to bring my colleagues round. What says the Military Classic (經)?—'Swoop down on the marketplace and drive the men off to fight' (敺市人而戰之). [This passage does not occur in the present text of Sun Tzŭ.] If I had not placed my troops in a position where they were obliged to fight for their lives, but had allowed each man to follow his own discretion, there would have been a general *debandade*, and it would have been impossible to do anything with them." The officers admitted the force of his argument, and said: "These are higher tactics than we should have been capable of." (See *Qien Han Shu*, chap. 34, ff. 4, 5.)

103. Danger has a bracing effect.

104. Cao Gong says: "Feign stupidity" 佯愚也—by an appearance of yielding and falling in with the enemy's wishes. Zhang Yu's note makes the meaning clear: "If the enemy shows an inclination to advance, lure him on to do so; if he is anxious to retreat, delay on purpose that he may carry out his intention." The object is to make him remiss and contemptuous before we deliver our attack.

105. I understand the first four words to mean "accompanying the enemy in one direction." Cao Gong says: "Unite the soldiers and make for the enemy" 并兵向敵. But such a violent displacement of characters is quite indefensible. Mei Yaochen is the only commentator who seems to have grasped the meaning: 隨敵一向然後發伏出奇. The *Tu Shu* reads 并力.

106. Literally, "after a thousand li."

107. Always a great point with the Chinese.

108. The *Tu Shu* has 是謂巧於成事, and yet another reading, mentioned by Cao Gong, is 巧攻成事. Capt. Calthrop omits this sentence,

after having thus translated the two preceding: "Discover the enemy's intentions by conforming to his movements. When these are discovered, then, with one stroke, the general may be killed, even though he be one hundred leagues distant."

109. 政舉 does not mean "when war is declared," as Capt. Calthrop says, nor yet exactly, as Cao Gong paraphrases it, "when your plans are fixed" 謀定, when you have mapped out your campaign. The phrase is not given in the *Peiwen yunfu*. There being no causal connection discoverable between this and the preceding sentence, 是故 must perforce be left untranslated.

110. 夷 is explained by Mei Yaochen as 滅塞.

111. The *locus classicus* for the tallies is *Chou Li*, XIV, fol. 40 (Imperial edition): 門關用符節貨賄用璽節道路用旌節. The generic term thus appears to be 節, 符 being the special kind used at city-gates and on the frontier. They were tablets of bamboo or wood, one half of which was issued as a permit or passport by the official in charge of a gate. (司門 or 司關. Cf. the "border-warden" 封人 of *Lunyu* III. 24, who may have had similar duties.) When this half was returned to him, within a fixed period, he was authorized to open the gate and let the traveler through.

112. Either to or from the enemy's country.

113. Show no weakness, and insist on your plans being ratified by the sovereign. 廊廟 indicates a hall or temple in the Palace. Cf. I. § 26. It is not clear if other officers would be present. Hardly anything can be made of 勵, the reading of the standard text, so I have adopted Du Mu's conjecture 厲, which appears in the *Tu Shu*.

114. Cao Gong explains 誅 by 治, and Heshi by 責成. Another reading is 謀, and Mei Yaochen, adopting this, understands the whole sentence to mean: Take the strictest precautions to ensure secrecy in your deliberations. Capt. Calthrop glides rather too smoothly over the rough places. His translation is: "conduct the business of the government with vigilance."

115. This looks a very simple sentence, yet Cao Gong is the only commentator who takes it as I have done. Mengshi, followed by Mei Yaochen and Zhang Yu, defines 開闔 as "spies" 間者, and makes 入 an active verb: "If spies come from the enemy, we must quickly let

them in." But I cannot find that the words 開闔 have this meaning anywhere else. On the other hand, they may be taken as two verbs, 或 開或闔, expressing the enemy's indecision whether to advance or retreat, that being the best moment to attack him. (Cf. *Daodejing*, chap. X: 天門開闔能為雌乎; also *Li Ji*, 曲禮, I. Ii. 25.) It is not easy to choose between this and Cao Gong's explanation; the fact that 敵人開 戶 occurs shortly afterwards, in § 68, might be adduced in support of either. 必 must be understood in the sense of 宜 or 當. The only way to avoid this is to put 開闔 between commas and translate: "If we leave a door open, the enemy is sure to rush in."

116. Cf. *supra*, § 18.

117. Capt. Calthrop hardly attempts to translate this difficult paragraph, but invents the following instead: "Discover what he most values, and plan to seize it." Chen Hao's explanation, however, is clear enough: "If I manage to seize a favorable position, but the enemy does not appear on the scene, the advantage thus obtained cannot be turned to any practical account. He who intends, therefore, to occupy a position of importance to the enemy, must begin by making an artful appointment, so to speak, with his antagonist, and cajole him into going there as well." 我若先奪便地而敵不至雖有其利 亦奚用之是以欲取其愛惜之處必先微與敵人相期誤之使 必至. Mei Yaochen explains that this "artful appointment" is to be made through the medium of the enemy's own spies, who will carry back just the amount of information that we choose to give them. Then, having cunningly disclosed our intentions, "we must manage, though starting after the enemy, to arrive before him" 我後人發先 人至 (VII. § 4). We must start after him in order to ensure his marching thither; we must arrive before him in order to capture the place without trouble. Taken thus, the present passage lends some support to Mei Yaochen's interpretation of § 47.

118. 墨 stands for "a marking-line" 繩墨, hence a rule of conduct. See Mencius VII. I. xli. 2. Cao Gong explains it by the similar metaphor "square and compasses" 規矩. The baldness of the sentiment rather inclines me to favor the reading 劃 adopted by Jia Lin in place of 踐, which yields an exactly opposite sense, namely: "Discard hard and fast rules." Jia Lin says: "Victory is the only thing that matters,

and this cannot be achieved by adhering to conventional canons" 惟勝是利不可守以繩墨而為. It is unfortunate that this variant rests on very slight authority, for the sense yielded is certainly much more satisfactory. Napoleon as we know, according to the veterans of the old school whom he defeated, won his battles by violating every accepted canon of warfare.

119. The last four words of the Chinese are omitted by Capt. Calthrop. Du Mu says: "Conform to the enemy's tactics until a favorable opportunity offers; then come forth and engage in a battle that shall prove decisive" 隨敵人之形若有可乘之勢則出而決戰.

120. As the hare is noted for its extreme timidity, the comparison hardly appears felicitous. But of course Sun Tzŭ was thinking only of its speed. The words have been taken to mean: You must flee from the enemy as quickly as an escaping hare; but this is rightly rejected by Du Mu. Capt. Calthrop is wrong in translating "rabbit" 兎. Rabbits are not indigenous to China, and were certainly not known there in the 6th century B.C. The last sixteen characters evidently form a sort of four-line jingle. Chap. X, it may be remembered, closed in similar fashion.

# CHAPTER 12

# The Attack By Fire
# 火攻篇第十二

1. Rather more than half the chapter (§§ 1-13) is devoted to the subject of fire, after which the author branches off into other topics.

2. So Du Mu. Li Quan says: "Set fire to the camp, and kill the soldiers" (when they try to escape from the flames) 焚其營殺其士卒也. Ban Chao, sent on a diplomatic mission to the King of Shanshan [see XI. § 51, note], found himself placed in extreme peril by the unexpected arrival of an envoy from the Xiongnu (the mortal enemies of the Chinese). In consultation with his officers, he exclaimed: "Never venture, never win! The only course open to us now is to make an assault by fire on the barbarians under cover of night, when they will not be able to discern our numbers. Profiting by their panic, we shall exterminate them completely; this will cool the King's courage and cover us with glory, besides ensuring the success of our mission.' The officers all replied that it would be necessary to discuss the matter first with the Intendant (從事). Ban Chao then fell into a passion: 'It is today,' he cried, 'that our fortunes must be decided! The intendant is only a humdrum civilian, who on hearing of our project will certainly be afraid, and everything will be brought to light. An inglorious death is no worthy fate for valiant warriors.' All then agreed to do as he wished. Accordingly as soon as night came on, he and his little band quickly made their way to the barbarian camp. A strong gale was blowing at the time. Ban Chao ordered ten of the party to take drums and hide behind the enemy's barracks, it being arranged that when they saw flames shoot up, they should begin drumming and yelling with all their might. The rest of his men, armed with bows and crossbows, he posted in ambuscade at the gate of the camp. He then set fire to the place from the windward side, whereupon a deafening noise of drums

and shouting arose on the front and rear of the Xiongnu, who rushed out pell-mell in frantic disorder. Ban Chao slew three of them with his own hand, while his companions cut off the heads of the envoy and thirty of his suite. The remainder, more than a hundred in all, perished in the flames. On the following day, Ban Chao went back and informed Guo Xun 郭恂 [the Intendant] of what he had done. The latter was greatly alarmed and turned pale. But Ban Chao, divining his thoughts, said with uplifted hand: 'Although you did not go with us last night, I should not think, Sir, of taking sole credit for our exploit.' This satisfied Guo Xun, and Ban Chao, having sent for Guang, King of Shanshan, showed him the head of the barbarian envoy. The whole kingdom was seized with fear and trembling, which Ban Chao took steps to allay by issuing a public proclamation. Then, taking the king's son as hostage, he returned to make his report to Dou Gu 竇固." (*Hou Han Shu*, chap. 47, ff. 1, 2.)

3. Du Mu says: "Provisions, fuel and fodder" 糧食薪芻. In order to subdue the rebellious population of Jiangnan, Gao Geng 高潁 recommended Wendi of the Sui dynasty to make periodical raids and burn their stores of grain, a policy that in the long run proved entirely successful. (隋書, chap. 41, fol. 2.)

4. An example given is the destruction of Yuan Shao's 袁紹 wagons and impedimenta by Cao Cao in 200 A.D.

5. Du Mu says that the things contained in 輜 and 庫 are the same. He specifies weapons and other implements, bullion and clothing. Cf. VII. § 11.

6. No fewer than four totally diverse explanations of this sentence are given by the commentators, not one of which is quite satisfactory. It is obvious, at any rate, that the ordinary meaning of 隊 ("regiment" or "company") is here inadmissible. In spite of Du Mu's note, 焚其行伍因亂而擊之, I must regard "company burning" (Capt. Calthrop's rendering) as nonsense pure and simple. We may also, I think, reject the very forced explanations given by Li Quan, Mei Yaochen, and Zhang Yu, of whom the last-named says: "Burning a regiment's weapons, so that the soldiers may have nothing to fight with" 焚其隊仗使兵無戰具. That leaves only two solutions open: one, favored by Jia Lin and Heshi, is to take 隊 in the somewhat uncommon sense of "a road" =

隧. The commentary on a passage in the 穆天子傳, quoted in *Kangxi*, defines 隊 (read *sui*) as "a difficult road leading through a valley" 谷中險阻道. Here it would stand for the "line of supplies" 糧道, which might be effectually interrupted if the country roundabout was laid waste with a fire. Finally, the interpretation that I have adopted is that given by Du You in the *Tongdian*. He reads 墜 (which is not absolutely necessary, *zhui* 隊 being sometimes used in the same sense), with the following note: "To drop fire into the enemy's camp. The method by which this may be done is to set the tips of arrows alight by dipping them into a brazier, and then shoot them from powerful crossbows into the enemy's lines" 以火墮敵營中也火墜之法以鐵籠火這着箭頭頸強弩射敵營中.

7. Cao Gong thinks that "traitors in the enemy's camp" 姦人 are referred to. He thus takes 因 as the efficient cause only. But Chen Hao is more likely to be right in saying: "We must have favorable circumstances in general, not merely traitors to help us" 須得其便不獨姦人. Jia Lin says: "We must avail ourselves of wind and dry weather" 因風燥.

8. 煙火 is explained by Cao Gong as 燒具 appliances for making fire." Du Mu suggests "dry vegetable matter, reeds, brushwood, straw, grease, oil, etc." 艾蒿荻葦薪芻膏油之屬. Here we have the material cause. Zhang Yu says: "vessels for hoarding fire, stuff for lighting fires" 貯火之器燃火之物.

9. A fire must not be begun "recklessly" 妄 or "at haphazard" 偶然.

10. These are, respectively, the 7th, 14th, 27th, and 28th of the 二十八宮 Twenty-eight Stellar Mansions, corresponding roughly to Sagittarius, Pegasus, Crater, and Corvus. The original text, followed by the *Tu Shu*, has 月 in place of 宿; the present reading rests on the authority of the *Tongdian* and *Yulan*. Du Mu says: 宿者月之所宿也. For 箕壁, both *Tongdian* and *Yulan* give the more precise location 戊箕東壁. Mei Yaochen tells us that by 箕 is meant the tail of the Dragon 龍; by 壁, the eastern part of that constellation; by 翼 and 軫, the tail of the 鶉 Quail.

11. 此四宿者 is elliptical for 月在此四宿之日. Xiao Yi 蕭繹 (afterwards fourth Emperor of the Liang dynasty, A.D. 552-555) is quoted by Du You as saying that the days 丙丁 of spring, 戊巳 of summer, 壬

癸 of autumn, and 甲乙 of winter bring fierce gales of wind and rain.

12. I take 五 as qualifying 變, not 火, and therefore think that Zhang Yu is wrong in referring 五火 to the five methods of attack set forth in § 1. What follows has certainly nothing to do with these.

13. The Yulan incorrectly reads 軍 for 旱.

14. The original text omits 而其. The prime object of attacking with fire is to throw the enemy into confusion. If this effect is not produced, it means that the enemy is ready to receive us. Hence the necessity for caution.

15. Cao Gong says: "If you see a possible way, advance; but if you find the difficulties too great, retire" 見可而進知難而退.

16. Du Mu says that the previous paragraphs had reference to the fire breaking out (either accidentally, we may suppose, or by the agency of incendiaries) inside the enemy's camp. "But," he continues, "if the enemy is settled in a waste place littered with quantities of grass, or if he has pitched his camp in a position which can be burnt out, we must carry our fire against him at any seasonable opportunity, and not wait on in hopes of an outbreak occurring within, for fear our opponents should themselves burn up the surrounding vegetation, and thus render our own attempts fruitless" 若敵居荒澤草穢或營棚可焚之地即須及時發火不必更待內發作然後應之恐敵人自燒野草我起火無益. The famous Li Ling 李陵 once baffled the 單于 leader of the Xiongnu in this way. The latter, taking advantage of a favorable wind, tried to set fire to the Chinese general's camp, but found that every scrap of combustible vegetation in the neighborhood had already been burnt down. On the other hand, Bocai 波才, a general of the Yellow Turban rebels 黃巾賊, was badly defeated in 184 A.D. through his neglect of this simple precaution. 'At the head of a large army he was besieging Changshe 長社, which was held by Huangfu Song 皇甫嵩. The garrison was very small, and a general feeling of nervousness pervaded the ranks; so Huangfu Song called his officers together and said: 'In war, there are various indirect methods of attack, and numbers do not count for everything. (The commentator here quotes Sun Tzǔ, V. § 5, 6 and 10.) Now the rebels have pitched their camp in the midst of think grass (依草結營), which will easily burn when the wind blows. If we set fire to it at night, they will be

thrown into a panic, and we can make a sortie and attack them on all sides at once, thus emulating the achievement of Tian Dan.' (See p. 126.) That same evening, a strong breeze sprang up; so Huangfu Song instructed his soldiers to bind reeds together into torches and mount guard on the city walls, after which he sent out a band of daring men, who stealthily made their way through the lines and started the fire with loud shouts and yells. Simultaneously, a glare of light shot up from the city-walls, and Huangfu Song, sounding his drums, led a rapid charge, which threw the rebels into confusion and put them to headlong flight." (*Hou Han Shu*, chap. 71, f. 2 r°.)

17. Zhang Yu, following Du You, says: "When you make a fire, the enemy will retreat away from it; if you oppose his retreat and attack him then, he will fight desperately, which will not conduce to your success" 燒之必退退而逆擊之必死戰則不便也. A rather more obvious explanation is given by Du Mu: "If the wind is in the east, begin burning to the east of the enemy, and follow up the attack yourself from that side. If you start the fire on the east side, and then attack from the west, you will suffer in the same way as your enemy."

18. Cf. Laozi's saying: "A violent wind does not last the space of a morning" 飄風不終朝. (*Daodejing*, chap. 23.) Mei Yaochen and Wang Xi say: "A day breeze dies down at nightfall, and a night breeze at daybreak. This is what happens as a general rule." The phenomenon observed may be correct enough, but how this sense is to be obtained is not apparent.

19. Du Mu's commentary shows what has to be supplied in order to make sense out of 以數守之. He says: "We must make calculations as to the paths of the stars, and watch for the days on which wind will rise, before making our attack with fire" 須籌星之數守風起之日乃可發火. Zhang Yu seems to take 守 in the sense of 防: "We must not only know how to assail our opponents with fire, but also be on our guard against similar attacks from them."

20. I have not the least hesitation in rejecting the commentators' explanation of 明 as = 明白. Thus Zhang Yu says: ". . . will *clearly* (i.e. obviously) be able to gain the victory" 灼然可以取勝. This is not only clumsy in itself, but does not balance 強 in the next clause. For 明 "intelligent," cf. *infra*, § 16, and *Lunyu* XII. 6.

21. Capt. Calthrop gives an extraordinary rendering of the paragraph: ". . .if the attack is to be assisted, the fire must be unquenchable. If water is to assist the attack, the flood must be overwhelming."

22. Cao Gong's note is: "We can merely obstruct the enemy's road or divide his army, but not sweep away all his accumulated stores" 但可以絕敵道分敵軍不可以奪敵蓄積. Water can do useful service, but it lacks the terrible destructive power of fire. This is the reason, Zhang Yu concludes, why the former is dismissed in a couple of sentences, whereas the attack by fire is discussed in detail. Wuzi (chap. 4) speaks thus of the two elements: "If an army is encamped on low-lying marshy ground, from which the water cannot run off, and where the rainfall is heavy, it may be submerged by a flood. If an army is encamped in wild marsh lands thickly overgrown with weeds and brambles, and visited by frequent gales, it may be exterminated by fire" 居軍下濕水無所通霖雨數至可灌而沉居軍荒澤草楚幽穢風飆數至可焚而滅.

23. This is one of the most perplexing passages in Sun Tzǔ. The difficulty lies mainly in 不修其功, of which two interpretations appear possible. Most of the commentators understand 修 in the sense (not known to Kangxi) of "reward" 賞 or "promote" 舉, and 其功 as referring to the merit of officers and men. Thus Cao Gong says: "Rewards for good service should not be deferred a single day" 賞善不踰日. And Du Mu: "If you do not take opportunity to advance and reward the deserving, your subordinates will not carry out your commands, and disaster will ensue." 費留 would then probably mean "stoppage of expenditure" 留滯費耗, or as Jia Lin puts it, "the grudging of expenditure" 惜費. For several reasons, however, and in spite of the formidable array of scholars on the other side, I prefer the interpretation suggested by Mei Yaochen alone, whose words I will quote: "Those who want to make sure of succeeding in their battles and assaults must seize the favorable moments when they come and not shrink on occasion from heroic measures: that is to say, they must resort to such means of attack as fire, water, and the like. What they must not do, and what will prove fatal, is to sit still and simply hold on to the advantages they have got" 欲戰必勝攻必取者在困時乘便能作為功也作為功者修火攻水攻之類不可坐守其利也坐守其利

者凶也. This retains the more usual meaning of 修, and also brings out a clear connection of thought with the previous part of the chapter. With regard to 費留, Wang Xi paraphrases it as 費財老師 "expending treasure and tiring out (*lit.*, ageing) the army." 費 of course is expenditure or waste in general, either of time, money, or strength. But the soldier is less concerned with the saving of money, than of time. For the metaphor expressed in "stagnation" I am indebted to Cao Gong, who says: 若水之留不復還也. Capt. Calthrop gives a rendering which bears but little relation to the Chinese text: "Unless victory or possession be obtained, the enemy quickly recovers, and misfortunes arise. The war drags on, and money is spent."

24. As Sun Tzŭ quotes this jingle in support of his assertion in § 15, we must suppose 修之 to stand for 修其功 or something analogous. The meaning seems to be that the ruler lays plans that the general must show resourcefulness in carrying out. It is now plainer than ever that 修 cannot mean "to reward." Nevertheless, Du Mu quotes the following from the 三略, chap. 2: "The warlike prince controls his soldiers by his authority, knits them together by good faith, and by rewards makes them serviceable. If faith decays, there will be disruption: if rewards are deficient, commands will not be respected" 霸者制士以權結士以信使士以賞信衰則士疏賞虧則士不用命.

25. 起, the *Yulan's* variant for 動, is adopted by Li Quan and Du Mu. Sun Tzŭ may at times appear to be over-cautious, but he never goes so far in that direction as the remarkable passage in the Daodejing. chap. 69: "I dare not take initiative, but prefer to act on the defensive; I dare not advance an inch, but prefer to retreat a foot" 吾不敢為主而為客不敢進寸而退尺.

26. Again compare Laozi, chap. 68: 善戰者不怒. Zhang Yu says that 慍 is a weaker word than 怒, and is therefore applied to the general as opposed to the sovereign. The Tongdian and Yulan read 軍 for 師, and the latter 合 for 致.

27. This is repeated from XI. § 17. Here I feel convinced that it is an interpolation, for it is evident that § 10 ought to follow immediately on § 18. For 動, the *Tongdian* and *Yulan* have 用. Capt. Calthrop invents a sentence that he inserts before this one: "Do not make war unless victory may be gained thereby." While he was about it, he might have

credited Sun Tzŭ with something slightly less inane.

28. According to Zhang Yu, 喜 denotes joy outwardly manifested in the countenance, 悅 the inward sensation of happiness.

29. The Wu State was destined to be a melancholy example of this saying. See p. 98.

30. 警, which usually means "to warm," is here equal to 戒. This is a good instance of how Chinese characters, which stand for ideas, refuse to be fettered by dictionary-made definitions. The *Tu Shu* reads 故曰, as in § 16.

31. It is odd that 全軍 should not have the same meaning here as in III. § 1, *q.v.* This has led me to consider whether it might not be possible to take the earlier passage thus: "to preserve your own army (country, regiment, etc.) intact is better than to destroy the enemy's." The two words do not appear in the *Tongdian* or the *Yulan*. Capt. Calthrop misses the point by translating: "then is the state secure, and the army victorious in battle."

# CHAPTER 13

# The Use Of Spies
# 用間篇第十三

1. 間 is really a vulgar form of 閒, and does not appear in the *Shuowen*. In practice, however, it has gradually become a distinct character with special meanings of its own, and I have therefore followed my edition of the standard text in retaining this form throughout the chapter. In VI. § 25, on the other hand, the correct form 閒 will be found. The evolution of the meaning "spy" is worth considering for a moment, provided it be understood that this is very doubtful ground, and that any dogmatism is out of place. The *Shuowen* defines 閒 as 隟 (the old form of 隙) "a crack" or "chink," and on the whole we may accept Xu Jie's 徐鍇 analysis as not unduly fanciful: "At night, a *door* is shut; if, when it is shut, the light of the *moon* is visible, it must come through a *chink*" 夫門夜閉閉而見月光是有閒隟也. From this it is an easy step to the meaning "space between," or simply "between," as for example in the phrase "to act as a secret spy between enemies." 往來閒諜. Here 諜 is the word which means "spy;" but we may suppose that constant association so affected the original force of 閒, that 諜 could at last be dropped altogether, leaving 閒 to stand alone with the same signification. Another possible theory is that the word may first have come to mean 覸 "to peep" (see 博雅, quoted in Kangxi), which would naturally be suggested by "crack" or "crevice," and afterwards the man who peeps, or spy.

2. 怠於道路, which is omitted by the *Yulan*, appears at first sight to be explained by the words immediately following, so that the obvious translation would be "[enforced] idleness along the line of march." (Cf. *Daodejing*, chap. 30: "where troops have been quartered, brambles and thorns spring up" 師之所處荊棘生焉.) The commentators, however, say that 怠 is here equivalent to 疲—a meaning

that is still retained in the phrase 倦怠. Du Mu refers 怠 to those who are engaged in conveying provisions to the army. But this can hardly be said to emerge clearly from Sun Tzŭ text. Zhang Yu has the note: "We may be reminded of the saying: 'On serious ground, gather in plunder' (XI. § 13). Why then should carriage and transportation cause exhaustion on the highway?—The answer is, that not victuals alone, but all sorts of munitions of war have to be conveyed to the army. Besides, the injunction to 'forage on the enemy' only means that when an army is deeply engaged in hostile territory, scarcity of food must be provided against. Hence, without being solely dependent on the enemy for corn, we must forage in order that there may be an uninterrupted flow of supplies. Then, again, there are places like salt deserts (磧鹵之地), where provisions being unobtainable, supplies from home cannot be dispensed with."

3. Mei Yaochen says: "Men will be lacking at the plough-tail" 廢於耒耜. The allusion is to 井田 the system of dividing land into nine parts, as shown in the character 井, each consisting of a 夫 or 頃 (about 15 acres), the plot in the center being cultivated on behalf of the State by the tenants of the eight. It was here also, so Du Mu tells us, that their cottages were built and a well sunk, to be used by all in common. [See II. § 12, note.] These groups of eight peasant proprietors were called 鄰. In time of war, one of the families had to serve in the army, while the other seven contributed to its support (一家從軍七家奉之). Thus, by a levy of 100,000 men (reckoning one able-bodied soldier to each family) the husbandry of 700,000 families would be affected.

4. "For spies" is of course the meaning, though it would spoil the effect of his curiously elaborate exordium if spies were actually mentioned at this point.

5. Sun Tzŭ argument is certainly ingenious. He begins by adverting to the frightful misery and vast expenditure of blood and treasure which war always brings in its train. Now, unless you are kept informed of the enemy's condition, and are ready to strike at the right moment, a war may drag on for years. The only way to get this information is to employ spies, and it is impossible to obtain trustworthy spies unless they are properly paid for their services. But it is surely false economy to grudge a comparatively trifling amount for this purpose, when

every day that the war lasts eats up an incalculably greater sum. This grievous burden falls on the shoulders of the poor, and hence Sun Tzŭ concludes that to neglect the use of spies is nothing less than a crime against humanity.

6. An inferior reading for 主 is 仁, thus explained by Mei Yaochen: 非以仁佐國者也. This idea, that the true object of war is peace, has its root in the national temperament of the Chinese. Even so far back as 597 B.C., these memorable words were uttered by Prince Zhuang 莊 of the Chu State: 夫文止戈為武 ... 夫武禁暴戢兵保大定功安民和眾豐財者也 "The character for 'prowess' (武) is made up of 'to stay' 止 and 'a spear' 戈 (cessation of hostilities). Military prowess is seen in the repression of cruelty, the calling in of weapons, the preservation of the appointment of Heaven, the firm establishment of merit, the bestowal of happiness on the people, putting harmony between the princes, the diffusion of wealth." (*Zuozhuan*, 宣公 XII. 3 *ad fin.*)

7. That is, knowledge of the enemy's dispositions, and what he means to do.

8. "By prayers or sacrifices" 以禱祀, says Zhang Yu. 鬼 are the disembodied spirits of men, and 神 supernatural beings or "gods."

9. Du Mu's note makes the meaning clear: 象, he says, is the same as 類 reasoning by analogy; "[knowledge of the enemy] cannot be gained by reasoning from other analogous cases" 不可以他事比類而求.

10. Li Quan says: "Quantities like length, breadth, distance, and magnitude, are susceptible of exact mathematical determination; human actions cannot be so calculated" 夫長短闊狹遠近小大即可驗之於度數人之情偽度不能知也.

11. Mei Yaochen has rather an interesting note: "Knowledge of the spirit-world is to be obtained by divination; information in natural science may be sought by inductive reasoning; the laws of the universe can be verified by mathematical calculation: but the dispositions of an enemy are ascertainable through spies and spies alone" 鬼神之情可以筮卜知形氣之物可以象類求天地之理可以度數驗唯敵之情必由間者而後知也.

12. 道 is explained by Du Mu as "the way in which facts leak out and dispositions are revealed" 其情泄形露之道.

13. 為 is the reading of the standard text, but the *Tongdian*, *Yulan* and *Tu Shu* all have 謂.

14. Capt. Calthrop translates 神紀 "the Mysterious Thread," but Mei Yaochen's paraphrase 神妙之網紀 shows that what is meant is the control of a number of threads.

15. "Cromwell, one of the greatest and most practical of all cavalry leaders, had officers styled 'scout masters,' whose business it was to collect all possible information regarding the enemy, through scout and spies, etc., and much of his success in war was traceable to the previous knowledge of the enemy's moves thus gained."[1]

16. 鄉間 is the emended reading of Jia Lin and the *Tu Shu* for the unintelligible 因間, here and in § 7, of the standard text, which nevertheless reads 鄉間 in § 22.

17. Du Mu says: "In the enemy's country, win people over by kind treatment, and use them as spies."

18. 官 includes both civil and military officials. Du Mu enumerates the following classes as likely to do good service in this respect: "Worthy men who have been degraded from office, criminals who have undergone punishment; also, favorite concubines who are greedy for gold, men who are aggrieved at being in subordinate positions, or who have been passed over in the distribution of posts, others who are anxious that their side should be defeated in order that they may have a chance of displaying their ability and talents, fickle turncoats who always want to have a foot in each boat (飜覆變詐常持兩端之心者). Officials of these several kinds," he continues, "should be secretly approached and bound to one's interests by means of rich presents. In this way you will be able to find out the state of affairs in the enemy's country, ascertain the plans that are being formed against you, and moreover disturb the harmony and create a breach between the sovereign and his ministers." The necessity for extreme caution, however, in dealing with "inward spies," appears from an historical incident related by Heshi: "Luo Shang 羅尚, Governor of Yizhou 益州, sent his general Wei Bo 隗伯 to attack the rebel Li Xiong 李雄 of Shu 蜀 in his stronghold at Pi 郫. After each side had experienced a number of

---

[1] "Aids to Scouting," p. 2.

victories and defeats, Li Xiong had recourse to the services of a certain Potai 朴泰, a native of Wudu 武都. He began by having him whipped until the blood came, and then sent him off to Luo Shang, whom he was to delude by offering to co-operate with him from inside the city, and to give a fire signal at the right moment for making a general assault. Luo Shang, confiding in these promises, marched out all his best troops, and placed Wei Bo and others at their head with orders to attack at Potai's bidding. Meanwhile, Li Xiong's general, Li Xiong 李驤, had prepared an ambuscade on their line of march; and Potai, having reared long scaling-ladders against the city walls, now lighted the beacon-fire. Wei Bo's men raced up on seeing this signal and began climbing the ladders as fast as they could, while others were drawn up by ropes lowered from above. More than a hundred of Luo Shang's soldiers entered the city in this way, every one of whom was forthwith beheaded. Li Xiong then charged with all his forces, both inside and outside the city, and routed the enemy completely." (This happened in 303 A.D. I do not know where Heshi got the story from. It is not given in the biography of Li Xiong or that of his father Li Te 特, *Jin Shu*, chap. 120, 121.)

19. By means of heavy bribes and liberal promises detaching them from the enemy's service, and inducing them to carry back false information as well as to spy in turn on their own countrymen. Thus Du You: 因厚賂重許反使為我間也. On the other hand, Xiao Shixian 蕭世誠 in defining the 反間 says that we pretend not to have detected him, but contrive to let him carry away a false impression of what is going on (敵使人來候我我佯不知而示以虛事). Several of the commentators accept this as an alternative definition; but that it is not what Sun Tzŭ meant is conclusively proved by his subsequent remarks about treating the converted spy generously (§ 21sqq). Heshi notes three occasions on which converted spies were used with conspicuous success: 1) by Tian Dan in his defense of Jimo (see supra, IX: 24); 2) by Zhao She on his march to Eyu (see VII: 4); and by the wily Fan Ju 范雎 in 260 B.C., when Lian Po was conducting a defensive campaign against Qin. The King of Zhao strongly disapproved of Lian Po's cautious and dilatory methods, which had been unable to avert a series of minor disasters, and therefore lent ready ear to the reports of

his spies, who had secretly gone over to the enemy and were already in Fan Ju's pay. They said: "The only thing which causes Qi anxiety is lest Zhao Gua 趙括 should be made general. Lian Po they consider an easy opponent, who is sure to be vanquished in the long run." Now this Zhao Gua was a son of the famous Zhao She. From his boyhood, he had been wholly engrossed in the study of war and military matters, until at last he came to believe that there was no commander in the whole Empire who could stand against him. His father was much disquieted by this overweening conceit, and the flippancy with which he spoke of such a serious thing as war, and solemnly declared that if ever Gua was appointed general, he would bring ruin on the armies of Zhao. This was the man who, in spite of earnest protests from his own mother and the veteran statesman Lin Xiangru 藺相如, was now sent to succeed Lian Po. Needless to say, he proved no match for the redoubtable Bo Qi and the great military power of Qin. He fell into a trap by which his army was divided into two and his communications cut; and after a desperate resistance lasting 46 days, during which the famished soldiers devoured one another, he was himself killed by an arrow, and his whole force, amounting, it is said, to 400,000 men, ruthlessly put to the sword. (See 歷代紀事年表, chap. 19, ff. 48—50).

20. 傳 is Li Quan's conjecture for 待, which is found in the *Tongdian* and the *Yulan*. The *Tu Shu*, unsupported by any good authority, adds 間也 after 敵. In that case, the doomed spies would be those of the enemy, to whom our own spies had conveyed false information. But this is unnecessarily complicated. Du You gives the best exposition of the meaning: "We ostentatiously do things calculated to deceive our own spies, who must be led to believe that they have been unwittingly disclosed. Then, when these spies are captured in the enemy's lines, they will make an entirely false report, and the enemy will take measures accordingly, only to find that we do something quite different. The spies will thereupon be put to death." Capt. Calthrop makes a hopeless muddle of the sentence. As an example of doomed spies, Heshi mentions the prisoners released by Ban Chao in his campaign against Yarkand. (See p. 155) He also refers to Tang Jian 唐儉, who in 630 A.D. was sent by Taizong to lull the Turkish Khan Jieli 頡利 into fancied security, until Li Jing was able to deliver a crushing blow against him.

Zhang Yu, says that the Turks revenged themselves by killing Tang Jian, but this is a mistake, for we read in both the Old and the New Tang History (chap. 58, fol. 2 and chap. 89, fol. 8 respectively) that he escaped and lived on until 656. Li Yiji 酈食其 played a somewhat similar part in 203 B.C., when sent by the King of Han to open peaceful negotiations with Qi. He has certainly more claim to be described as a 死間; for the King of Qi being subsequently attacked without warning by Han Xin, and infuriated by what he considered the treachery of Li Yiji, ordered the unfortunate envoy to be boiled alive.

21. This is the ordinary class of spies, properly so called, forming a regular part of the army: "Your surviving spy must be a man of keen intellect, though in outward appearance a fool; of shabby exterior, but with a will of iron. He must be active, robust, endowed with physical strength and courage; thoroughly accustomed to all sorts of dirty work, able to endure hunger and cold, and to put up with shame and ignominy" 生間者必取內明外愚形劣心壯趫健勁勇閑於鄙事能忍饑寒垢恥者為之. Heshi tells the following story of Daxi Wu 達奚武 of the Sui dynasty: "When he was governor of Eastern Qin, Shenwu 神武 of Qi made a hostile movement upon Shayuan 沙苑. The Emperor Taizu (?Gaozu) sent Daxi Wu to spy upon the enemy. He was accompanied by two other men. All three were horseback and wore the enemy's uniform. When it was dark, they dismounted a few hundred feet away from the enemy's camp and stealthily crept up to listen, until they succeeded in catching the passwords used by the army. Then they got on their horses again and boldly passed through the camp under the guise of night watchmen (警夜者); and more than once, happening to come across a soldier who was committing some breach of discipline, they actually stopped to give the culprit a sound cudgeling! Thus they managed to return with the fullest possible information about the enemy's dispositions, and received warm commendation from the Emperor, who in consequence of their report was able to inflict a severe defeat on his adversary." With the above classification it is interesting to compare the remarks of Frederick the Great:[1] "Es giebt vielerley Sorten von Spions: 1. Geringe

---

[1] "Unterricht des Königs von Preussen an die Generale seiner Armeen," cap. 12 (edition of 1794).

Leute, welche sich von diesem Handwerk meliren. 2. Doppelte Spions. 3. Spions von Consequenz, und endlich 4. Diejenigen, welche man zu diesem unglücklichen Hankwerk zwinget." This of course is a bad cross-division. The first class ("Bürgersleute, Bauern, Priesters, etc.") corresponds roughly to Sun Tzǔ's "local spies," and the third to "inward spies." Of "Doppelte Spions" it is broadly stated that they are employed "um dem Feinde falsche Nachrichten aufzubinden." Thus they would include both converted and doomed spies. Frederick's last class of spies does not appear in Sun Tzǔ's list, perhaps because the risk in using them is too great.

22. The original text and the *Tu Shu* have 事 in place of the first 親. Du Mu and Mei Yaochen point out that the spy is privileged to enter even the general's private sleeping-tent. Capt. Calthrop has an inaccurate translation: "In connection with the armies, spies should be treated with the greatest kindness."

23. Frederick concludes his chapter on spies with the words: "Zu allem diezem füge noch hinzu, dass man in Bezahlung der Spions freygebig, ja verschwenderisch seyn muss. Ein Mench, der um eures Dienstes halber den Strick waget, verdienet dafür belohnet zu werden."

24. Du Mu gives a graphic touch: 出口入耳也, which is to say, all communications with spies should be carried on "mouth-to-ear." Capt. Calthrop has: "All matters relating to spies are secret," which is distinctly feeble. An inferior reading for 密 is 審. The following remarks on spies may be quoted from Turenne, who made perhaps larger use of them than any previous commander: "Spies are attached to those who give them most, he who pays them ill is never served. They should never be known to anybody; nor should they know one another. When they propose anything very material, secure their persons, or have in your possession their wives and children as hostages for their fidelity. Never communicate anything to them but what it is absolutely necessary that they should know."[1]

25. Mei Yaochen says: "In order to use them, one must know fact from falsehood, and be able to discriminate between honesty and double-dealing" 知其情偽辨其邪正則能用. Wang Xi takes 聖 and

---

[1] "Marshal Turenne," p. 311.

智 separately, defining the former as "intuitive perception" 通而先
識 and the latter as "practical intelligence" 明於事. Du Mu strangely
refers these attributes to the spies themselves: "Before using spies we
must assure ourselves as to their integrity of character and the extent
of their experience and skill" 先量間者之性誠實多智然後可用
之. But he continues: "A brazen face and a crafty disposition are more
dangerous than mountains or rivers; it takes a man of genius to penetrate such" 厚貌深情險於山川非聖人莫能知. So that we are left
in some doubt as to his real opinion on the passage.

26. Zhang Yu says that 仁 means "not grudging them honors and
pay;" 義, "showing no distrust of their honesty." "When you have at-
tracted them by substantial offers, you must treat them with absolute
sincerity; then they will work for you with all their might."

27. Mei Yaochen says: "Be on your guard against the possibility of
spies going over to the service of the enemy." The *Tongdian* and *Yulan*
read 密 for 妙.

28. Cf. VI. § 9: 微乎微乎. Capt. Calthrop translates: "Wonderful
indeed is the power of spies."

29. The Chinese here is so concise and elliptical that some expansion is necessary for the understanding of it. 間事 denotes important information about the enemy obtained from a surviving spy. The
subject of 未發, however, is not this information itself, but the secret
stratagem built up on the strength of it. 聞者 means "is heard"—by
anybody else. Thus, word for word, we get: "If spy matters are heard
before [our plans] are carried out," etc. Capt. Calthrop, in translating
"the spy who told the matter, and the man who repeated the same" 間
與所告者, may appeal to the authority of the commentators; but he
surely misses the main point of Sun Tzǔ's injunction. For, whereas you
kill the spy himself "as punishment for letting out the secret" 惡其
泄, the object of killing the other man is only, as Chen Hao puts it, "to
stop his mouth" 以滅口 and prevent the news leaking any further. If it
had already been repeated to others, this object would not be gained.
Either way, Sun Tzǔ lays himself open to the charge of inhumanity,
though Du Mu tries to defend him by saying that the man deserves
to be put to death, for the spy would certainly not have told the secret
unless the other had been at pains to worm it out of him. The *Tongdian*

and *Yulan* have the reading 先聞其間者與, etc., which, while not affecting the sense, strikes me as being better than that of the standard text. The *Tu Shu* has . . . 聞與所告者, which I suppose would mean: "the man who heard the secret and the man who told it to him."

30. 左右 is a comprehensive term for those who wait on others, servants and retainers generally. Capt. Calthrop is hardly happy in rendering it "right-hand men."

31. 謁者, literally "visitors," is equivalent, as Du You says, to "those whose duty it is to keep the general supplied with information" 主告事者, which naturally necessitates frequent interviews with him. Zhang Yu goes too far afield for an explanation in saying that they are "the leaders of mercenary troops" 典賓客之將.

32. 闍吏 and 守舍之人.

33. 守將, according to Zhang Yu, is simply "a general on active service" 守官任職之將. Capt. Calthrop is wrong, I think, in making 守將 directly dependent on 姓名 ("the names of the general in charge," etc.).

34. As the first step, no doubt, towards finding out if any of these important functionaries can be won over by bribery. Capt. Calthrop blunders badly with: "Then set the spies to watch them."

35. 必索 is omitted by the *Tongdian* and *Yulan*. Its recurrence is certainly suspicious, though the sense may seem to gain by it. The *Tu Shu* has this variation: . . . 敵間之來間吾者, etc.

36. 舍 is probably more than merely 居止 or "detain" 稽留. Cf. § 25 *ad fin.*, where Sun Tzǔ insists that these converted spies shall be treated well. Zhang Yu's paraphrase is 館舍.

37. Du You expands 因是而知之 into "through conversion of the enemy's spies we learn the enemy's condition" 因反敵間而知敵情. And Zhang Yu says: "We must tempt the converted spy into our service, because it is he that knows which of the local inhabitants are greedy of gain, and which of the officials are open to corruption" 因是反間知彼鄉人之貪利者官人之有隙者誘而使之. In the *Tongdian*, 鄉 has been altered to 因, doubtless for the sake of uniformity with § 9.

38. "Because the converted spy knows how the enemy can best be deceived" (Zhang Yu). The *Tongdian* text, followed by the *Yulan*, has here the obviously interpolated sentence 因是可得而攻也.

39. Capt. Calthrop omits this sentence.

40. I have ventured to differ in this place from those commentators—Du You and Zhang Yu—who understand 主 as 人主, and make 五間之事 the antecedent of 之 (the others ignoring the point altogether). It is plausible enough that Sun Tzŭ should require the ruler to be familiar with the methods of spying (though one would rather expect "general" 將 in place of 主). But this involves taking 知之 here in quite a different way from the 知之 immediately following, as also from those in the previous sentences. 之 there refers vaguely to the enemy or the enemy's condition, and in order to retain the same meaning here, I make 主 a verb, governed by 五間之事. Cf. XI. § 19, where 主 is used in exactly the same manner. The sole objection that I can see in the way of this interpretation is the fact the 死間, or fourth variety of spy, does not add to our knowledge of the enemy, but only misinforms the enemy about us. This would be, however, but a trivial oversight on Sun Tzŭ's part, inasmuch as the "doomed spy" is in the strictest sense not to be reckoned as a spy at all. Capt. Calthrop, it is hardly necessary to remark, slurs over the whole difficulty.

41. As explained in §§ 22-24. He not only brings information himself, but makes it possible to use the other kinds of spies to advantage.

42. Sun Tzŭ means the Shang 商 dynasty, founded in 1766 B.C. Its name was changed to Yin by Pan Geng 盤庚 in 1401.

43. Better known as Yi Yin 伊尹, the famous general and statesman who took part in Cheng Tang's campaign against Jie Gui 桀癸. Lü Shang 呂尚, whose "style" was 子牙, rose to high office under the tyrant Zhou Xin 紂辛, whom he afterwards helped to overthrow. Popularly known as 太公, a title bestowed on him by Wen Wang, he is said to have composed a treatise on war, erroneously identified with the 六韜.

44. There is less precision in the Chinese than I have thought it well to introduce into my translation, and the commentaries on the passage are by no means explicit. But, having regard to the context, we can hardly doubt that Sun Tzŭ is holding up Yi Zhi and Lü Ya as illustrious examples of the converted spy, or something closely analogous. His suggestion is, that the Xia and Yin dynasties were upset owing to the intimate knowledge of their weakness and shortcomings that these

former ministers were able to impart to the other side. Mei Yaochen appears to resent any such aspersion on these historic names: "Yi Yin and Lü Ya," he says, "were not rebels against the Government (非叛 於國也). Xia could not employ the former, hence Yin employed him. Yin could not employ the latter, hence Zhou employed him. Their great achievements were all for the good of the people." Heshi is also indignant: "How should two divinely inspired men such as Yi and Lü have acted as common spies? Sun Tzǔ's mention of them simply means that the proper use of the five classes of spies is a matter which requires men of the highest mental caliber like Yi and Lü, whose wisdom and capacity qualified them for the task. The above words only empha-size this point" 伊呂聖人之耦豈為人間哉今孫子引之者言五間之用須上智之人如伊呂之才智者可以用間蓋重之之辭耳. Heshi believes then that the two heroes are mentioned on account of their supposed skill in the use of spies. But this is very weak, as it leaves totally unexplained the significant words 在夏 and 在殷. Capt. Calthrop speaks, rather strangely, of "the province of Yin...the country of Xia...the State of Zhou...the people of Shang."

45. Chen Hao compares § 15: 非聖智不能用間 He points out that "the god-like wisdom of Cheng Tang and Wu Wang led them to em-ploy Yi Yin and Lü Shang" 湯武之聖伊呂宜用. The *Tu Shu* omits 惟. Du Mu closes with a note of warning: "Just as water, which carries a boat from bank to bank, may also be the means of sinking it, so reli-ance on spies, while productive of great results, is oft-times the cause of utter destruction" 夫水所以能濟舟亦有因水而覆沒者間所以能成功亦有憑間而傾敗者.

46. The antecedent to 此 must be either 間者 or 用間者 under-stood from the whole sentence. Jia Lin says that an army without spies is like a man without ears or eyes.